Samuel Leavitt

Our Money Wars

The Example and Warning of American Finance

Samuel Leavitt

Our Money Wars
The Example and Warning of American Finance

ISBN/EAN: 9783744669580

Printed in Europe, USA, Canada, Australia, Japan

Cover: Foto ©Suzi / pixelio.de

More available books at **www.hansebooks.com**

OUR MONEY WARS

THE EXAMPLE AND WARNING OF AMERICAN FINANCE

BY

SAMUEL LEAVITT

AUTHOR OF "PEACEMAKER GRANGE," ETC.

BOSTON
ARENA PUBLISHING COMPANY
COPLEY SQUARE
1894

CONTENTS.

CHAPTER I.
1600 TO 1700.

CHAPTER II.
1700 TO 1776.

CHAPTER III.
1776 TO 1786.

CHAPTER IV.
1786 TO 1796.

CHAPTER V.

1796 to 1806.

CHAPTER VI.

1806 TO 1816.

CHAPTER VII.

1816 TO 1826.

CHAPTER VIII.

1826 TO 1836.

CHAPTER IX.

1836 TO 1846.

CHAPTER X.

1846 TO 1856.

CHAPTER XI.

1856 TO 1861.

CONTENTS.

CHAPTER XII.

1861 TO 1866.

WAR

CHAPTER XIII.

1866 TO 1873.

CONTRACTION.   ---

CHAPTER XIV.

1873 TO 1880.

SEVEN YEARS OF FAMINE IN A LAND OF PLENTY.

CHAPTER XV

1880 TO 1885.

THE TRIUMPH OF THE PLUTOCRATS.

CHAPTER XVI.

1885 TO 1893.

THE BEGINNING OF THE END.

OUR MONEY WARS.

CHAPTER I.

1600 to 1700.

THE FIRST AMERICAN MONEY.—Indian money or wampum was used in New England almost universally, as late as 1635. For a long time, the intercourse between the Indians and the colonists was more important, in an economic sense, than has commonly been supposed. The native was a producer, not only for himself, but, through his surplus, for the white settler. In his furs he furnished the chief staple of exchange with Europe. But he did more than this, he supplied corn and other food products to the colonists, he labored for the planters on the latters' farms—unsteadily, it is true, but such help as he was willing to give was indispensable. It is also to be noted that at the first, contact with the colonists benefited the Indian from an industrial point of view. A Sachem would sell a tract of land for a certain number of hoes, and, according to Governor Bradford, these iron implements, substituted for the wooden spade, or clam shell of the squaws, produced more corn on an acre, and yielded a surplus for sale. Thus the Narragansetts were enabled to sell from 500 to 1,000 bushels at a time.

But for the trade which soon opened up, a medium of exchange was needed; and the relative importance of the parties to the commercial transactions, is indicated by the fact that it was the money not of the colonists, but of the Indians, which became the common currency. The aborigines of New England had a true money in wampum.

This name was given to the white beads made from
the stems or inner whorls of a sea-shell found on all the
south coast of New England.   When strung they were
called *wampum-peage*, meaning strings of white beads.
Color was the basis of nomenclature, as well as of difference in value.   The black beads, which were called *Sacki*
and were made from the dark part of the common quahog,
or round clam shell, were generally worth twice as much
as the white.

What at first especially contributed to recommend wampum as a currency to the colonists, was the fact that it
was exchangeable, or, so to speak, redeemable in furs,
and above all, in the highly-prized skins of the beaver.
Wampum was the magnet which drew the beaver out of
interior forests, and sent it to Europe, thus starting the
revolving commerce between the New and the Old World.
In calculating wampum, the unit of measure was theoretically a string of beads a fathom long, but in practice
the length varied.   After 1643 a fathom was always
worth sixty pence; but as the colonists received beads
sometimes at four, and sometimes six a penny, the number of beads in a fathom would vary from 240 to 360.   We
refer, of course, to white beads; the black beads were rated
by colonial statutes at twice the value.   The strong hold
upon colonial life secured by wampum, is shown by a long
course of colonial legislation respecting it.   In 1641 Massachusetts made the shell beads a legal tender at six a penny
up to £10, a large sum in the transactions of that date.   Two
years later the legal tender limit was reduced to 40 shillings.
At that time wampum was a universal currency, exchangeable for merchandise, for labor and for taxes.   In 1641,
when the trade in wampum was farmed out in Massachusetts,
the lessees stipulated to redeem from Harvard College all the
accumulations of peage or string beads, in its treasury, under
£25.   By 1645 the inventories of deceased colonists commonly contained items of peage, and frequently there was
no other money.   Judgments of the courts were made payable in strings of beads.   It is interesting to learn that in
1648 a process analogous to coinage was applied to wampum in Massachusetts.   At President Dunster's suggestion
it was enacted that the beads should be strung in eight
different parcels; 1d., 3d., 12d., in white beads; 2d., 6d.,

2s. 6d., and 10s. in black. Taken together, these parcels formed a complete assortment of change or small coin.

About the date last mentioned, however, the circulation of wampum began to decline. In 1649, a Massachusetts statute prohibiting the receipt of beads for taxes—a statute which before had been inoperative, was re-enacted and enforced. There were several causes for the decline; for instance, labor had become better organized, and coin was more abundant among the colonists; but the main cause was the falling off in the supply of beavers. The colonists would have received the beads as readily in 1660 as 1640, if the same facility of redemption in beaver had existed; for the continued use of wampum as an accessory currency shows that it was convenient and desirable. In the remote districts of New England, wampum still circulated in the beginning of the eighteenth century. Madam Knight found wampum classed as currency on the southern shore of Connecticut in 1704. In 1693 the shell beads were recognized in the definite rates of the Brooklyn ferry.

In 1652 a mint was set up in Boston to coin silver into what was called "Pine Tree" money. Considerable silver was then coming from the West India trade—our rulers in England only busying themselves in stealing from us any good money we could get hold of. Singularly enough, we depended for coin, then, largely upon another class of pirates—the Buccaneers of the Spanish Main—who spent most of their plunder on our shores, where were the nearest civilized ports. This was a great blessing—"a blessed providence"—to our Puritan ancestors, and the gold-bug economists of that time.

Yet barter prevailed generally, on account of the scarcity of money. An act of 1654 provides that all contracts in kind shall be so satisfied.

In 1655, a constable brought cattle to the treasurer for taxes, which were so poor that the latter would not receive them.

In 1657, another constable prayed for relief because, having taken boards for taxes, the treasurer would not allow him as much as he allowed for them.

In 1658, it was ordered that no man should pay taxes in "lank" cattle.

"In fact the barter continued general," says Prof. Wm. G.

Sumner of Yale College, in his "History of American Currency." And yet this same learned pundit, who is one of those who never let conditions or facts bother them when "a theory is confronting them," says, in the first page of his first chapter: "Every community will have so much of the precious metals as it needs for its exchanges." This sublime British Bullion-Report dogma he calmly maintains throughout his book.

THE FIRST BANK-NOTES.—It will not seem surprising that money was scarce, at this period, when we consider that it was about 1660 when the first regular bank-note was printed by Palmstruck of Sweden. He met the usual fate of great inventors, and reformers. He became so unpopular, that he got into difficulties; and was finally obliged to leave his country. But soon afterward, the Government of Sweden decided that, after all, the bank-note was not such a very bad thing. So they took possession of the bank which Palmstruck had abandoned; and that bank, to-day, is the great central bank of Sweden.

THE BRITISH DEBT.—Foreign facts that have a special bearing upon American finance will be presented here in chronological order. For instance, we are informed by Hume, the historian, that the British public debt had reached only the small sum of £1,054,925 on March 20, 1689. But the rulers found making public debts "a great scheme"; and by 1697 the French war had raised the debt to £50,-000,000. The French war, before our Revolution, raised it to £140,000,000; our Revolution to £240,000,000, and the Napoleonic war to £800,000,000, in 1815, where it has stuck ever since.

FIRST AMERICAN PAPER MONEY.—In 1690 the first issue of paper money was made by Massachusetts. This was the year before the establishment of the Bank of England. An expedition had been sent out against the French in Canada; and returning without the hoped-for plunder, and in a state of misery, the soldiers were clamorous for their pay. So £7,000 were issued, in notes from 5 shillings to £5. The form of these notes or bills was as follows: "This indentured bill, of ten shillings, due from the Massachusetts colony to the possessor shall be in value equal to money; and shall be accordingly accepted by the treasurer and receivers subordinate to him, in all public payments, for any stock at any time in the Treasury." They circulated at par with coin for 20 years until redeemed.

The "Century Magazine," in 1891, is printing a lot of false statements about money to tickle its monopoly readers. Here is what the "Twentieth Century," said about one of its screeds.—In "Topics of the Time" we are treated to a review of the "Century's" own tirades against "cheap money." The land bank of 1696 failed. The land bank of Rhode Island failed. John Law's bank failed. The notes of the Argentine republic failed. *Argal*, all cheap money schemes must fail. The series is liable to several criticisms. *Imprimis*, it does not embody half the cheap money experiments which have been made. The "Century" is aware of this, and though it says it has not noticed numerous criticisms because they were answered in subsequent papers, threatens a fresh series to fill up the voids. The statement, quoted this month from the Buenos Ayres "Standard," that John Law lived to see his error, is false. But, passing over these minor points—the land bank of 1696 failed—that is, it never came into working existence, not as the "Century" man says, because the capitalists, those gods of the bourgeois idolatry, would not buy the stock of an institution avowedly intended to break them down, but because the rate at which it could lend was arbitrarily fixed at 3 ½ per cent., while the current rate was 6 per cent., an arrangement which could only have been intended to defeat the scheme (Macaulay "History of England," vol. iv., pp. 553, 560, Boston edition, 1856). John Law's bank did not fail until the Mississippi scheme was added to it. That there ever was a Mississippi scheme was due to the plethora of capital seeking investment, which in turn was due to Law's success.

CHAPTER II.

1700 to 1776.

MORE PAPER MONEY.—In 1703, South Carolina began to issue paper money. In that year, also, Massachusetts made a second issue of £15,000; which was made a legal tender for private debts.

In 1716, another issue to the amount of £150,000 was authorized to be distributed among the different counties of the province; and to be put into the hands of five trustees in each county, to be appointed by the Legislature : *to be let out on real estate security in the county*, in specific sums, for the space of ten years, at five per cent. per annum. Another act for £50,000 in bills was passed in 1720, which resulted in *clearing Massachusetts of debt* in 1773; though the currency was usually much below par in coin.

In 1709, Connecticut began to issue bills. We must here diverge to get some facts from Europe.

THE TRUTH ABOUT JOHN LAW.—In answer to questions, I printed in the *Chicago Express*, in August, 1891, the following : "The History of John Law. Law, a Scotchman, Was King of French Finance for Many Years. Made Mistakes, but Was ' a Financier Without a Parallel.' "

We are asked about John Law, the noted financier, and reply: He was born in Scotland in 1671. His father was a goldsmith and banker. The son was a brilliant scholar with a great head for finance. After some years spent in travel he returned home. A book printed in Scotland in 1701 called, "Proposals and Reasons for Constituting a Council of Trade in Scotland," was reprinted in his name in 1751; but that book, though right in his line of work, was evidently written by Wm. Paterson, founder of the Bank of England. It suggested a central board to manage great commercial undertakings like the East India Company, that flourished so long in India, and to furnish occupation for the poor, to encourage mining, fishing and manufactures, and to bring about a reduction in the rate of interest. It is plain that from this book Law got the first hint of the ideas that he afterward carried out in Mississippi and France.

In 1715, Law went to France, when the Duke of Orleans, with whom he was a favorite, became Regent. The late monarch had run up the public debt to three milliard (three thousand million) livres, and national bankruptcy was talked of. A squeeze of creditors reduced the debt one-half. Then, in the old style of inflation, practiced by kings, the coin was called in and re-issued at the rate of 120 for 100. This was a great boon to foreign coiners. The notes issued on this basis at once sank 75 per cent. below their nominal value.

It was when French affairs were in this wretched state that Law proposed one of his vast schemes to the Regent. The latter let him try a part of it. By an edict of May 2, 1716, a private bank called the General Bank was founded, with Law for manager. The capital was six million livres, divided into 1200 shares of 5,000 livres each, payable in four installments, one-fourth in cash, three-fourths in the " billets d'état," the national notes, that were at such discount. It was to perform the usual work of a bank, and could issue notes payable at sight ; in the weight and value of the money mentioned at the day of issue.

The bank was a great and immediate success. By providing for the absorption of part of the state paper it raised to some extent the credit of the Government. The notes were a most desirable medium of exchange, for they had the element of fixity of value, which was, owing to the arbitrary mint decrees of the Government, wanting in the coin of the realm. They were also found the most convenient instruments of remittance between the capital and the provinces, and they thus developed and increased the industries of the latter. The rate of interest, previously enormous and uncertain, fell first to 6 and then to 4 per cent. ; and when another decree (April 10, 1717) ordered collectors of taxes to receive notes as payment (like our Demand Notes) and to change them for coin at request, the bank so rose in favor that it had soon an issue of 60 million livres. Law now gained the full confidence of the Regent, and was allowed to proceed with the development of the " system."

Remember in reading what follows that this was near 200

years ago, when experiments in finance were more fantastic, numerous and dangerous than those with the steam engine.

The trade of the French possessions in Louisiana, etc., all called Mississippi, had been granted to a speculator named Crozat. He found the undertaking too large and was glad to give it up. Law was allowed to establish the "West Indies Company," and endow it with privileges amounting to sovereignty. The capital was 100 million livres, divided into 200,000 shares of 500 livres. The payments were to be one-fourth in coin, and three-fourths in National notes. On these last the Government was to pay 3 million livres interest yearly to the company. As the state paper was depreciated the shares fell much below par. The rapid rise of Law had made him many enemies, and they took advantage of this to attack the system. D'Argenson, the former chief of police, and head of the Council of Finance, with the brothers Paris of Grenoble, famous tax farmers of the day, formed what was called the "Anti-System." The farming of the taxes was let to them, under an assumed name, for 48 1-2 million livres a year.

That was a worse state of things than we have here now. If Law had been as wise as Solon, but without Solon's dictator power, he could not have straightened French finance.

The Anti-Law party formed a company the exact counterpart of the Mississippi Company. The payments were to be entirely in money. The returns from the public revenue obtained by these tax farmers were sure; those from the Mississippi scheme were not. Hence the shares of the latter were for some time out of favor. Law proceeded unmoved with the development of his plans. December 4, 1718, the bank became a Government institution called The Royal Bank. Law was manager and the king guaranteed the notes. The shareholders were repaid in coin, and to widen the influence of the new institution, the transport of money between towns where it had branches was forbidden.

It thus appears that Law was the founder of the Bank of France, which has kept up in various forms until now. He is generally depicted by bullionists as an addlepated inflationist, bringing ruin and destruction by all his schemes. He certainly made many mistakes and saw many things wrong. But here is what the sober old Cyclopedia Britannica says about him : "Notwithstanding the faults of his system, it cannot be denied that its author was a financial genius of the first order. He had the errors of his time; but his writings show that he first propounded many truths as to the nature of currency and banking then unknown to his contemporaries. The marvelous skill which he displayed in adapting the theory of the system to the actual condition of things in France, and in carrying out the various financial transactions rendered necessary by its development is *absolutely without parallel.*"

Before continuing his story we will give briefly what his system was as described in his " Money and Trade Considered." He thoroughly appreciated the need of an abundance of money, though he bungled about getting it. He was too much like our bankers in fondness for credit money. He said that " credit if it have a circulation has all the beneficial effects of money. To create and increase instruments of credit is the function of a bank." If he had strictly followed his next rule he would have done better : " Let such be created then, and let its notes be only given in return for land sold as pledged." He was, as will be shown, swept away by a tide of speculators and politicians, and could not do this.

He dimly saw the need of a Government currency, and partly succeeded in getting it. But he could do nothing moderately. Like the Bellamyites of to day, seeing the evil of private monopolies and the farming of the taxes, he proposed to unite foreign trade and internal finance in one huge monopoly managed by the state for the people.

Now for the rest of his story, ending in a grand smash.

We left him in 1718 with the king guaranteeing his bank-notes. The paper issue now reached 110 millions. Then he agreed to take Mississippi shares at par at a near date. The shares rose. The next move was to merge the " Oriental India " and the " China " companies, founded respectively in 1664 and 1713, with his new one into " The Company of the Indies." The fact that those companies had been running so long though feebly, shows that this " South Sea Bubble " was not formed of such ephemeral material as generally supposed. But the French have no genius for ruling colonies. They have not the iron grip of John Bull, that made a success of the East India Company financially, by grinding the Hindoos to death.

For the amalgamated company 25 million livres capital was issued. The payment was spread over twenty months. It required four of the old shares and a premium of 50 livres to obtain a new one. All these 500 livre shares rose rapidly to 750.

Law now tried to get new powers. July 25, 1719, an edict gave the company control of the mint for 9 years for 5 million livres. For this, new 500 livre shares were issued with a premium of 500. Five of the old shares went for one of these; 12 per cent. per annum dividends were promised on these.

Again Law's enemies tried to ruin him by a run for coin. But now, having kingly power, he ordered a reduction in the value of coins at a given date. This brought the coin back on the run. August 27, 1719, brought an edict giving his company the farming of the revenues for 9 years for 52 million livres. His enemies lost it. This floored them. Law now tackled the national debt of 1500 million livres. He issued notes to that amount. The creditors were paid in a certain order. The company issued shares to correspond, and as these were the chief investment available the creditors bought them with the notes as fast as they were paid. Government paid 3 per cent. on the loan shares. It had before to pay 80 millions on the debt per annum. It was now 50 millions. The shares were so eagerly taken that often others got them when Government creditors could not. October 2 the shares sold at 8,000 livres on the Bourse.

Law had now more than regal power. The exiled Stuarts paid court to him. The proudest European aristocracy humbled themselves before him. Our Nick Biddle, 100 years later, "was not a patch to him." He was made controller general of the finances; and the Bank was united in name as well as in reality with the Company.

Dec. 1719, was high-water. The 500 livres shares had reached 20,000 livres. But then decay began. The same madness of speculation that prevailed in England at that time seized France. Men rushed to Paris to speculate.

Then some began to think. The market value of the shares was 12 milliards. 500 million revenue was needed for an annual 5 per cent. on this. The company could only pay 5 per cent. on 1 milliard, 677 million the original capital. The commercial undertakings had only begun to pay. Much time would be needed for an East India Co. success; the French were " not in it " when colony squeezing was called for.

People began to sell the shares and buy coin, houses, land, anything stable. Law knew what was needed—general scaling down, as had been done with the debt. But he dare not do it. He issued violent edicts. The notes must be at a premium over coin. Big premiums were promised. It was useless. Coin fled the country. Prices rose. Distress prevailed. Law lost his influence. His enemy stampeded him, and demolished his system. A vast number of the shares found in the bank were destroyed. The notes were reconverted into Government debt. The " system " had disappeared with French haste by November, 1720.*

Law left France in Dec., 1720, poor as he came. He had never grasped at private wealth. Montesquieu pathetically describes him as he found him in Venice, still planning commercial prosperity for France. He died there March 21, 1729.

It will be seen from the above that Law was the founder of the Bank of France. But observe in the following the timidity of an authority usually so good as Appleton's Cyclopedia, in making no mention of the fallen hero. It says :

" In 1716 a bank was founded in Paris under this name—which was, two years later, changed to the Royal Bank, Under this organization, it remained until 1803 ; when, having been unsuccessful, it was placed upon its present organization as the Bank of France, with a capital of 45,000,000 francs, which was, in 1806, increased to 90,000,000 francs. At present the capital is 182,500,000 francs, and the charter of the bank extends to Dec. 31, 1897. It is a bank of deposit, discount, and circulation ; issuing its own notes, and having an exclusive monopoly of this privilege for the whole country. It is, in one sense, a Government institution, the Government appointing a governor and two deputy governors—all of whom must be stockholders in the bank.

" The affairs of the institution are managed by a council-

---

* Sometimes a few lines of inside history are worth whole books of that usually printed. There is nothing more certain than that a chief reason why Law could not save his system was found in the fact that the king's mistresses had invested heavily in the " shares," and absolutely stopped him from scaling them down as he knew should be done.

general of 20 members, who are elected by 200 of the
principal stockholders. No bills are discounted having more
than three months to run; and, as a general thing, they
must be guaranteed by three approved signatures, though in
some instances two are accepted. The Governor makes an
annual report. The annual dividends are limited to five per
cent; all profits over that amount being invested in five per
cent. consolidated stock; to be divided among the stockholders at the expiration of the charter. In 1848, all the
banks in other great cities were consolidated with it; and it
now has 62 branches."

The three following items show that our Judge Warwick
Martin, from whom they were taken, did not know that he
was speaking of the work of his great fellow-worker John Law.

THE BANK OF FRANCE.—In 1720, the notes of the Royal
Bank of France were at a premium over coin of 50 per cent.
At the time the bank was established the notes were made
payable in coin of the standard fineness of the French Government of that period. But the Government added 50 per
cent. to the alloy, in their coins, in the good old style of
inflation, and reduced the fineness to that extent; while
the notes of the bank continued to be paid in the fine coin
called for in the notes. Until the edict of the Government
compelled the bank—a private corporation—to pay in current
coin, the notes were worth 50 per cent. over the coin of the
nation.

SPECULATIONS IN FRANCE IN 1720.—The suspension of the
Royal Bank of France in 1720 was caused by speculations
of the most gigantic character, both in the Eastern and
Western hemispheres. Money was furnished by this bank
to purchase the companies of the East and of the West, the
Senegal Company and the Company of the Indies. The
parties purchasing these companies engaged in all kinds of
speculation, with the intention of controlling the business of
the world. When the bank made loans and advances to
these speculators, it was not only in profession but in reality
a specie-paying bank. The bank was compelled to suspend
specie payments; but let it not be forgotten that all the
money to engage in and sustain these speculations was advanced by the bank before suspension, *not after*. When the
bank suspended the speculators and the speculations failed.
The suspended bank did not aid them.

SPECULATIONS IN ENGLAND IN 1720, OR ABOUT THAT TIME.
—These speculations equaled those of France. More than
two hundred speculative companies were gotten up and put
into operation in England alone. Large premiums were
paid for the privilege of subscribing to the stock of many of
these companies, so great was the speculative prospects of
large fortunes therefrom. The people were deranged by the
immediate prospects of immense gains. But let it be remembered that the money by which these grand schemes were
carried on was not suspended bank-notes or irredeemable
paper money of a nation, or irredeemable paper of any kind.
The notes and credits of the Bank of England, which bank
then professed to pay coin for all liabilities, did the work.
The bank was ultimately compelled to suspend ; but the
money to conduct these speculations was furnished while the
bank professed to pay coin.

PAPER IN THE COLONIES.—In 1720, bills were issued by
the colony of Rhode Island, and were made legal tender for
all debts.

In 1723, Pennsylvania began to issue money.

In this year, a great crisis occurred in England. The bank
was suspended. The coin of the American colonies was
required, and drawn over, in England's peremptory fashion
—to prepare the bank for resumption. All coin left Pennsylvania ; though the State passed laws raising its value.
Then the State issued treasury notes, and kept them in use
until 1773. when Parliament finally made all such issues void
(after prohibiting them in 1751). The money was made legal
tender. It was redeemed by the payment of taxes, without
loss to any one. This is the familiar history of Pennsylvania, and the statement of Franklin.

Benjamin Franklin, on p. 185 of his autobiography, said :
" I remember well that when I first walked about the streets
of Philadelphia, eating my roll, I saw most of the houses of
Walnut Street, between Second and Front Streets, with bills
on their doors To Let, and many likewise on Chestnut Street ;
which made me think that the inhabitants of the city were
deserting it one after another. Our junta debates possessed
me so fully of the subject that I wrote and printed an anony-
mous pamphlet on ' The Nature and Necessity of a Paper
Currency.' It was well received by the common people in
general ; but the rich men disliked it, for it increased as well

as strengthened the clamor for more money; and they happened to have no writer among them that was able to answer it. Their opposition slackened, and the point was carried by a majority in the House. The utility of this currency became, by experience, so evident as never to be much disputed; so that it grew soon to be £55,000, and in 1779 to £80,000, since which it rose to £350,000—trade, buildings, and inhabitants all the while increasing." Again he said, in 1764, when in England, that the paper money of New York, New Jersey, and Pennsylvania was "a chief cause of their great increase in settlements, numbers, buildings, improvements, agriculture, shipping, and commerce."

Maryland began to issue money in 1733.

Delaware began in 1739.

Virginia began in 1755—though England prohibited such issues in 1751.

Dr. Franklin visited England, and protested against the act, that was caused by the English jealousy of the prosperity and growing independence of the colonies. Franklin stated to the British authorities, that before the issue of colonial money, the colonies were stripped of gold and silver. That there were great difficulties for want of money, as trade had to be carried on by the extremely inconvenient method of barter. But that the introduction of colonial money had given new life to business, and promoted greatly the settlement and development of the country. Whereby the provinces had greatly increased in inhabitants, and their exports had been increased tenfold. This Parliamentary prohibition, more than anything else, led to the discontent which resulted in the Revolution.

The people of Massachusetts made a desperate effort to get currency by establishing a Land Bank about 1740. Sumner of Yale shows what a Tory he would have been, had he lived then, by this talk about it: "The Governor made war on this bank, with all his energy, as unlawful and pernicious, contrary to the act of Parliament and to his instructions. Finding that some civil and military officers were engaged in it, he removed them. This called forth a protest from Samuel Adams and John Choate, as an invasion of personal liberty. There can be no doubt that the bitterness engendered by this conflict was one great cause of the Revolution. Two great economic errors were amongst the causes of that war. One, the attempt of the colonies to issue paper, in which they were in error as to the question of political expediency'; the other, the attempt by England to carry out the 'colonial system,'" etc., etc.

So we see Sumner *versus* the Revolutionary Fathers. He makes the same objection to Continental money, though he gives no shadow of a method by which they could have fought the war without paper money. It would be in the style of this extraordinary person to say : " They should not have rebelled if they could not do it without paper money."

Governor Shirley, of Massachusetts, now took it in his head to capture Louisburg, on Cape Breton ; which, by help of other colonies, and a succession of strange and lucky accidents, was accomplished, June 28, 1745. There was much plunder and glory. Yet the chief good was the excuse for a quantity of paper money. But to the delight of Sage Sumner of Yale, Parliament was so tickled by this bit of honest industry, that it resolved to ransom Louisburg from the colonies with hard silver and copper. Here was a case where Sumner's justly celebrated "laws of nature" provided Massachusetts with " just the coin it needed." But the Boston Puritan Fathers got so large a share of the buccaneering plunder, that the other colonies were out in the cold. Massachusetts called in its "paper promises to pay," and went proudly on to a " sound honest money basis." Miss Bay State turned up her nose at the other colonies—obscured them in passing, with her gorgeous silvery parasol ; and never spoke as she passed them by, as they lay floundering " in the soup." Sumner— usually so sour over all financial affairs but those of England —is, for once, radiantly happy over this conservative policy. Being a thorough Calvinist, he believes that the ruin it wrought on the other colonies "served them right." He thus briefly disposes of them :

"The only 'shock' was to Rhode Island and New Hampshire, who found their trade transferred to the 'silver colony,' and their paper heavily and suddenly depreciated."

> " But things like that, you know, must be
> In every glorious victory ! "

The West India trade of Massachusetts had been largely done through Newport. It was now transferred to Salem and Boston. "None but the brave deserve the fair !" Selah !

Much general sudden bankruptcy ensued, on account of this glorious providential "resumption :" but Sumner—with that tender mercy of a Torquemada for which he is noted—coolly remarks, in opposition to those who recommended a slower process: "A bankruptcy could not be too sharply and definitely accomplished when resolved upon."

In 1764, before the Stamp Act was proposed in Parliament (which was passed the next year, and repealed the year following), Dr. Franklin, writing in England in defense of the paper money of the colonies, says : "*On the whole, no method has, hitherto, been framed to establish a medium of trade in lieu of money, equal, in all its advantages, to bills of credit, founded on sufficient taxes for discharging them, or land securities of double the value for repaying them at the end of the term, and in the mean time made a general legal tender.* The experience of now nearly half a century in the middle colonies (New York, New Jersey, and Pennsylvania) has convinced them of it among themselves, by the great increase of their settlements, numbers, buildings, improvements, agriculture, shipping, and commerce. And the same experience has satisfied the British merchants who trade thither, that it has been greatly useful to them, and not in a single instance prejudicial."

In 1764, the British Board of Trade objected to the use of legal-tender paper money in the colonies (doubtless because it rendered the people of the colonies independent of the money power of Great Britain), on the ground that "every medium of exchange should have an intrinsic value; which paper money had not." Dr. Franklin replied : "However fit a particular thing may be for a particular purpose, whenever that thing is not to be had, or not to be had in sufficient quantity, it becomes necessary to use something else,—the fittest that can be got,—in lieu of it. * * * Bank bills and bankers' notes are daily used here [England] as a medium of trade; and, in large dealings, perhaps, the greater part is transacted by their means. And yet they have no intrinsic value; but rest on the credit of those that issued them,—as paper bills in the colonies do on the respective settlements there. These (bank bills) being payable in cash, upon sight, by the drawer is, indeed, a circumstance that cannot attend the colony bills ; for the reason just above mentioned,—their cash (bullion) being drawn from them by the British trade. But the legal tender being substituted in its place, is rather a greater advantage to the possessor; since he need not be at the trouble of going to a particular bank or banker, to demand the money.

" At this time, even the silver money in England is obliged to the legal tender for a part of its value; that part which is the difference between its real weight and its denomination. Great part of the shillings and sixpences now current are, by wearing, become five, ten, twenty, and some of the sixpences, even fifty per cent. too light. For this difference between the real and the nominal, you have no intrinsic value. You have not so much as paper: you have nothing. It is the legal tender,—with the knowledge that it can easily be re-passed *for the same value,*—that makes three pennyworth of silver pass for sixpence." *Franklin's Works:* Duane's edition, vol. iv., 1809.

Another extract from Franklin's works gives this version of the colonial money :—

" The Assembly of Pennsylvania, by an act passed in 1739, authorized the issue of paper money to the amount of eighty thousand pounds sterling ($400,000). This was to be emitted to the several borrowers from a loan office, established for that purpose. Five persons were nominated trustees of the loan office, under whose care and direction the bills or notes were to be emitted.

" They were to lend out the bills on real security of at least double the value for a term of sixteen years, to be paid with interest. One-sixteenth part of the principal was yearly paid back into the office, which made the payment easier to the borrower. The interest was applied to public services; the principal during the first ten years let out again to fresh borrowers.

" The borrowers, from year to year, were to have the money only for the remaining part of the term of sixteen years, re-paying by fewer, and of course, proportionately large install-ments, and during the last six years of the sixteen the sums paid in were not emitted, but the notes burnt and destroyed, so that at the end of sixteen years the whole might be called in and burnt, and the accounts completely settled.

" Lest a few wealthy persons should engross all the money, which was intended for more general benefit, no one person,

2

whatever security he might offer, could borrow more than one hundred pounds.

" Thus numbers of poor settlers were accommodated and assisted with money to carry on their settlements, to be repaid in easy yearly payments, as the yearly products of their lands should enable them."

It bore no promise of redemption in coin, but a pledge that it should be received for all dues. It rested wholly upon the credit of the commonwealth, the taxpayers and producers, and it was loaned to the extent of the demand, upon " land and plate."

It passed through no banker's hands, but was loaned to the people direct, thus saving banking toll, and banking restriction of volume ; nor are there any panics or fluctuations recorded.

Thomas Powell, M.P., of England, who had acted as governor and commander-in-chief of all provinces, in a book written by him in 1768, says in regard to this colonial system of money :

" I will venture to say that there never was a wiser or better measure, never one better calculated to serve the uses of an increasing country, and never was a measure more steadily pursued or more faithfully executed for forty years together than the loan office in Pennsylvania, formed and administered by the assembly of that province.

" In a country under such circumstances money lent upon interest to settlers creates money. Paper money thus lent upon interest will create gold and silver principal, while the interest becomes a revenue that pays the charges of the government. This currency is the true Pactolean stream which converts all into gold that is washed by it."

As a result of this system, Dr. Franklin says : " Between the years 1740 and 1775, while abundance reigned in Pennsylvania and there was peace in all her borders, a more happy and prosperous population could not perhaps be found on this globe. In every home there was comfort. The people generally were highly moral, and knowledge was extensively diffused."

Franklin, in vol. 4, p. 85, of his works, says : " Gold and silver are not intrinsically of equal value with iron. Their value rests chiefly on the estimation they happen to be in among the generality of nations. Any other well-founded credit is as much an equivalent as gold and silver. Paper money, well-founded, has great advantages over gold and silver; being light and convenient for handling large sums, and *not likely to have its volume reduced by demands for exportation.*"

David Hume, the historian, says in substance : " In Pennsylvania the land itself is coined. A planter, immediately he purchases land, can go to a public office, and receive notes to the amount of half his land, which notes he employs in all payments : and they circulate through the colony by convention. No more than a certain sum is issued to one planter ; and each must pay back into the public treasury, every year, one tenth of his notes. When they are all paid back, he can repeat the operation." This brought a pros-.perity that Burke said was "unparalleled."

In an evil hour, the British Government took away from America its "representative money ;" commanded that "no more paper bills of credit should be issued ; and that they should cease to be a legal tender ;" and collected the taxes in hard silver. This was in 1773. The contracting of the circulating medium paralyzed all the industrial energies of the people. Ruin seized upon these once flourishing colonies ; the most severe distress was brought home to every interest and every family; discontent was urged on to desperation ; till, at last, "human nature," as Dr. Johnson phrases it, "arose and asserted its rights."

THE MONEY OF THE POOR.—In 1775 the Parliament of Great Britain passed an act providing that "all promissory or other notes, bills of exchange or drafts or undertakings in writing, being negotiable or transferable, for the payment of any sum or sums of money less than the sum of 20 shillings in the whole * * shall be and the same are hereby declared to be absolutely void and of no effect." Two years after, this was followed by an act extending these provisions to all sums under five pounds. To us, at the present time, this appears to be an act of flagrant tyranny, upon the part of the strong against the weak. Why may not a poor man give his note for 19 shillings or for four pounds, as well as the rich for larger sums.

CONTINENTAL MONEY.—The act of June 25, 1775, was passed more than one year before independence was declared. It authorized the issue of $2,000,000 of notes, which read as follows : "This note entitles the bearer to receive —— Spanish mill dollars, or the value thereof in gold or silver, according to the resolution of Congress of the 10th of May, 1775."

We need not say that this was neither money nor a promise to pay money emanating from any individual State or nation. The note authorized the party holding it to receive therefor Spanish mill dollars, or their equivalent in gold or silver ; but it did not obligate any person, State or nation, to pay said dollars, or other coin.

We point out the defects in this money, and show the causes of its depreciation in the following manner :—

1. The States were contending with the greatest nation on earth. Her armies had generally been victorious on land. She was conceded to be the mistress of the seas. The States were poorly prepared for war with such a power. They had no army, no navy, no fortifications, no arms, no ammunition, no credit, no money. The odds were immensely against them, viewed from a military standpoint. The contest was not only doubtful, but from any standpoint, excepting justice and right, was overwhelmingly in favor of Great Britain. Under these circumstances it would have been difficult to maintain a State paper circulation at par, had Congress adopted the best method of doing it. But with the means adopted, it is astonishing that any success attended their efforts to keep the Government circulation at par.

2. At the time $6,000,000 of this money were issued independence had not been declared. The States were still colonies, and the people and Congress subjects of Great Britain, styling themselves in their communications to the throne, "Your Majesty's most faithful subjects." They were engaged in petitioning for and demanding their rights as " British subjects." They were also preparing to defend their rights and maintain them if denied to them by the mother country. To raise and equip an army for that purpose was at first their only object in issuing these bills of credit. At that time the United States were not a nation. The power delegated to Congress by the States extended only to soliciting and demanding a restoration of rights, and to prepare for war, if need be. Congress were little else than an advisory counsel to the States. They possessed no power to impose and collect taxes or duties, and did not attempt it. They enacted that the States should impose taxes

and collect them; but the States could comply with the wishes of Congress in this behalf, or neglect to do so, and some of them did the latter.

3. The bills of credit emitted by Congress were not made legal tender in payment of private debts, and were not made receivable for debts due Congress or the colonies. Congress had no debts due them. They collected no duties on imports or internal revenue. These impositions and collections were confined to the States. To Congress it was all outgo and no income. They made their own money, and paid it out to equip and sustain the army and to support a limited civil service. There was but one means through which the money issued and paid out by the Continental treasurer could get back into his hands. Of this we shall speak hereafter.

. 4. Previous to 1779 the faith of the States, as expressed by Congress, was pledged for the redemption of the bills emitted; but the faith of Congress, or of a national Government of any kind, was not pledged. The law did not, at any time, read that Congress would pay, or that the treasurer would pay, but that the States as individuals, not collectively, would pay. Everybody knew that the duty of paying or redeeming the bills devolved upon the States in their individual capacity. not upon Congress or a nation. Each State was bound only for its portion. The debt was divided among the States according to population. This fact, at the beginning of 1779, or thereabout, was extensively circulated among the people, to the prejudice of Congress, and to the depreciation of the bills. Congress noticed the charge, and pledged the faith of the United States for the redemption of the bills, and soon after commenced giving certificates of indebtedness bearing interest for them.

5. But another most fatal mistake in the issue of this money was in making it payable not only in coin, but in that which was at a premium over other coin. It should not have been redeemable in coin of any kind; it should have been made legal tender—lawful money. The States had only about $5,000,000 of coin all told. It was impossible to make the redemption in coin, and no such promise should have been given. If no coin had been promised in the law or in the notes, no one would have expected coin, and it would not have been demanded. But the law expressly promised coin. When the people presented the notes at the treasury

of a State, or that of Congress, and demanded the fulfill-
ment of the promise, and learned that the coin could not be
paid, the credit of the notes was injured ; though the people
stood the disappointment, and continued to receive and pay
the money until another injurious circumstance occurred.

6. Very unwisely, the Continental money was not made as
though intended to circulate as money. For the purpose of
giving it credit above other notes, it was made payable in
coin, which was at a premium. The failure to pay coin for
it, as promised, reduced it somewhat in value ; and the failure
of the States to redeem it, as provided by law, reduced it still
lower. The extension of time in which the States were to
redeem the notes, from four years after 1779 to nineteen
years after that time, had a still greater depressing effect.

7. The fact that the printing of the notes was, of necessity,
poorly done, caused them to be counterfeited in large quantities ; so that few persons could know the good notes from
the counterfeits. The people feared to receive them. This
counterfeiting was a trick of the enemy to destroy the money.

8. At the time these notes began to depreciate it was the
darkest in the Revolution. Our armies had not been successful in battle. The British had been reinforced. The
contest, with men of weak faith, was doubtful. The people
did not need to be told that if the cause failed the money
would be worthless. The cause of the colonies depended
upon sustaining the money of the colonies. Great Britain
knew this ; and for the purpose of destroying the Revolution,
the armies of the Crown, with the aid of British gold and
silver, and their allies, the Tories, used all their powers to
cut off from the colonies the sinews of war, and thus to destroy the American cause. Much of the depreciation of the
bills of credit was owing to these efforts.

9. Had this money been both issued and redeemable by the
nation or Government ; had the Government possessed the
power to impose duties on imports and internal taxes, and to
collect them ; had the bills been made, by the act creating them,
legal tender in payment of all private debts and receivable for
debts due the nation and individuals, with power in the general
Government to make its authority respected ; had nothing
been said in the law or in the notes about paying in specie, as
was done on the issue of our Treasury notes ; and no provision
been made for the States to redeem them in coin, which

they failed to do, not more than $50,000,000 need to have been issued. The money paid out would have returned to the Treasury for taxes and duties, and could have been repaid out. This would have obviated the necessity of issuing three-fourths of the bills issued, and kept those out at par, or nearly so, with coin. But whether par with coin or not, they would have been a sure, sound, and safe circulation, with which the loyal people would have been satisfied. Had these bills from the beginning been convertible into three, four, or five per cent. interest-bearing certificates or bonds, at the will of the holder, and reconvertible into bills, when desired, this, with their reception for all debts due the nation and people, would have insured their good standing among the people, and made them a first-class currency.

CHAPTER III.

1776 to 1786.

CONTINENTAL MONEY (CONTINUED).—That great financier, Albert Gallatin, said : "The Continental money carried the United States through the most arduous and perilous stages of the war, and * * * it cannot be denied that it saved the country."

JEFFERSON TO EPPS, 1813.—"In the Revolutionary War, the old Congress and the United States issued bills without interest and without tax. They occupied the channels of circulation very freely; until those channels were overflowed by an excess beyond the calls of circulation. But although we have so improvidently suffered the field of circulating medium to be filched from us by private individuals ; yet I think we may recover it, in part, and even in the whole, if the States will co-operate with us * * * It is not easy to estimate the obstacles which, in the beginning, we should encounter, in ousting the banks from the possession of circulation."

Again Jefferson said : "Continental money expired without a single groan. Not a murmur was heard among the people. On the contrary, universal congratulations took place on their seeing the gigantic mass,—whose dissolution had threatened convulsions which should shake their infant confederacy to its centre,—quietly interred in its grave. Foreigners, indeed, who do not like the natives, feel indulgence for its memory,—as of a being which has vindicated their liberties, and fallen in the moment of victory,—have been loud, and still are loud, in their complaints. A few of them have reason ; but the most noisy are not the best of them. They are persons who have become bankrupt by unskillful attempts at commerce with America. That they may have some pretext to offer to their creditors, they have bought up great masses of this dead money of America,—where it is to be had at $5,000 for one ; and they show the certificates of their paper possessions as if they had died in their hands; and had been the cause of their bankruptcy."

Calhoun said: "Continental money is the ghost conjured up by all who wish to give the banks an exclusive monopoly of Government credit."

Birkey said in his "Money Question": "It is worthy of note that Continental bills were not issued in the form of paper money; such as was first introduced in Massachusetts, and subsequently adopted by many of the other colonies; but in the form of promises to pay specie, at certain specified times, which, under the circumstances, was a manifest impossibility. The gradual depreciation of Continental money, as it passed from hand to hand, inflicted a loss upon each successive holder; which cAme to be regarded in the nature of a tax, or *contribution toward the cause of independence*. The large sums held by individuals, after it ceased to circulate, were taken at its greatest depreciation; and no great loss was sustained. When, after it had seen the liberties of the people vindicated it sank, in the moment of victory, quietly into its grave, no commercial crash or money panic attended its fall."

Some wise man said, in 1878: "The Continental money was lost but once—by depreciation. The funded Greenbacks and other currency are lost once in every eleven years, in payment of interest on the bonds."

Judge Warwick Martin says:—

"Before we can fully understand and appreciate what the States did surrender to the Federal Government, we must know what powers they possessed previous to the adoption of the Constitution, and what they did relating to money. All the powers which they had relating to war, peace, duties on imports, coining money of gold and silver, or copper, or emitting bills of credit, and making them legal tender, they yielded up to Congress. Now, what did they possess and use? The history of the States and the journal of the Continental Congress show plainly that these States coined money of gold, silver, and copper, and regulated its value. They also regulated by law the value of foreign coins. They emitted their own Treasury notes or bills of credit, and made them legal tender in payment of all debts due the States and individuals therein. In entering the General Government as States, they renounced all these rights and privileges, and transferred them to the Federal Government,

which was created by and for the benefit of all the States.
It is, therefore, preposterous to suppose that the Federal
Government possesses less power relating to money than was
possessed by the States in their independent capacity. Yet
the theory that the United States are prohibited from doing
what each one of the States could do, and did, involves this
absurdity.

"For the benefit of those who may not believe that the
States did issue legal tender paper money before and during
the Revolution, we state that the Continental Congress, before and after the adoption of the Articles of Confederation,
did not issue, or pretend to issue, money of any kind. They
did issue what they called bills of credit : but they possessed
no power to make these bills legal tender, or to issue coin of
any kind. They saw the necessity of having their bills made
legal tender, to prevent their depreciation ; but they did not
possess the power to make them such. In 1778, when the
notes began to depreciate, Congress called upon the States
to make them legal tender, as they had done their own bills."

This was neglected. And, also, Franklin's proposition to
fund them.

Finally, as to Continental money, even "that inexpressible
specter," Prof. Sumner of Yale, has to admit that " on account
of the peculiar character of American society, there are few
family traditions of the Continental currency."

That is, none but the traitors of the period howled about it.

Again, as to this question of the authority given by Congress, Martin says : "No less than seven materials have
been used by Congress, in making money for the people ;
only two of which (gold and silver) are named in the Constitution. The other five are : copper, tin, zinc, nickel, and
paper, not one of which is named in the Constitution. But
we are told that the Constitution authorizes Congress to coin
but not to print money. The one is understood to apply
to metal, and the other to paper. But at this time, in all
Europe, coin and print mean the same thing. The two words
are used by all financial writers as interchangeable. They
both mean stamp, and nothing else."

Looking abroad in 1778, we find the first savings bank
founded in that year.

THE FIRST SAVINGS BANKS.—A committee of the French
Government has traced the history of these institutions in

various countries; showing that the first, on record, was
formed at Hamburg, in 1778, as a branch of a friendly society; that the example was followed in several German and
Swiss towns; and that, in 1798, Mrs. Wakefield established
a Poor Children's Savings Bank at Tottenham, England;
which in 1804 expanded into a regular savings bank, leading
to the creation of about 60 others before 1817, when an act
was passed to regulate them. In France, a *Bureau d'Econo-
mie* was founded in 1787. Feuchère afterward established a
Chambre d'Accumulation de Capitaux et d'Intérêts. An Act
of 1793 promised the foundation of a *Caisse Nationale de
Prevoyance;* and the Bank of France, in the year 1808, was
required to open a department for the receipt of deposits
above 50 francs; but the first real savings bank was only
formed in 1818. The deposits in all Europe, exclusive of
Russia and Turkey, recently amounted to 5,900,000,000
francs. They have, during the last few years, increased
largely in England and Switzerland, owing to the multiplica-
tion of banks; and also in Austria, owing to the precautions
adopted against a run on them during a financial crisis.
* * * During the last years of the French Empire a
modification of the rules was repeatedly demanded, and two
committees investigated the subject; that of 1869 recommending that a bank should be open on Sundays at every
mairie, and that the maximum should be raised to 3,000
francs.

SHAY'S REBELLION IN 1785.—Thousands of people have
heard of this, without knowing what it was about. It was
such a rebellion as we ought to have had between 1866 and
1874. It occurred in New England; and was an insurrec-
tion of debtors, who were suffering from an attempt to return
to specie payment. The people cried out for paper money.
It was put down by force of arms, but accomplished its immediate purpose, as Massachusetts passed a law delaying
the collection of debts. In Rhode Island the movement was
not riotous, but took the form of a political issue. The paper
money men carried the election in 1786, and more paper was
issued.

Some one should write a full, truthful account of this
affair, as the bullionists have published lying, garbled accounts of it—as a sort of John Law inflation. [The "Century,"
for May, 1891, has such a story.]

THE BANK OF NORTH AMERICA.—In 1781 came the Bank of North America. This bank was chartered by the Continental Congress in this last year of the war for independence, and gave very solid help. Robert Morris, of Philadelphia, where the bank was placed, suggested it. Its capital, at first, was $400,000. It was afterward increased to $2,000,000. Congress took a portion of the stock. The notes of the bank were made legal tender for all debts due the Government. This made them the notes of the Government. Owing to this, the demands upon the bank for coin were small and infrequent. No difficulty was experienced from such demands. The people preferred these notes to coin. At that time the coin in the country was estimated at $5,000,000. The notes of this bank, thus connected with the Government, brought the coin from its hiding-places. The estimated amount was soon $10,000,000. The people deposited the coin in the bank, and used the notes in place thereof in business. The coin greatly increased in amount, instead of diminishing. It was not needed except for change. It went into the Continental Treasury. The notes went into the hands of the people, and were retained. By these means, the coin known to exist was almost doubled. The Government was prepared for emergencies. The money continued in use after the war closed; and it was as useful in peace as in war. It was not costly, like loans. That bank still exists in Philadelphia.

CHAPTER IV.

1786 to 1796.

THE UNITED STATES BEGIN.—March 4, 1789, the United States Government, with its Constitution, as presented to Congress Sept. 19, 1788, went into operation.

Never until 1862 was the power of the Government to make its paper money, or that of the banks, legal tender for all payments to the United States denied. The power to make such money legal tender in payment of private debts was never fully adopted until 1862 ; when it was denied to the Government. The notes of the banks of the United States of 1791 and 1816, the notes of State banks from 1812 to 1814, the Treasury notes of the United States from 1812 to 1817, and the same from 1837 to 1861, had all been made legal tender for all debts due the Government, including duties on imports ; but they were not treated as legal tender to the people. In 1862, the powers of bankers over Congress, and especially in the Senate, was so great that this order was changed in relation to Treasury notes. They were made unlimited legal tender to the people, but of limited legal tender to the Government. This was done to insure their being at a discount for coin, the same as suspended bank notes.

The Supreme Courts of New York, Pennsylvania, Illinois, Ohio, Wisconsin, and all other States where any case has come up for decision, have decided the legal tender notes constitutional. There has never been any decision against them by any court as legal tender for all debts contracted since their issue. The only decision that they were not constitutional, for debts contracted before their issue, has been overruled by a subsequent decision.

The short method of meeting all so-called arguments against the constitutionality of legal tender notes is, to refer to the legislation of Congress from 1791 down to this time ; and demand the authority of the Constitution for alloying gold and silver coin; and for the issue of copper, tin, zinc, and nickel money, about which the Constitution says not one word. This will give them something to think of.

FRENCH ASSIGNATS.—As the failure of the French assignats is assigned by bullion advocates as a reason why legal-tender Treasury notes of the United States must fail, we will briefly consider these assignats in the light of history.

1. These assignats were issued by the Revolutionary Government of France in 1790, and after that time. They were not based upon the faith, credit, or revenues of the nation as our legal tenders are, but upon the confiscated estates of priests and nobles. These estates were assigned or set apart by the Government as security for circulating notes. They had no basis but these lands.

2. Up to 1792, only 1,200,000,000 of francs, or about $240,000,000 had been issued. This sum was not beyond the wants of business, and was not in excess of population. So long as the issue was not over this sum, the money never went below 90 cents in the dollar, notwithstanding the uncertainty as to the duration of the Government and the security upon which the notes were based.

3. But encouraged by the success attending the money, the Government supposed the issue could be extended to any amount. They therefore, issued 45,578,000,000 francs, or some $9,000,000,000, based upon the same security. So great was the confidence of the people in their leaders that with this immense issue, beyond the needs of the people, the money was worth 60 cents in the dollar for coin, and so remained for a considerable time.

4. But a large amount of the money was counterfeited by the enemies of the money, and circulated among the people. It was difficult to distinguish the genuine from the counterfeit. The revolutionary Government was becoming divided, and some of the leaders caused others to be put to death. It was apparent to all thinking minds that the Government must soon end, and the estates upon which the money was based would, it was supposed, be restored to those from whom they had been taken, and the money would, therefore, be of no value. These considerations caused the money to fall till it took $18 to pay for one of coin. The impending fall of the Government caused the money to depreciate still more. The Government issued an

edict requiring it to be received and paid at the price to
which it had fallen, and authorized the entry of all confiscated lands therewith at that price. This, with the other causes,
destroyed its credit altogether, and it went out of use in
1795. As authority for these facts, we refer to vol. ii. of the
American Cyclopedia, page 30, and to French history of
the times, which we think is a little colored against assignats.

The French Government issuing it was not only a revolutionary government, but it became a professed republic,
surrounded by monarchies. Had it been a true republic,
established upon proper principles, and administered by men
of prudence and moderation, it would not have been permitted to live long. The monarchies of Europe would have
combined for its overthrow. But when the French people
deposed their king, declared for a republic, and placed
themselves under the leadership of Robespierre, Danton, and
others, they exchanged their former despots for worse ones.
The reign of these men was one of terror and blood instead
of peace and justice, law, order, and liberty.

The basis of this money was real estate, which, if of the
right kind, with good titles, is the best of security for ulti-
mate payments, but not suitable for a basis of circulation, because it takes too long to convert it into money. But these
confiscated estates were really no security at all. The Government had no title to them, and could not confer one upon purchasers. These estates had been violently taken from those
having legal titles to them, who held them under vested
rights. Every reflecting man knew that as soon as the
Government was changed, the most of the estates would be
returned to their rightful owners. Who could expect money
based upon such a foundation to remain good? The matter
of astonishment is, not that this money went down, but that
it was current for any considerable length of time. The fact
known to all, that the estates had been unlawfully taken
from their owners by the men in power, was sufficient to
create the fear that they might, by the same men, be violently taken from those who purchased them.

THE FIRST UNITED STATES BANK.—The First Bank of
the United States, under the Constitution, was chartered
Feb. 25, 1791, by Congress. It was the work of the
Federals, who hated and wished to avoid Treasury notes.
But they were " hoist by their own petard "; for it was so

managed that its notes served nearly the same purpose as
Government legal tenders. The capital was $10,000,000.
One-fifth of the stock was owned by the United States, and
$8,000,000 by the people. Six of the $8,000,000 were
Government indebtedness, and $2,000,000 money.

The tenth section of the charter made the notes of the
bank those of the nation, by providing that for twenty years
they should be received for all dues to the Government. The
law placed the Government money in this bank, and there it
remained—subject to the warrants of the treasurer. The
bank received the Government revenues, and paid the
Government debts. In reality, the bank was the Treasury,
and, so far as finance was concerned, the Government was
the bank. The name and credit of the United States accom-
panied every note, throughout the world. All the copper,
silver, gold, and paper money of the nation was in the bank.
The Government kept no money at the Treasury. The
people who held and used the notes did not inquire whether
the bank paid or did not pay coin. It was a matter of in-
difference to them. They did not wish coin. The notes which
the Government had bound itself to receive for twenty years,
whether the bank paid coin or not, were satisfactory to them.
They did not look to or regard the bank. They confided in
the Government, which did not deceive them. In those days
the Government kept contracts made with the people, as well
as with nations and institutions. There was little or no demand for coin in business. It, therefore, went into the bank,
and into the Treasury, which was the bank. The notes went
out, the coin went in. [See "Example of France."] When
drafts of the treasurer upon the bank were presented, for
which coin could be demanded, the notes were generally paid
instead of coin, being preferred because of safety, uniformity,
and convenience. The coin remained in the bank ; the notes
went out among the people. The charter of this bank expired in 1811. When the era of State banks came, the above
style was reversed. The people, having small confidence in
the banks, got all the coin they could from them, so the notes
went into the banks, and the coin went out among the people.

The power to lay and collect taxes and duties implies the
power to provide the people the money in which to pay those
taxes and duties ; and also to say in what kind of money
they shall be paid. That the framers of the Constitution did

not intend that these taxes and duties should be paid in gold
and silver coin only, is evident from the fact that from 1791
to 1840 no law was ever passed by Congress requiring them to
be paid in gold and silver coin. From 1791 to 1811 taxes and
duties were paid in the notes of the Bank of the United
States, and so on. The law of 1840 was repealed in 1841.

Neither of the United States banks ever suspended. This
cannot be said of any other banks of issue in the world.

THE UNITED STATES MINT.—An Act of April 2, 1792,
created the Mint, and provided for the coining of gold, silver,
and copper coins of the United States. The relation between gold and silver created by this act was fifteen pounds
of silver to one of gold. Gold was made, by this law, 11–12
fine, the same as English gold. The silver coins were made
896½ parts pure and 103½ parts alloy, in the 1000 parts.
The silver dollar was made to contain 416 grains of this
compound : 371¼ grains being pure silver, and 43¾ grains
copper. Twenty-seven grains gold, 11–12 fine, were made
the value of the silver dollar of 416 grains. The dollar was
made the unit of value, and of the money of account ; in
which all proceedings in courts of justice were to be kept.
*Gold was not made a dollar, but 27 grains were made the
value of a dollar* and legal tender, at that valuation, the
same as silver. All coins of gold, silver, and copper were
made full legal tender.

When the question of the establishment of the Mint was
under consideration, by the founders of the Government,
Mr. Hamilton, in his communication to the House of Representatives, Jan. 28, 1791, said : "Upon the whole, it seems
to be most advisable, as has been observed, not to attach
the unit exclusively to either of the metals ; because this
cannot be done effectually without destroying the office and
character of one of them as money, and reducing it to the
situation of mere merchandise. * * * To annul either of the
metals as money is to abridge the quantity of circulating
mediums, and is liable to all the objections which arise
from the comparison of the benefits of a full, with the evils
of a scanty, circulation."

This is the way in which we "happened" to get our standard silver dollar : Mr. Hamilton had a number of the old
Spanish milled dollars, as then in circulation, assayed, and
they were found to contain 371¼ grains of pure silver, and

therefore the new dollar was made to contain that amount—
so that the money unit of the colonies, as at that time in circulation, was continued as the money unit under the new
constitution.

MONEY OF ACCOUNT.—What is called "The Money of
Account"—in our country, dollars, dimes, etc.—was estab-
lished here in 1792. In some countries it is only an idea.
The British pound is ideal.

From about 1660 until 1816, the pound sterling had no
corresponding piece of coin. The English guinea had been
intended to represent a pound. But it had not been properly adjusted; and, owing also to the fluctuations in the
price of gold, it varied in value until 1717, when its value
was fixed at 21 shillings. In 1816, after much deliberation,
it was decided to fix the weight of the sovereign at five pen-
nyweights, three grains, and 623 thousandths of a grain. It
is manifest that the whole difficulty was in establishing a
coin whose value should correspond to the unit of value of
the money of account carried in the minds of the people.
The English sovereign has since been changed several
times.

The people of the United States have undergone a similar
experience with pounds, shillings, and pence,—the pounds
varying in value in different States, from 4s. 8d. to 8s. to the
dollar.

There were no coins in existence corresponding to these
amounts. These different units of value had their origin in
various causes, which we will not stop to discuss : but when
industry and trade had become sufficiently advanced, they
became fixed. The trade of the colonies with the West Indies had introduced into the country a considerable amount
of Spanish coins. The names and values of these coins did
not correspond to the money of account of the people ; and
their value was estimated in the money of account of the
several colonies, *precisely as that of wheat*, or any other
commodity, is estimated. In 1792, an Act was passed by
Congress with a view to establishing a uniform money of account throughout the country. People reckoned in pounds,
shillings, and pence, and paid in Spanish dollars. It will be
remembered that Continental money was payable in "Spanish milled dollars, or the value thereof in gold or silver."
The Act of Congress of April, 1792, declared "That the

money of account of the United States shall be expressed in
dollars or units; dimes or tenths; cents or hundredths;
and mills or thousandths: * * * and that all accounts
in public offices, and all proceedings in the courts of the
United States, shall be kept and had in accordance with this
regulation." This is believed to be *the first time that a
money of account was established by law:*—money of account having in all other nations grown up in the minds of
·the people.

Sir James Stewart, in his work on Political Economy, says:
—Money which I call money of account, is no more than a
scale of equal parts invented for measuring the respective
values of things vendible. * * * Money of account per-
forms the same office, with regard to the value of things, that
degrees, minutes, seconds, etc., do with regard to angles; or
as scales do to geographical maps, or to plans of any kind.
In all these inventions, there are some denominations taken
for the unit. In angles it is the degree; in geography it is
the mile; in plans it is the foot or yard; in money it is the
pound, livre, florin, etc. The degree has no determinate
length; so neither has that part of the scale upon plans or
maps which marks the unit : the usefulness of these being
strictly confined to the marking of *proportions.* Just so the
unit in money can have no invariable determinate proportion
to any part of value. That is to say, it cannot be fixed in
perpetuity to any particular quantity of gold or silver, or any
other commodity. The value of commodities depends upon
circumstances,—their value ought to be considered as changing with respect to one another only. Consequently, *anything which troubles or perplexes the ascertaining of these
changes of proportion,—by the means of a general determinate and invariable scale, must be hurtful to trade;* and this
is the infallible consequence of every vice in the policy of
money or coin. * * * It does not follow from this adjusting
of the metals to the scale of value, *that they themselves
should therefore become the scale!*

THE VALUE OF FOREIGN COINS.—The Act of February 9,
1793, regulates the value of foreign coin in the United
States (as the Constitution provided Congress should do);
making them money of this country, at the valuation placed
upon them by this law—for the time stated in the law. Congress supposed that the Mint, which they had created, would

be able to coin into United States money all the gold and silver bullion and foreign coins in three years. This law, therefore, provided that foreign coins should not be money in the United States after that time.

THE FOREIGN LOANS.—The Act of March 3, 1795, provides for taking up the foreign loan made to us by France, Spain, and Holland during our Revolutionary struggle. How different was the course pursued by the Fathers of the Revolution, and the founders of the Republic, from that of our present so-called statesmen! Instead of making a foreign loan to pay off a home loan, Congress proposed to make a home loan to pay off this foreign loan, which was made as a necessity. Small bonds were made for that purpose; so that all the people could invest in them, and hold them as money. One-half per cent. was allowed the people at home, over and above what was being paid for the foreign loan. "In this way," Webster says, "Hamilton smote the rock, and the waters gushed forth." "He touched the dead body of credit, and it sprang to life."

CHAPTER V.

1796 to 1806.

THE BANK OF VENICE.—When the United States was beginning to feel its way toward the goal (not yet reached) of
a sensible system of money and finance, Napoleon was un-
wittingly destroying the wisest system ever known on this
earth. In 1797, he seized the Bank of Venice, of which the
following is a fair description :—

In 1171, when the gallant Republic of Venice singly with-
stood the shock of the Asiatic hordes, that threatened to
inundate Europe, Duke Vitale Michel II. called on the
wealthy citizens to contribute to a loan of 2,000,000 ducats,
for the defense of the State; the sums so loaned to be entered to the credit of the contributors on the books of the
Republic. These credits, being divisible and transferable,
grew into favor as a currency, performing all the functions
of money, and rose to a high premium above gold and silver
coin. Such was the origin of the earliest bank of history.
In 1423, a law fixed the *agio* or premium at 20 per cent., and
directed all payments, not otherwise agreed on, to be paid at
the Bank of Venice; while at the same time it discontinued
the four per cent. interest that had hitherto been promptly
paid on the credits. This per cent. *agio* added to the coin
ducat of Venice constituted a new unit of value, represented
by no coin, yet maintaining its ideal existence, as the ducat
of the Bank of Venice; and rose to an additional *agio*,—
termed a *sur agio*,—of 20 to 30 per cent. It continued the
favorite currency of the Adriatic for nearly 600 years; until
the remorseless march of Napoleonic despotism, in 1797,
crushed the Republic. A worthless booty was found in the
bank; for it had no coin or deposits, but only a faithful
record of the loans that more than 600 years before the
citizens of Venice had made, to preserve the life of the
Republic. France repaid the citizens; but the bank and the
Republic were no more. There was the money of a republic

having no foundation but credit on the books of a department in its treasury; with no coin in its vaults, and not bound to make that credit good in later times, by any payment of interest or any redemption whatever; which yet stood for hundreds of years at a high premium over gold and silver coin. Plain and open in all its progress, there was no peculation or steal in any of its processes.

Stephen Colwell, in his great work "Ways and Means of Payment," gives a digest of fourteen authorities about that bank. He says that this credit money amounted to $16,-000,000 when Napoleon seized the bank, and that the interest alone saved on each million of ducats was $6,250,-000,000,000—at four per cent. for four hundred years, savings bank interest. He adds: "If credits had been convertible at will into the precious metals, the *agio* would never have originated, much less have attained so high a point. For the moment holders of credits advanced the price, specie, *if a legal tender*, would have become the medium of payment, as the cheaper medium. If the same mode of adjusting debts were resorted to now, the result would be that inconvertible credits would go, frequently, to a high premium over gold and silver."

FOREIGN COINS.—The mint had not come up to the expectation of Congress. The Act of Feb. 1, 1798, therefore extended the legality of foreign coins for three years longer; and some of the valuations thereof were changed, adding to their legal tender value.

SMALL COINS.—The Act of April 24, 1800, provides for the purchase of copper to coin into cents and half cents, which were unlimited legal tender. Copper is not named in the Constitution.

CHAPTER VI.

1806 to 1816.

FOREIGN COINS.—The Act of April 10, 1806, renewed the legality of foreign coins, changing the value of many of them. These laws show that law makes and unmakes money. These gold and silver coins were money, in the United States, at the values fixed by law; and they differed in value under the different laws, showing the control of law over them.

WILD-CAT BANKS.—By this time wild-cat State banks were in full bloom.

In March, 1809, a legislative committee of the State of Rhode Island made an examination into the affairs of the Farmers' Exchange Bank of Gloucester; and it was found that the bank had $580,000 of its notes in circulation, and only $86.16 in its vaults for their redemption. Before the end of the year, a general suspension of the banks of New England took place. It was discovered that nearly all were in the same condition,—no specie, and nothing to show but worthless notes of speculators.

FLUCTUATION OF GOLD IN ENGLAND.—Currency matters of Europe become now of immense interest, in connection with the Napoleonic wars. Worshipers of gold, "the invariable unit," are invited to consider the following statement of its variations from 1810 to 1820 in gold-worshiping England :—

The act known as the Peel Act of 1844 made gold receivable at the Bank of England at the rate of £3 17s. 10½d. per ounce of pure metal. Doubleday's Financial History of England, p. 277, has the following statement of the fluctuations of gold in that country, for the ten years from 1810 to 1820, compared with the present standard price, by the Peel Act of 1844.

1810	£4	5s.	0d.	1816	£3	18s.	6d.
1811	4	17s.	1d.	1817	4	0s.	0d.
1812	5	8s.	0d.	1818	4	1s.	5d.
1813	5	10s.	0d.	1819	4	3s.	0d.
1814	5	1s.	0d.	1820	3	17s.	10½d.
1815	4	12s.	9d.				

1811.

STATE BANKS.—In this year, our State banks (that are always ready in their seraphic wisdom and cherubic unselfishness to furnish us just what currency is "needed," according to certain "laws of nature," known only to them) were spreading themselves again. That terrible hard hitter, Bryant of Boston, in his book on "Money," gives them this rap :—

Some who are ignorant and many who are knaves assert that the law of "supply and demand" is the true and adequate governor of this question. That the assertion is absolute nonsense is shown by the following actual facts of our financial history. In 1811 the volume of money issued and circulated, by the old system of State banks, was $28,000,000. In 1816 it had risen to $110,000,000; in 1818 it had fallen to $40,000,000; in 1832 it stood at $60,000,000; in 1837 it reached $150,000,000; in 1843 it had sunk to $58,000,000; in 1847 it was $105,000,000; in 1857 $215,000,000; in 1858 it had fallen to $150,000,000; in 1865, the legal tender and bank note circulation was $1,199,565,231 among 27,000,000 people (rebel States excluded); and in 1875 was $700,000,000 among 45,000,000 people. When we look at these figures, and see how the volume of our money, under the law of "supply and demand," has bobbed up and down, and then consider that it is the *inevitable* law that values must, of necessity, swell and sink, just as the volume of dollars rises or sinks ; and then call to mind the widespread ruin and bankruptcy in which the country was thereby plunged ;—is it not evident that no one but an idiot can have anything further to say about the law of supply and demand ?

1812.

When the war with England began, the State banks were, of course, less reliable than ever. The first Bank of the

United States went out of existence in 1811, Congress refusing to grant it a new charter. Many State banks were
established during the life of this national bank, and hundreds grew up all over the country soon after the re-charter
of this bank was refused. The notes of the State banks
were then the principal money of the United States. These
banks attempted to supply the money to carry on the war,
agreeing to take in exchange for their notes 6 per cent. bonds
of the United States at 75 and 80 cents on the dollar. The
banks then professed to pay coin. To some extent the
Government received money from the banks upon these conditions; but through the influence of Mr. Jefferson, then in
private life, the Government was induced to issue Treasury
notes, which bore interest, but were receivable for all debts
due the United States. The misfortune with most of those
Treasury notes was that they were issued in sums too large
to use as money. The consequence was, the acts authorized
the Government to sell these Treasury notes to banks, and
to have the amount thereof placed to the credit of the
United States, to be paid to the Government in the notes of
the banks. The banks, therefore, as a general rule, held the
Treasury notes and received the interest, while the Treasury
held and paid out the bank notes. This act was against the
people.

INTEREST-BEARING TREASURY NOTES.—The Act of June 3,
1812, authorized the issue of $5,000,000 Treasury notes, to
run one year, bearing 5 and 2-5th, per cent. interest. They
were made receivable for all debts due the Government, and
were to be paid to such public creditors, and other persons,
as were willing to receive them. They might also be used
to procure loans; or might be placed to the credit of the
Treasury, in banks, at par and accrued interest.

THE ACT OF JUNE 30, 1812, provided that the moneys of
the Government might be deposited in State banks; and they
were so deposited. The banks then professed to pay coin—
a profession which was a false pretense.

From 1812 to 1816 business was sustained by legal tender
Treasury notes, that were not a tender to the people.

Judge Warwick Martin, speaking of notes that are a legal
tender to the Government, but not to the people, shows the
absurdity of this, once for all, as follows: " Unless a part is

greater than the whole, what is a tender to the whole people, as embodied in the Government, should be a tender to individuals."

From 1812 to 1862, when the exception was put in the legal tender act, Treasury notes were received the same as gold and silver, at our custom-houses. Those of 1812, '13. '14, '15. '37, '38, '39, '40, '41, '42, '43, '45, '46, '47, '48, '57 and '60 were so received.

1813.

It was in this year that Jefferson, writing to Epps, defended Continental money and Treasury notes. See 1776.

THE ACT OF FEB. 25, 1813, authorized the issue of 10.000.-000 in Treasury notes, similar to those under the Act of June 3, 1812.

1814.

JEFFERSON DISGUSTED.—On January 16, 1814, previous to the crisis of that year, Jefferson wrote as follows: " Everything predicted by the enemies of the banks in the beginning is now coming to pass. We are to be ruined by the deluge of bank paper, as we were formerly by the old Continental paper. It is cruel that such revolutions in private fortunes should be at the mercy of avaricious adventurers, who, instead of employing their capital—if any they have—in manufacture, commerce, and other useful pursuits, make it an instrument to burden all the exchanges of property with their swindling profits,—profits which are the price of no industry of theirs. * * * And what have we purchased by this tax of $200,000,000, which we are to pay by wholesale, but usury, swindling, and new forms of demoralization."

SUSPENSION OF THE BANKS.—In the early part of 1814, the banks being called upon for further loans to the Government declined to make them unless permitted to suspend specie payments. To the disgrace of the United States, these conditions were submitted to. The banks suspended. The Treasury was soon filled with suspended bank paper, while the banks were filled with Treasury notes. The latter were as good as coin. The former were nearly worthless. This condition of things caused a great demand among bondholders and capitalists for a bank of the United States. Jefferson and those agreeing with him insisted that instead

of chartering a new bank the Government should issue
Treasury notes, as the permanent money of the country, and
should ignore all banks.

THE ACT OF MARCH 4, 1814, authorized $10,000,000 in
Treasury notes, similar to those of 1812 and 1813. No
charge was to be made to the Government by the banks
which credited these notes.

THE ACT OF MARCH 14, 1814, authorized the placing of
Treasury notes, to the credit of the Government in State
banks, at their face and accrued interest; though the banks
were then suspended.

AN ORIGINAL GREENBACKER.—Many beside Jefferson already began to see the true light.

On November 12, 1814, Mr. Hall, of Georgia, introduced
into the House of Representatives the following: 1 *Resolved*, That the Committee of Ways and Means be directed
to inquire into the expediency of authorizing the Secretary
of the Treasury to issue notes convenient for circulation, to
the amount of —— million of dollars, under such checks
as may be thought best calculated to prevent counterfeits;
in which alone, and gold and silver, shall be paid all taxes,
duties, imports, or debts due, or which hereafter may become due to the United States. 2. *Resolved*, That the
Treasury notes which may be issued as aforesaid shall be a
legal tender in all debts due, or which may hereafter become
due, between a citizen of the United States and a citizen or
subject of any foreign State or kingdom.

Two more follow, which provide for the funding after
twelve months, and redeeming in coin. This system was
discarded because it was thought to be too expensive; and
a National Bank, with a capital of $35,000,000 established,
with what results everybody knows.

LEGAL TENDER TO GOVERNMENT.—The Act of December
26, 1814, authorized the issue of $25,000,000 in Treasury
notes, in place of a loan of that amount previously authorized. Ten millions of these notes were to be applied to the
payment of ten millions previously borrowed. The notes
were to run one year, and were to bear five 2-5ths interest.
They were made legal-tender for all obligations to the
Government, and to be otherwise like those previously issued.

How Banks are Created.—Notwithstanding the constitutional prohibition against emitting bills of credit, charters incorporating private institutions authorized to emit bills of credit (bank notes) were granted by the Legislatures of the several States in large numbers; in utter disregard of the Constitution, as well as of the public good. In Pennsylvania, for example, 25 charters, incorporating specie basis banks of issue, were granted during the session of 1813; but were vetoed by the Governor. At the next session of the Legislature, in 1814, a bill was passed, over the veto of the Governor, chartering 41 banks, with a capital of $17,-000,000 : 37 of them went into operation at once, and six months afterward suspended specie payment. The manner of obtaining a charter was very simple. A petition setting forth " the wants of the people," in the locality where the bank was to be established, was all that was required; political influence and intrigue accomplished the rest.

1815.

A Fight Against Treasury Notes.—The Act of February 14, 1815, authorized the issue of $25,000,000 Treasury notes, in addition to other issues. Up to this time, the Secretaries of the Treasury, Mr. Gallatin and Mr. Crawford, had complained that the Treasury notes, so far issued, were made too large for common circulation, though their standing among the people was good; and the people were desirous of having them. They say Treasury notes had taken the place of coin, and equalized the exchange throughout the country. To meet the wishes of these Secretaries and of Jefferson and Madison, as well as of the people, these $25,000,000 Treasury notes for circulation were authorized and issued. The most of them were required to be less than $100 in denomination, and to be payable to bearer; while those of $100 and over were to be made payable to order and to pass by indorsement, and were to bear five 2-5ths interest ; but the smaller ones were to bear no interest. They were also, for the first time, made receivable for six per cent. interest bonds. They were made to circulate as money and to have the characteristics of coins, but they were not redeemable therein. This was the first time the United States ever issued such Treasury money. In addition to being convertible into bonds, it was made legal tender for all debts due the United States. The interest notes were convertible into bonds also.

The banks had suspended before this act was passed. It, therefore, provides that if any of the interest-bearing Treasury notes were sold to banks and credited to the Treasury, the credits must be in coin. Upon these terms the banks did not want them. These notes, after being paid into the Treasury, were to be reissued. All notes previously issued were, under the laws creating them, to be canceled, after being received in the Treasury. They were not to be paid out again. But these notes, made specially to circulate as money, were to be paid out to all who were willing to receive them, which included all the people.

One peculiarity in all the Treasury notes issued in 1812, 1813, 1814, and 1815, was that although the Government was compelled to receive them for all dues and demands, the people were not compelled under the laws to receive them. The laws made it optional with them whether to receive them or not. But that the people preferred them to bank notes is proved by the fact that, though not compelled by law to receive them, they did gladly receive and hold them.

But so long as Treasury notes of the Government bore interest and were receivable for all debts due the United States, and were sold to the banks, and payment therefor made in bank notes, both before and after the suspension, the banks and bankers were very well satisfied with them. The banks had the most of these Treasury notes and were making the interest, while the Government and the people were compelled to receive the bank notes, and to use them. The Treasury notes were actually better than coin. The bank notes proved to be almost worthless. But when these $25,000,000 Treasury notes of small denominations were made to circulate as money and to bear no interest, the indignation of all the banks in the country was aroused. They saw that if these notes went out among the people, and became the money of the country, there would be an end to the circulation of bank notes. Such was the truth. There was, therefore, a general combination in New England, New York, Delaware and Pennsylvania, to kill off these Treasury notes which bore no interest. The old Bank of the United States, chartered in 1791, the charter of which expired and

was not renewed in 1811, was then, as the law allowed, closing up its affairs.   The debts of the people to this bank were
very large.   The Bank was pressing for payment.   The
people presented these Treasury notes which did not bear
interest in payment.   The Bank, to destroy the credit of the
notes, and to force the recharter of a National bank, refused
to receive the notes of the Government in payments to the
Bank.   As the Bank would not receive the notes from the
merchants, the merchants were, reluctantly, compelled to
refuse to receive them for debts due them and for goods
sold.   The New England banks and those in Delaware were,
also, as deeply involved in this conspiracy to destroy the
credit of these Treasury notes as they are now.   The em-
bargo and non-intercourse laws of Jefferson and Madison
had destroyed the carrying-trade of New England, and had
caused a suspension of the New England banks in 1809 and
1810.   The people of New England were, therefore, greatly
opposed to the war with England.   They did all they could
to cripple the Government in carrying it on.   They refused
all loans, even of bank notes, and were very hostile to all
Treasury notes, especially to those intended to take the
place of bank notes, as those of 1815 were.

By a general combination between State banks, the old
National Bank, bondholders, and bullion brokers, these notes
of the United States were forced to a discount for a short
time.   One of the strongest arguments in favor of having all
Treasury notes made full legal tender is here presented.
Had they been legal tender to the people, as well as to the
Government, all the efforts of the banks and brokers to re-
ject them, and reduce their value, would have been fruitless.
If the legal character were removed from the present notes,
the National banks would at once discredit them.

Immediately after these efforts of the banks to discredit
Treasury notes, an application was made to Congress for a
charter of a national bank, which proposed to take from the
Government, as part of its capital, $15,000,000 of these same
Treasury notes, to withdraw them from competition with
bank notes.

Mr. Madison vetoed the bill, principally on account of this
provision.   But $28,000,000 of bonds were substituted for
Treasury notes, as capital of the Bank ; and by a combination of the Federal party and a few Democrats, the Bank

was chartered. The charter provided that no other such bank should be chartered by Congress for 20 years. This implied, also, that all Treasury notes intended to circulate as money should be withdrawn, and that this Bank should furnish all the national paper circulation for 20 years. For this privilege the Bank paid $1,500,000. This contract, on the part of the Government, was disgraceful; but having been made, it had to be carried out; and it was carried out.

AN OLD STORY.—The Act of February 25, 1815, gave that same old authority to the Secretary of the Treasury as to selling Treasury notes to State banks, and having the proceeds placed to his credit therein. When the banks suspended in 1814, they were well supplied with Treasury notes, and the Treasury was well filled with bank notes. The former were good beyond doubt: the latter were very doubtful, and proved mostly worthless in the end.

MADISON ON TREASURY NOTES.—In his message of December 5, 1815, President Madison said, speaking of the need of a stable and sufficient currency: "If the operation of the State banks cannot produce this result, the proper operation of a National bank will merit consideration; and if neither of these expedients is deemed effectual, it may be necessary to ascertain the terms upon which the notes of the Government (no longer required as an instrument of credit) shall be issued, *upon motives of general policy, as a common medium.*"

In 1815, Jefferson gave the following statement of the number of banks which had been established up to that time:

"In 1781 we had 1 bank, capital $ 1,000,000
" 1791 " " 6 " " 13,500,000
" 1794 " " 17 " " 18,642,000
" 1796 " " 24 " " 20,472,000
" 1803 " " 34 " " 29,112,000
" 1804 " " 66 " " not known

And at this time (1815) we have probably 100 banks."

PAPER MONEY BROKE THE POWER OF THE FIRST NAPOLEON AT LEIPSIC.—Waterloo, in 1815, could not be reached by coin. According to Sir Archibald Alison, the historian, "By a decree on September 30, 1813, from Peterswalden, in Germany, the allied sovereigns issued paper notes, which soon passed as cash from Kamschatka to the Rhine; and produced the currency which brought the war to a successful termination."

Before Geo. S. Coe, the Professor Sumner of Wall Street, writes that proposed book on Finance, he had better read up on the history of Europe. Poor, the railroad statistician, who has written a big book upon money and dedicated it to Coe, quotes him at p. 551 as making the following misstatement : " The capital of the New York banks thus associated [in 1862] made an aggregate of 120 millions, an amount greater than the Bank of England and the Bank of France combined : each of whose institutions had been found sufficient for the gigantic struggle of those great nations, from time to time, in conflict with all Europe."

CHAPTER VII.

1816 to 1826.

1816.

THE SECOND UNITED STATES BANK. — The Act of April 10, 1816, chartered the second Bank of the United States, with a capital of $35,000,000 composed of $21,000,-000 United States bonds, and $7,000,000 coin and bank notes. The Government made up the balance by taking $7,000,000 of the stock ; and had five directors in the institution. The notes of the Bank were made legal tender for all dues to the United States. The charter extended 20 years. The Bank, as was said, paid $1,500,000 for its charter. Our modern National banks don't see things in that way. This bank had some Democrat backing ; but none from Jefferson and Madison.

CURRENCY THEORIES.—Dallas, Secretary of the Treasury, in his report in 1816, says, " Whenever the emergency occurs that demands a change of system, it seems necessarily to follow that the authority which was alone competent to establish the national coin, is alone competent to create a national substitute."

President Madison said, in his Message of December 3, 1816, " For the interests of the community at large, as well as for the purposes of the Treasury, it is essential that the nation should possess a currency of equal value, credit, and use, wherever it may circulate. The Constitution has intrusted Congress exclusively with the power of creating and regulating a currency of that description."

FOREIGN COINS.—The Act of February 20, 1816, renews the value of foreign coins, for three years again, as it is found impossible to run them through the mint in spite of their " intrinsic value." It is strange that Congress was constantly changing the value of these coins ; and limiting the time in which they should be money. If gold and silver were the best money, and depended not upon law but upon

4

weight for their value, why all these laws changing their money value?

1817.

TESTING TREASURY NOTES.—As the Bank of the United States had purchased of the Government, for $1,500,000, the monopoly of making legal-tender paper money for twenty years; and as many of the Treasury notes of 1813, 1814 and 1815 still remained in the hands of the people, the Bank claimed that the permitting of said Treasury notes to remain out was a violation of contract on the part of the United States; and Congress, in obedience to the wishes of the Bank, in 1817, called in all of said notes, providing that they should not be received at any place but in the Treasury. But the people knew that Congress possessed no such power as they had attempted to exercise. They, therefore, held on to the Treasury notes, as they now do to legal-tender notes.

In 1818, a firm in Boston tendered said Treasury notes in payment for duties on imports, for which they had previously been received. The banks in Boston then had, as they now have, a deadly hostility to all paper money issued by the Government. The district attorney in Boston was glad of the opportunity, which the law gave him, to instruct the collector of the port not to receive Treasury notes for duties. They were, therefore, refused at the custom-house. The Government brought suit for the duties. The merchant pleaded a tender of payment in Treasury notes. The Government responded that Treasury notes were not legal tender.

The case was heard by Judge Story, in 1819. His review of the case occupies eighteen pages. He gave judgment for the defendants. His decision is that "Treasury notes were and are legal tender for everything for which the law makes them receivable." (2 Mason, pp. 1 to 18.) The Government had made these notes receivable for all debts due the United States. The Government could not, therefore, go back on its own contract. The result of this decision was to keep the Treasury notes in the hands of the people, the Bank to the contrary notwithstanding.

Congress endured the censure of the Bank until 1822, when, upon the 3d of May of that year, they passed another act to discredit Treasury notes ; so that the people might be compelled to surrender them ; which they did not wish to do.

1818.

A legislative committee of the State of New York made the following report in 1818: "Of all aristocracies none more completely enslaves a people than that of money ; and, in the opinion of your committee, no system was ever better devised to perfectly enslave a community than that of the present mode of conducting banking establishments. Like the siren of the fable, they entice to destroy. They hold the purse-strings of society ; and by monopolizing the whole of the circulating medium of the country, they form a precarious standard by which all property in the country— houses, lands, debts and credits, personal and real estate of all descriptions—are valued."

1819.

LEGAL TENDER DISCUSSIONS.—Judge Story declared the Treasury notes legal tender. Sumner, of Yale, says that this decision was as great an outrage as the Dred Scott decision. See 1817.

1820.

Wm. H. Crawford, Secretary of the Treasury, in his report, February, 1820, said : "All intelligent writers on currency agree that when the currency is decreasing in amount, poverty and misery must prevail."

The ACT OF MAY 15, 1820, and the ACT OF MARCH 3, 1821, repealed the law prohibiting the Bank of the United States (private) from loaning the Government sums over $100,000 ; and authorized the Secretary of the Treasury to borrow of said bank $8,000,000 at five per cent.

PEEL'S RESUMPTION.—In 1820 came Peel's Resumption of Specie in England, after 25 years without coin payments. The elder Peel had built up the family by cotton spinning, and was a wise, practical old man. When his son performed his "great and only" Resumption Act, the father said, "My son, you have enriched your family and your class, but you have nearly ruined your country." Ricardo, the Jew banker and economist, was largely responsible for this terrible deed. When specie was only five per cent. premium, he argued that a forced specie resumption would cause only a five per cent. reduction of values, while Sir William Heygate contended that it would be at least five times as much. Events proved that Sir William was right, and Ricardo frankly confessed as much when he said (See "Duncan's History of the Bank Charter," p. 110): "Ay, Heygate, you and the few others who opposed us on cash [specie] payments have proved right. I said the difference would be only five per cent., and you said at the least it would be 25 per cent."

And yet, our college professors and other so-called teachers of political economy continue to peddle out, in the interest of the usurer, the discarded theories of Ricardo and other mischievous sophists, as scientific truths; while carefully suppressing—also in the interest of the usurer—their disavowal and denial of the same. One consequence of this was seen in the fact that our American financial quacks made the same false statement when our Greenbacks had nearly reached parity with gold; and their persistence in Resumption produced the same awful effects.

This same Ricardo, in one of his "lucid intervals," uttered the following, to the shame and confusion of all our Sumners and Shermans: "A regulated paper currency is so great an improvement in commerce that I should greatly regret if prejudice should induce us to return to a system of less utility. The introduction of the precious metals for the purposes of money may, with truth, be considered as one of the most important steps toward the improvement of commerce and the arts of civilized life. But it is no less true that, with the advancement of knowledge and science, we discover that it would be *another improvement* to banish them again from the employment to which, during the less enlightened period, they had been so advantageously applied."

A word more from Sumner's description of Peel's Resumption, before I give the real facts from Sir A. Alison, Doubleday and Miss Martineau. He says of the debates before the bill was passed, that it was opposed by "the practical bankers and city men, and the great mass, *who did not understand the matter.* * * * The city men had a theory of their facts. It was really one theory against another; the one drawn from a narrow routine [business experience, S. L.], the other *a philosophical and scientific generalization, from a broad range of facts.*" O Lord, how long?

Here are the facts. During the wars with Napoleon, and after they were over, for nearly 20 years, the Bank of England suspended specie payments. But in 1819, after four years of peace, the value of paper currency rose to be only six per cent. below coin. Peel and Ricardo urged upon Parliament resumption in four years. They said, as some said here, in 1875 : "We are almost at the point of resumption ; we have already discounted our sufferings. It is only a question of three per cent." Ricardo said : "The whole difficulty would be in raising the value of the currency three per cent."

Though wise business men protested, though the Governor and directors of the Bank of England warned Parliament of the danger of contracting the currency—as they must be compelled to do to resume in four years—such was the influence of Peel and Ricardo, that they carried "Peel's Resumption Act" through the House of Commons by a unanimous vote. But one man stood out against it ; and they even persuaded him to leave the chamber when the vote was taken, so that it would appear unanimous.

Sir Archibald Alison, in his history, tells the sad story of the result : "The effect of this extraordinary piece of legislation was soon apparent. The industry of the nation was speedily congealed, as a flowing stream is by the severity of an Arctic winter. * * * The entire circulation of England fell from $232,545,000 in 1818 to $142,757,000 in 1821. The effects of this sudden and prodigious contraction of the currency were soon apparent ; and they rendered the next three years a period of ceaseless distress and suffering in the British Islands." The discounts in the Bank of England, —which in 1810 had been $115,000,000, and in 1815 not less than $103,000,000,—sank, in 1820, to $23,360,000, and in 1821 to $13,610,000. The effect upon prices was not less immediate and appalling. The rate of wages fell one-half. "From the tremendous reduction in the price of land," says Doubleday, "which now took place, the estates barely sold for as much as would pay off the mortgages ; and the owners were stripped of all, and made beggars."

Resumption in England is thus described in Doubleday's History :—We have already seen the fall in prices produced by the immense narrowing of paper circulation. The distress, ruin and bankruptcy which now took place were universal,—affecting the great interests both of land and trade ; but especially among land-owners,—whose estates were burdened by mortgages, settlements, legacies, etc.,—the effects were most marked, and out of the ordinary course. Before the close of the year 1819, the distress became insufferable. Great meetings were held throughout England and Scotland, during the summer. In August, 60.000 people,—men, women and children,—assembled near Manchester. A collision occurred between the people and the troops, in which a number were killed and many wounded. This created intense excitement, and the meetings of the people, held in Liverpool, York, Leeds, and various other cities, were attended by vast multitudes of suffering people, demanding vengeance. Serious riots occurred, which were only quelled by military force. In 1820, a conspiracy was discovered, which had for its object the murder of all the King's ministers : and which was only frustrated through the cowardice of one of the conspirators, who betrayed his associates. Military training went on among the people, and the Government was obliged to provide a large military force, to prevent an outbreak.

"On Sunday morning." says Alison, " a treasonable proclamation was found placarded all over the streets of Glasgow, Paisley, Stirling and the neighboring towns and villages : *in the name of a provisional government* calling on the people to desist from labor ; on all manufacturers to close their workshops ; and on all the friends of their country to come forward and effect a revolution by force, with a view to the establishment of an entire equality of civil rights. Strange to say, this proclamation—unsigned and proceeding from an unknown authority—was widely obeyed. Work immediately ceased ; the manufactories closed from the desertion of workmen ; the streets were filled with anxious crowds, eagerly expecting news from the South. The sounds of industry were no longer heard ; and 200,000 persons, in the busiest districts of the country, were thrown into a state of compulsory idleness, by the mandates of an unseen and unknown power."

5,000 troops were immediately assembled at Glasgow, and the insurgents were overawed. Before the end of the year, the Government had increased its volunteer force to 35,000 men. "Without doubt," says Alison, "this power-

ful volunteer force, organized especially in the manufacturing districts, at this period,—and the decisive demonstration
is afforded of moral and physical strength on the part of the
Government,—was the chief cause through which Great
Britain escaped an alarming convulsion."

The preparatory steps taken for this consolidation of the
money power—which were attended with almost incon-
ceivable horrors—are thus delineated by Miss Harriet
Martineau : " It is not he who sees from afar the clouds of
dust from an earthquake, and who faintly hears the mur-
murs of confused sounds,—and who knows that so many
churches and so many dwellings, and even so many people,
have perished,—that can feel the deepest horror of the scene.
It is rather he, who, in some narrow street, meets the
spectacle of the writhing of a crushed sufferer here, a child-
less mother there, a surviving lover, a forlorn infant, wailing
among the ruins and flames, who has the best understanding of what has befallen. And so it was with this social
convulsion in England. There are some, now, of the most
comfortable middle-class order, who cannot think of that year
without bitter pain. They saw many parents grow white-
haired in a week's time ; lovers parted on the eve of mar-
riage ; light-hearted girls sent forth from the shelter of home,
to learn to endure the destiny of the governess or the seam-
stress ; governesses too old for a new station, going actually
into the workhouse ; rural gentry quitting their lands, and
whole families relinquishing every prospect in life, and
standing as bare under the storm as Lear and his strange
comrades on the heath. They saw something even worse
than all this. They saw the ties of family honor and har-
mony snapped by the strain of cupidity at first, and discontent afterward, and the members falling off from one
another as enemies. They saw the hope of the innocent, the
faith of the pious, the charity of the generous, the integrity
of the trusted, give way. They saw the most guilty re-
warded, and the most virtuous involved as deeply as any in
the retribution. But it would be an endless task to adduce
the sorrows of that time ; nor can their issue ever be recognized. Still, the depression did pass away. Our ships were,
once more, abroad upon the sea ; and the clack of the loom
and the roar of the forge were again heard in our towns.

But the heart-wounds of such a time can no more be healed than the whitened hair can resume its color."

A Parallel.—The following description of the condition in the United States in 1820, reminds one of the way in which specie was resumed in 1879, at the corner of Wall and Nassau Streets, only, in sums of $50 and upward. In the South the banks still pretended to pay specie. But this account of the way in which they did business in some localities would hardly justify the pretension. Here is the style. It was first started at Darien, Ga. "One who presented a bill had to make oath, in the bank, that the bill was his own, and that he was not an agent for any one. He was required to make this oath before the cashier and *five directors !* and had to pay $1.37½ expenses on each bill."

1822.

Act of May 3, 1822, tries again to call in Treasury notes. See 1817.

CHAPTER VIII.

1826 to 1836.

1828.

THE STEADY CURRENCY OF FRANCE.—As early as 1828, the steadiness of French money was being noticed in England. Huskisson said: " If they wish to prove the value of a steady and unchangeable currency they had it in the history of France : that country had been twice invaded by a foreign army, her capital had been twice taken possession of, and she was obliged to pay large sums to foreign countries; but they had a steady metallic currency ; and however situations might have affected the rest,—however the extensive contractor might have been injured or ruined,—the body of the population remained unoppressed. This was attributed to the permanent footing upon which the currency of the country had been established."

Huskisson did not see that it was abundance of Government money, and doing business with money instead of checks and notes, that kept the French safe.

1829.

GEN. JACKSON TAKES HOLD.—There is a curious lack of Governmental financial events and Congressional acts about money from 1820 to the time when President Jackson's strong hand gets hold. The United States Bank has meanwhile had its own way—a pretty aristocratic way for a private corporation.

In his Message of December 8, 1829, President Jackson alleged that the United States Bank had failed to furnish a sound and uniform currency ; and he proposes that the Treasury shall do what the Bank has failed to do. He says :

" The charter of the Bank of the United States expires in 1836 ; and its stockholders will, most probably, apply for a renewal of their privileges. In order to avoid the evils resulting from precipitancy in a measure involving such important principles and such deep pecuniary interest, I feel that

I cannot, in justice to the parties interested, too soon present it to the deliberation of the Legislature and the people. Both the constitutionality and the expediency of the law creating this bank are well questioned by a large portion of our fellow-citizens. And it must be admitted by all, that it has failed in the great end of establishing a uniform and sound currency. Under these circumstances, if such an institution is deemed essential to the fiscal operations of the Government, I submit to the wisdom of the Legislature, whether a NATIONAL ONE, FOUNDED UPON THE CREDIT OF THE GOVERNMENT AND ITS REVENUES, might not be devised ; which would avoid all constitutional difficulties, and at the same time secure all the advantages to the Government and country that were expected to result from the present Bank."

1832.

Instead of rechartering the Bank in 1829, 1830, 1831 and 1832, General Jackson insisted upon the Government issuing its own money, making its own exchanges, and keeping its own deposits. But the weakness of Congress was again apparent, when contending with the money power. They surrendered to that power, and rechartered the National Bank in 1832. Jackson vetoed the bill, and a two-thirds vote could not be obtained to pass it over the veto. Here was a good opportunity to carry out the plans of Jefferson and Madison, which had been defeated by the banks in 1816.

General Jackson used all his great power to induce Congress to have the money of the nation based upon the revenues and credit of the nation ; but the bank power controlled Congress, and they would not listen to his advice or adopt his measures in favor of a national currency, issued by the nation, expecting to force him to sign a United States Bank bill. But Jackson was not the man to be forced. He remained firm.

The Bank had four years to operate, after the veto, before its charter expired. The Government was to pay off the national debt and have some $40,000,000 surplus money on hand, which was in the Bank of the United States.

The Bank, immediately after the veto, commenced issuing its own money and that of the Government to subsidize the press, to control the election of President, then about to take

place, so as to insure a renewal of its privileges for twenty
years. To permit money of the Government to be thus used
would have been treason to the United States. This was
something of which Andrew Jackson could not be guilty.
There was but one way to prevent it, which was the removal
of the deposits from said Bank. No one but the Secretary
of the Treasury could do this. Mr. Duane, then Secretary,
was ordered to do it, but he refused. He was at once removed, and Mr. Taney was appointed in his place. *He
removed the deposits,* Oct. 1, 1833.

When the U. S. Bank sought a recharter, Old Hickory was
firm, unyielding and uncompromising. He gathered his
little Democratic band around him; and when the second
campaign opened he sent them out to educate and save the
people—according to his best light. He made no conces-
sions and formed no coalitions with either of the old parties.
Benton, in his "Thirty Years in Congress," said that the
Bank spent $3,000,000 in bribing and subsidizing members
of Congress, newspaper editors, politicians, brokers, jobbers
and men of influence, to defeat Jackson, and purchase a recharter. But justice and Jackson prevailed: the Bank power
was destroyed.

JACKSON'S VETO MESSAGE, JULY 10, 1832.—It is maintained by some that the Bank is a means of executing the
constitutional power "to coin money and regulate the value
thereof." Congress have established a mint to coin money,
and passed laws to regulate the value thereof. The money
so coined, with its value so regulated, and such foreign coins
as Congress may adopt, are the only currency known to the
Constitution. But if they have other power to regulate the
currency, it was conferred to be exercised by themselves,
and *not to be transferred to a corporation.* If the Bank be
established for that purpose, with a charter unalterable without its consent, Congress have parted with their power for a
term of years, during which the Constitution is a dead letter.
It is neither necessary nor proper to transfer its legislative
powers to such a bank, and therefore unconstitutional. * * *
Unauthorized by the Constitution, subversive of the rights
of the States and dangerous to the liberties of the people
* * * when the laws undertake to grant gratuities and exclusive privileges to make the rich richer and the potent

more powerful, the humbler members of society,—the farmers, mechanics and laborers, who have neither the time nor the means of securing like favors for themselves,—have a right to complain of the injustice of the Government.

1833.

JACKSON'S MESSAGE, DEC. 3, 1833.—It being thus established by unquestionable proof, that the Bank of the United States was converted into a permanent electioneering engine, it appeared to me that the path of duty, which the Executive Department of the Government ought to pursue was not doubtful. As by the terms of the Bank charter, no officer but the Secretary of the Treasury could remove the deposits, it seemed to me that this authority ought to be at once exerted, to deprive that great corporation of the support and countenance of the Government, in such a use of its funds and such an exertion of its powers. In this point of the case, the question is distinctly presented, whether the people of the United States are to govern through representatives chosen by their unbiased suffrages, or whether the power and money of a great corporation are to be secretly exerted to influence their judgment and control their decisions. It must now be determined whether the Bank is to have its candidates for all offices in the country,—from the highest to the lowest,—or whether candidates on both sides of political questions shall be brought forward, as heretofore, and supported by the usual means.

THE ACT OF APRIL 11, 1833, provided that the Bank of the United States should no longer act as the Commissioner of Loans for the United States, the President having vetoed its recharter. A commissioner of loans was no longer needed; as the United States did not wish to make any loans—the debt being nearly paid off.

1834.

THE ACT OF JUNE 25, 1834, makes the silver dollar of Mexico, Peru, Brazil and Central America lawful money of the United States. They remained such until 1857. They were not money in the United States until made such by law.

THE CHANGE OF RATIO.—In 1834, came our change of ratio between silver and gold. Judge Warwick Martin, writing in 1880, said :—

The legal relation between silver and gold in Great Britain, France, and other European countries is to-day 15½ pounds of silver to 1 of gold. This is still the legal relation in England. Notwithstanding this and the fact that $75,-000,000 of the reserves of the Bank of England are in silver, this bank has [1880] forced the discount on silver to 15 per cent., and makes large amounts of money out of it. England wishes the United States to agree to this discount so that the bondholders will not be compelled to receive silver in payment for their bonds, and that the Bank may continue to make 21 per cent. upon silver purchased by the Bank. But what is the situation of the United States in connection with this matter? From 1792 until 1834, the relation created by law between silver and gold in the United States was 1 pound of gold to 15 pounds of silver. The English took advantage of this and purchased all our gold, paying 15 pounds of silver for 1 pound of gold ; and thus making one-half pound of silver by every pound of gold thus purchased from us. We then made our coin 11-12 fine. Our bonds were, up to 1834, yet unpaid, and they were payable in coin at this standard fineness. The fineness could not therefore be changed by law at that time. Our honesty and regard for the national credit compelled us to permit England to depredate upon us until our debt was paid.

In June, 1834. every dollar of the money owing by the United States was placed in bank, in the money for which the bonds called, to pay them on presentation. We were then out of debt. The time had come when we could, in justice to all, change the relation between silver and gold and the standard fineness of both.

On the 28th of June, 1834, the act was passed changing the relation of silver and gold and making the legal relation 16 pounds of silver to 1 of gold, and the standard fineness 9-10 instead of 11-12, as it had been. This was the only time in our history when we could have made these changes, owing to previous debts. It is to be greatly regretted that 15½ to 1 had not been adopted instead of 16 to 1. But the English did not neglect the opportunity which this law gave to depredate upon us. They had, under our old law, taken away nearly all our gold and given us nearly all their silver. They were able, after the law of 1834, to purchase nearly all our silver, and to pay for it in gold, 1 pound of gold for 16 pounds of silver—thus making one-half pound of silver upon every pound of gold they sold us. . . . . It will be seen, therefore, that unless nations can agree upon the same unit of value and of the money of account, and upon the legal relation which gold and silver shall sustain to each other, and also upon a common standard of fineness, they never can have international metallic money. Upon these three things they never can agree. An agreement among nations to adopt such a coinage, would make it necessary to recoin and change all the coins of the world. This will never be done.

But there is no necessity for anything of the kind. As nations do not pay debts to each other in money, but in commodities, it matters not to one nation what the money of another nation is. As we have no money of the world, and can have no international money, we beg our statesmen to permit us to attend to our business instead of to the business of other nations. We want money for the United States, not for other nations. Let our money be made by Congress of that which costs us least, and will best answer the business demands of the country.

[It is about time that honest rustic, Uncle Sam, stopped allowing England—the bunco-steerer of the world—to play him for a flat.—L. S.]   _____

Here is a technical description of the law of June 28, 1834; showing its effect on the relations of gold and silver: The United States were out of debt. They had in bank the money to pay off every obligation. They could, therefore, without being charged with bad faith, change the standard fineness of their coins: which they then did. This act changed the relation between silver and gold from 15 to 1 to 16 to 1, and the standard fineness of gold from 11-12 to 9-10. This made 25.8 grains gold, 9-10 fine, correspond with the silver dollar of 371¼ grains pure silver, instead of 27 grains 11-12 fine, as under the law of 1792. The gold dollar did not exist under either of these laws; but 27 grains gold, under the former law, and 25.8 grains, under the latter, were made the value of a dollar. The so-called gold dollar of 1792 contained 24.75 grains pure gold, and under the acts of 1834 and 1837, 23.22 grains pure gold, a difference of 1.53 grains in the dollar. The law of 1792 made a pound of gold

worth 15 pounds of silver. The law of 1834 makes a pound
of gold worth 16 pounds of silver. There is 1⅔ per cent.
difference in the metallic values of gold coins, of the same
denomination, under these two laws. Their legal or money
value is the same under both laws—being $2.50, $5.00,
$10.00, and no more. Law makes and unmakes money.
The gold eagle, under the law of 1792, contained 15½
grains more pure gold than the eagle under the laws of 1834
and 1837.

———

The second Act of June 28, 1834, changed the valuation
of foreign gold coins in the United States to make them correspond with the law of June 28, 1834, changing the
standard fineness of gold in the United States. This shows
how completely metallic money, as well as other money, is
made and controlled by law. Law makes and unmakes
money. Why were so many coin laws passed by Congress
in one month? There is a history in this worthy of being
known.

———

Profound lessons have been drawn, by some real economists, from the effect of the change of ratio in 1834, upon
the financial relations of England and the United States.

Henry C. Carey wrote in 1875 :—Of all American writers
whose attention was then given to monetary questions, there
was, I think, none whose opinions in relation thereto, were
held in more respect than were those of my friend, Mr.
Condy Raguet, from whose work, published in 1839, I
take the following passage : " Prior to the passage of the
gold bill above referred to, the metallic currency of the
United States had been virtually, as above stated, a currency
of silver, since the establishment of the Government—gold
very rarely appearing—while that of Great Britain was of
gold. The consequence was, that the currency of each was
independent of the other ; and the contraction or expansion of
each did not necessarily act upon the other. The contraction in England, which preceded the resumption of specie
payments, in 1821, after a long suspension of 24 years, produced no convulsion on this side of the Atlantic. Nor did
our contraction, distressing and durable as it was, after the removal of the public deposits from the Bank of the United
States, on October 1, 1833—which brought down the prices of

stock from 20 to 50 per cent., and led to the importation of $3,793,293 in silver from England alone, during the year ending September 30, 1834,—produce any convulsion in that country. Such would have continued to be the case, had the mint regulations remained without alteration. But no sooner was gold, by a change in its relative value to silver, rendered the most profitable of the two metals to import, than we found the currency of England disturbed to a degree that rendered necessary an immediate reduction of her paper-issue; although the amount of gold drawn from her between the passage of the law, in June, 1835, and September 30 of the same year, was but $1,922,960. To our importation of gold in the years 1835 and 1836, instead of silver, may be ascribed that further contraction of the British currency, which led to the crisis of the latter year that was so fatal to American credits and American cotton; by which millions of dollars were lost to the country.

"Now as like causes will produce like effects, it behooves us to examine well into this matter; and if we find that we have committed an error, it is our duty to retrace our steps. Thus far very little progress has been made toward introducing gold into actual circulation: notwithstanding that a large amount has been imported. Still, a long perseverance in the law will give us a gold currency: but it will be most dearly purchased. It will so closely ally our fortunes with those of Great Britain, that no convulsion can take place in the currency of that country that will not act directly and powerfully upon ours: while, on the other hand, none can take place on our side that will not act directly upon hers; and in so doing break down the prices of cotton and tobacco, and other American products, in the market of Europe, to the great injury of our planting interest."

1835.

BANKING IN THE NORTHWEST.—The following shows how things were working at this time in the great Northwest. Mr. John Johnston, Alexander Mitchell's son-in-law, said at the Bankers' Convention in Saratoga, in 1880:

"The first bank in what is now Wisconsin was chartered in 1835, by the Legislature of the Territory of Michigan. In

1836, three other banks were started, with a possible circulation of $1,800,000, by a legislature representing 20,000 people,
scattered over 266,000 square miles. This area has now
600 banks. The panic of 1837 greatly discredited the circulation of the existing banks. In 1838, Wisconsin was reduced to its present limits of 54,000 square miles. From
1836 to 1840, its population had increased 250 per cent.,
largely in consequence of the crisis of 1837. In 1839,
George Smith and Alexander Mitchell came from Aberdeen,
Scotland, to the western shores of Lake Michigan, as pro-
moters of the Scottish Land Improvement Co., but they fell
into the practice of banking. Their Wisconsin Marine and
Fire Insurance Co. issued certificates of deposit as small as
one dollar, and in volume up to $1,000,000. Wisconsin having
been cleared of paper currency by the recent financial hurri-
cane, these certificates of deposit had a great mission to perform. The company encountered both adverse legislation
and repeated runs. These runs were organized by the bankers
and brokers of the other States. In 1844, the Legislature
repealed the company's charter. The spirited young Scotch-
men issued a declaration that this action could not affect
their rights, and that their notes would continue to be redeemed in Milwaukee, Chicago, Galena, St. Louis, Detroit
and Cincinnati. This strengthened them in the eyes of the
public. The Peninsular Bank of Michigan often sent by
steamboat large amounts of the company's circulation for
redemption. The coin was always ready. The worst run of
all was organized by Chicago brokers in 1849. Mr. Mitchell
sent for coin to meet the raid, both by lake and land. The
wagon broke down on the way, but the run was met. Its
depositors never ran the company. Farmers, hearing that
Mr. Mitchell was being run, would leave their crops to bring
him what coin they had on hand."

All this is natural enough. Though it is quite deplorable,
we can't blame Mitchell, if this fool people made him the
King of the Northwest,—its richest millionaire,—by neglect-
ing to provide a suitable amount of Government paper
money.

SPECULATIONS IN ENGLAND IN 1834, 1835 AND 1836.—
When the 800 State banks professing to pay coin for all liabilities were, in 1833, 1834, 1835 and 1836, supplying the
people of the United States with money to engage in all

5

kinds of speculations, the banks of Great Britain, including the Bank of England, also professing to pay coin, were doing the same thing for the people of England ; and in the monetary crisis which followed, the Bank of England would have suspended but for aid received by her from the Bank of France [as usual]. These speculations were not caused or sustained by Government paper, or irredeemable money of any kind. Banks professing to pay coin were their supporters.

CHAPTER IX.

1836 to 1846.
1836.

THE BANKS IN LUCK AGAIN.—The Act of June 23. 1836, provides that the deposits of the United States should be made in State banks, and that said banks should do and perform for the Treasury all that the United States banks had done and performed. These banks obligated themselves to at all times pay coin, and to pay the Government two per cent. interest for certain deposits. They were to report their condition to the Secretary of the Treasury at certain periods. Thus it seems that,—strange as it may appear,—Congress had not learned wisdom, by their experience with State banks in 1812, '13, '14 and '15. The two per cent. bait was a big inducement. But in less than one year after the act was passed, these banks all suspended, with a large amount of Government money on deposit—forty million dollars. The Treasury being without funds, Treasury notes were again resorted to ; and by them the business of the country and the Mexican war were sustained. The Government again came out a large loser by deposits in State banks. This led to the divorcing of the Government from all banks ; and excluding all bank notes from the Treasury, by the law of 1846.

WISDOM OF SARSAPARILLA TOWNSEND.—Notable echoes from this Jackson epoch are found in the pamphlets issued, from 1862 to 1864, by that wise and earnest patriot, S. P. Townsend, of sarsaparilla fame and fortune. He brings in an element not elsewhere considered, "The Albany Regency." For instance, here :—

In the days of the old United States Bank, the Democracy broke the Bank and bankrupted the country, and succeeded in ruining the Whig party : because they made it appear that it was the Bank that destroyed the people [partly true, S. L.] : when the fact was the disaster was caused by destroying the institution. It is due to the great Jackson to say that he never contemplated cessation of a national banking insti-

tution : for he said in his veto message, " Had the Executive
been called upon to furnish the plan for a bank, the duty
would have been cheerfully performed." It was the corrupt
Albany Regency, and their pet Safety-fund banking system,
headed by Martin Van Buren, and the Albany *Argus*, that
destroyed and brought into contempt and banished the
national constitutional money; and filled the land with worthless shin-plasters. These, having no foundation, soon van-
ished ; or kept shifting and drifting like the sands of the
desert, until, under Buchanan's administration, the people
became so impoverished that it was with difficulty the Government could negotiate a loan of a few millions at twelve
per cent. per annum. This same party, led on by the same
Albany *Argus*, are pursuing exactly the same course in regard to the legal tender Treasury notes. They have—in
tens of thousands of speeches and editorials—predicted that
the use of these notes would ruin the country ; and clamored that they may be withdrawn ; which, if done, will as
assuredly destroy business and credit, and bankrupt the
country, as did the destruction of the old United States Bank.
But what would be most unfortunate of all, these unprincipled
politicians would come into power again ; raised from the ruin
they had caused, aided by the weakness of Unionists, who
are actually alarmed at prosperity !

1837.

According to an Act of 1836, the surplus in the United
States Treasury was to be distributed among the States,
in proportion to their population, beginning Jan. 1, 1837.

THE ACT OF JANUARY 18, 1837, changed the alloy in silver
coins from 103½ to 100 parts in the 1000 parts ; making both
gold and silver coins, in the United States, 9·10 fine ; and
reducing the alloy in the silver dollar 3½ grains ; but leaving the silver therein 371¼ grains, the same as in the law
of 1792. The dollar, under the law of 1837, is 412½ grains,
instead of 416 grains, as under the law of 1792. Be it remembered that the Constitution says nothing about alloying gold
and silver coins. Did Congress violate the constitution by
so doing ? We think not.

PANIC OF 1837.—March 4, 1837, Martin Van Buren became President.

May 10, 1837, all the New York banks suspended. Sumner, of Yale, thus describes this matter:

In March, a meeting was held in New York, which was addressed by Mr. Webster. He ascribed the distress to the interference of the Government with the currency, and to the "Specie Circular" [demanding that public lands be paid for in specie only]. A committee of fifty was sent to Washington, to ask for the rescinding of the circular. In the address to the President (Van Buren), they said: "The value of our real estate has, within the last six months, depreciated more than forty millions." "Within the last two months there have been more than 250 failures." "A decline of $20,000,000 has occurred in our local stocks." "The immense amount of merchandise in our warehouses, has, within the same period, fallen in value at least thirty per cent." "Within a few weeks, not less than 20,000 individuals depending on their daily labor for their daily bread have been discharged by their employers; because the means of retaining them were exhausted." They ascribe all this, as they say, not to an undue extension of mercantile enterprise, but to the attempt to substitute a metallic for a paper currency, the removal of the deposits and the specie circular.

The President did nothing.

The banks all suspended May 10.

Nearly all the banks made money out of the suspension, and paid large dividends during the year.—History of Am. Currency: W. G. Sumner.

This last item is very significant—coming from such a gold idolater!

Tom Benton on Currency.—There were lively discussions in Congress on currency in 1837. Thomas Benton said, in the Senate: "The Government ought not to delegate this power if it could. It was too great a power to be trusted to any banking company whatever, or to any authority but the highest and most responsible which was known to our form of government. The Government itself ceases to be independent,—it ceases to be safe,—when the national currency is at the will of a company. The Government can undertake no great enterprise—either of war or peace—without the consent or co-operation of that company. It cannot count its revenues for six months ahead, without referring to the action of that company,—its friendship or its en-

mity, its concurrence or opposition,—to see how far that company will permit money to be scarce or plentiful; how far it
will let the money system go on regularly, or throw it into
disorder; how far it will suit the interests or policy of that
company to create a tempest or suffer a calm in the moneyed
ocean.

"The people are not safe when such a company has such a
power. The temptations are too great, the opportunity too
easy, to put up and down prices; to make and break fortunes;
to bring the whole community on its knees to the Neptunes
who preside over the flux and reflux of paper. All property
is at their mercy. The price of real estate, of every growing
crop, of every staple article in the market, is at their command. Stocks are their plaything—their gambling theatre—
on which they gamble daily, with as little secrecy and as little morality, and far more mischief to fortunes, than common
gamblers carry on their operations."

Speaking of the acts of the Bank charter, by Jackson, and
of De Toqueville's mistake about it, Benton says :—De
Toqueville speaks of the well-informed classes who rallied
around the Bank; and the common people, who had formed
no rational opinion about it, and who had joined General Jackson. Certainly the great business community, with few exceptions,—comprising wealth, ability and education,—went
for the Bank, and the masses for General Jackson. But which
had formed the rational opinion is seen by the event. The
" well-informed " classes have bowed not merely to the decision but to the intelligence of the masses. They have
adopted their opinion of the institution—condemned it—
repudiated it as an "obsolete idea "; and of all of its former
advocates not one now exists. All have yielded to that in-
stinctive sagacity of the people, which is an overmatch for
book-learning; and which, being the result of common-sense,
is usually right; and being disinterested, is usually honest.

CALHOUN ON CURRENCY.—John C. Calhoun, in his speech
in the Senate, in 1837, when the banks were suspending,—
with the public money in their vaults,—made the following
remarks :—It is, then, my impression that, in the present condition of the world, a paper currency in some form * * *
is almost indispensable in financial and commercial operations of civilized and extensive communities. In many respects it has a vast superiority over a metallic currency; es-

pecially in great and extended transactions,—by its greater cheapness, lightness, and the facility of determining the amount. It may throw some light on this subject to state that North Carolina, just after the Revolution, issued a large amount of paper, which was made receivable in dues to her. It was also made a legal tender; but which, of course, was not made obligatory after the adoption of the Federal Constitution. A large amount—say between $400,000 and $500,-000—remained in circulation after that period, and continued to circulate for more than 20 years, at par with gold and silver during the whole time, with no other advantage than being received in the revenue of the State, which was much less than $100,000 per annum.

No one can doubt but that the Government credit is better than that of any bank; more reliable ; more safe. Why, then, should it mix up with the less perfect credit of those institutions? Why not use its own credit to the amount of its own transactions? Why should it not be safe in its own hands, while it shall be considered safe in the hands of 800 private institutions, scattered all over the country, and which have no other object but their own private profit; to increase which, they extend their business to the most dangerous extremes? And why should the community be compelled to give six per cent. discount for the Government credit, blended with that of the bank, when the superior credit of the Government could be furnished separately without discount, to the mutual advantage of the Government and the community?

But whatever may be the amount that can be circulated, I hold it clear, that to that amount it would be as stable in value as gold and silver itself, provided the Government be bound to receive it exclusively with those metals in all its dues, and that it be left perfectly optional with those who have claims on the Government, to receive it or not.

Again he said : We are told the form I suggested is but a repetition of the " old Continental Money," a ghost that is ever conjured up by all who wish to give the banks an exclusive monopoly of Government credit. There is not the least analogy between them. The one is a promise to pay when there is no revenue ; and the other a promise to receive, in the dues of the Government, when there is abundant revenue.

ONE MILL PER ANNUM.—Judge Warwick Martin says of
the Act of October 12, 1837 :—The banks had all suspended,
with nearly $40,000,000 Government funds. Not one year
before, the law had made these banks public depositories,
with their promise that they would always pay coin for all
liabilities. The Government had, in 1835, paid off the last
dollar of the national debt. The surplus then in the Treasury was near $40,000,000. This was in the banks. The
Government had no money to pay ordinary expenses, unless
the Treasury used suspended bank notes. This Mr. Van
Buren, then President, refused to do. He called Congress
together to meet the emergency. Their remedy for the
emergency was to issue Treasury notes, which Jefferson says
are the only reliance of a nation. This Act of October 12,
1837, provided for the issue of $10,000,000 Treasury notes,
in denominations not less than $50, running one year. The
law left the interest which they were to bear discretional
with the President and the Secretary of the Treasury ; but in
no case was it to exceed six per cent. Congress appeared
too timid to make these notes money, bearing no interest.
They did not authorize the Secretary to so make them.
They did, however, leave the rate of interest which the notes
were to bear discretionary with him. He, knowing that the
people needed them as money, complied with the law, by causing many of these notes to bear one mill interest per annum.
As such, they circulated freely as money, and the people
were delighted to get and use them. They answered all the
purposes of coin, and equalized the exchanges throughout
the country. The banks did not at that time possess sufficient power to injure them. The writer was then in the mercantile business in Pittsburg, Pa., and he often saw and received them in business. They were made legal tender for
all debts due the United States ; and were payable to creditors of the Government, as all the other Treasury notes had
been. They, like the notes of the Bank of England, were,
under this law, never to be paid out of the Treasury but
once. Upon returning they were all canceled.

THE ACT OF OCTOBER 16, 1837—(Statutes 5, p. 206) authorized the Secretary of the Treasury to settle with the deposit
banks upon the best terms he could—said banks having all
suspended, owing the Government some $40,000,000, which
they could not pay, excepting in their suspended bank paper.

A THINKER CRIES " EUREKA ! "—1837 brought out a great thinker and writer on finance, from among the New York merchants,—Edward Kellogg.

Edward Kellogg was a prosperous merchant ; but the panic of 1837 dragged him into the whirlpool of financial ruin ; he had become bankrupt, through no fault of his. He studied the question of panics, in all its bearings, and lay awake many a night pondering over the causes of hard times. And one night, in 1843, after lying awake, as he had often done before, he jumped up, exclaiming, in the very words of the old Greek philosopher, " Eureka " ! and sat down to write out the points of his discovery. He had " found it ". The whole trouble lay in the fallacy that placed money, the life-blood of the world's industries, under the control of the few, and made it a monopoly. As a matter of course, the first pamphlet he wrote was incomplete. But he wrote more, and rewrote the first one. His gifted daughter, Mary, was his valuable and trusted assistant ; and soon, as a result of their joint labors, we had his book, " A New Monetary System," which has been a text-book and guide for labor and currency reformers ever since.

1838.

THE ACT OF MAY 21, 1838.—This act authorized the re-issue of the $10,000,000 Treasury notes issued under the Act of 1837, which that act provided should be canceled on their return to the Treasury. It was unwise in Congress not to provide that these Treasury notes, which bore no interest, should remain uncanceled until worn out ; when new notes should have been given for them. It has taken time and a great war to open the eyes of the people, and Congress, to see what Jefferson saw in 1813.

ALBERT GALLATIN, when president of the Bank of North America, of New York City, in 1838, said at a bank convention : " We all know that while a bank note bears upon its face a promise to pay the amount of its denomination in coin, it carries with it the implied condition that it be not asked for."

Many years later, that great philosopher, Henry C. Carey, quoted this, and said :—In other words, he might have said, Whenever British banks and bankers are inflating the currency,, British manufacturers flood our markets with goods

to be sold at long credits. Money and credit then abound
among ourselves. Specie not being needed, our banks follow
suit, largely extending their loans, and thus inducing their
customers to enlarge their business, to build ships and
houses, and to make new roads. A year or two passes, and
we enjoy what is called prosperity. Then, however, comes
from across the Atlantic a chilling frost, in the form of
refusal of new credits, and withdrawal of old ones, and in
all other of the usual accompaniments of a crisis. The little
specie we then have on hand is drawn out,—the gold for
Britain, and the silver for France or Germany,—compelling
us to insist upon payment by our customers; most of whom,
unable to pay, become bankrupt. We, ourselves, then, after
fruitless efforts, resort to suspension, in the hope and belief
that State legislators may manifest their pity for us, by
legalizing, for a year or two, the violation of the laws to
which we have been driven. Such is the true financial history of the country, throughout seventy years that we were
making believe to use machinery of exchange like that in
use in France, England, and other manufacturing countries
of Europe. At intervals of half-a-dozen years, our monetary bag has been inflated from abroad; the balloon then
rising, to be suddenly collapsed at the will of foreign bankers,—with ruin to all who have been led to go in debt; leaving
them, and their families, to start in the world anew; with the
stain of bankruptcy clinging to them in all the future.

IN 1838, HENRY C. CAREY printed his great book, "The
Credit System in France, Great Britain and the United
States." He announced the then novel doctrine that, among
the many vices of the credit and banking systems of England
and America,—which always have been so closely related,
as to be almost, if not absolutely identical,—the most destructive was that which permitted banks to lend, without
restriction, money or credits deposited with them for safe-
keeping. He was, thus, the first to thoroughly expose the
sham and evil hidden under "bank deposits and loans," which
are largely the mere moonshine of inflated bank credits—
alias debts.

1839.

One financial event of this year was the book on Money
printed by Condy Raguet, much quoted by H. C. Carey and
others.

THE PHILA. BANK OF THE UNITED STATES (NICK BIDDLE'S) stopped October 10, 1839, followed by nearly all the banks of the South and West. It finally closed February 4, 1841. The great deserted palace of a bank building stood there on Third Street in 1860, and later—a monumental warning against too much "private enterprise."

1840.

THE ACT OF MAY 31, 1840 (STATUTES 5, p. 370).—This law renews the Act of 1837, relating to the issue of Treasury notes, and makes the following modifications : 1. That they were to be issued in place of those redeemed ; not to exceed in this issue $5,000,000. 2. They were to be redeemed in less than a year, if the Treasury was in a condition to redeem them. 3. When ready to redeem them, the Secretary of the Treasury was to give notice. 4. After due notice, the notes should cease to bear interest, if they remained out. This act was to continue only one year. It is evident that Congress supposed the necessity for issuing Treasury notes would soon cease, but they were mistaken.

THE ACT OF JULY 4. 1840, was the first independent Treasury act of the days of Mr. Van Buren. The money of the Government was to be kept by the Government, instead of the banks, in mints, custom-houses, post-offices and the Treasury building. The main feature of the bill was that after January 3, 1843, no payment should be made to the Government in anything but gold and silver coin. The banks were then suspended. The Government was being sustained by Treasury notes. But still this law provided that after January, 1843, Treasury notes should be excluded from the Treasury, as well as bank-notes—an insane procedure. An appeal was made to the people, that year, upon this law ; and they repudiated it by electing Gen. Harrison president. This law provided penalties for any Government official who sold gold and silver for paper money, and paid the debts of Government therein. It also prohibited Government drafts from being sold as money. This was an epoch to delight the soul of Sumner of Yale, and warm the cockles of his frigid heart.

Judge Warwick Martin says of this singular effort :—

From 1837 until 1840 the first effort of the Democratic party, and of any considerable number of the American people, to obtain coin only for the Treasury was made.

Then it was advocated by Mr. Van Buren and Mr. Benton.
At first, their object was simply to separate Government
money from that of individuals, by divorcing the Government and all banks, by the establishment of the Sub-Treasury. But the question came up naturally, what kind of
money shall be received and held in the Treasury? The
leaders of this branch of the Democratic party did not think
of providing a reliable, sound, uniform currency for the
people. They left the State banks to supply this currency.
All Mr. Van Buren and Mr. Benton aimed at was to furnish
money for the Government. They induced a majority of
Congress in 1840 to pass an act making gold and silver coin,
only, the money of the Government, receivable for taxes and
duties. Though the Government was then being sustained
by Treasury notes, this law excluded them from the Treasury
also. Mr. Calhoun nobly defended Treasury notes; showing
their equality with coin whenever they had been tried, and
their great superiority over bank notes, whether State or
National. But the hard money prevailed this one time. As
Treasury notes then in the hands of the people, provided
upon their face and in the laws enacting them, that they
should be received for all debts due the Government, the
law of 1840, which excluded them from the Treasury, was a
violation of the Constitution in that behalf, and treated it as
such; and the Treasury notes continued to be received the
same as before this law passed. No law ever passed by
Congress, excepting the sedition law of John Adams, was so
unpopular as this law. The people had not called for it.
It made a distinction between the money of the Government
and that of the people. The people must be satisfied with
State bank notes. The Government officials must have hard
money, which was generally at a premium over our bank
notes. Mr. Van Buren went before the people on hard
money and was defeated, with all the office-holders to aid
his election. This was the only opportunity the people of
the United States ever had to vote upon hard money, and
they rejected it and its advocate and author.

1841.

President Harrison Died in April, and Mr. Tyler
became president. One of the first acts of the Whigs
was to authorize the issue of $12,000,000 of six per cent.

bonds, to take up the Democratic Treasury notes ; though the people were satisfied with them, and they bore little or no interest. This was an act to benefit the capitalists, and to injure the people, by depriving them of $12,000,000 of the best money, which they greatly needed, and imposing upon them an annual payment of $720,000 for no good purpose. But the great object of the Whigs was to establish a National bank ; and the scarcer they made the money of the country, for the time being, the greater would be the demand for the bank. An agent was sent to Europe to sell the $12,000,000 of bonds ; but he failed to sell them ; and the Whigs, though they did it reluctantly, were compelled to issue Treasury notes to run the Government. But Congress were, as usual, ready to carry out the wishes of the money power. They, therefore, chartered a bank of the United States, with a capital of $50,000,000, which was vetoed by Mr. Tyler. Another bank was chartered, called. "The Fiscal Corporation," which was also vetoed.

THE ACT OF AUGUST 13, 1841, repealed the Democratic Act of June, 1836, excluding the notes of the Bank of the United States from the Treasury ; and provided that said notes should, thereafter, be received therein ; though the bank was then a only State bank. That same year the bank made its disastrous failure. This act also repealed the act of 1840, called the First Sub-Treasury Act ; and provided that bank notes should be received in the Treasury.

RELIEF NOTES.—In 1841, Pennsylvania was on the verge of bankruptcy. The State was unable to pay interest on the public debt ; or even pay the wages of laborers for work done on the public improvements. Corporations were bankrupt, and merchants were in nearly as bad a situation. There was no money ; and, consequently, trade and production were completely paralyzed. The State of Pennsylvania, in this crisis, issued $3,100,000 of what was called "Relief Notes", bearing simply a promise that they would be received by the Treasury of the State, in payment of all taxes and other obligations due to the State. These were taken greedily by the people. Banks inserted in the front of their books an agreement that the depositor should receive on check the same kind of money he deposited, and then took these notes. They discounted paper with them. The wheels of industry were set in motion by these notes, which promised nothing but that they would be received in payment of State taxes. The State paid her domestic creditors; and these hastened to pay theirs, or to supply their wants by purchase; crops, for which there had been no market, moved. The loom and the spindle were heard again. Labor—lifted from despair—found work and wages. With the great resources of Pennsylvania under full and free development, she was soon exporting more than she imported. Gold and silver—as usual when not needed—flowed in upon her; and the broken banks resumed specie payment.

INDIANA TREASURY NOTES.—Judge Warwick Martin says that, in 1841, the State of Indiana required money to complete her public works, and issued Treasury notes to meet the demand. These notes bore interest, and were paid out by the State to those to whom the State was indebted. At first banks and bankers turned up their financial noses at them; but both the principal and the interest were receivable for all taxes due the State; and it was not long until they were at a premium everywhere. "The writer speaks from personal knowledge upon this subject, having received and paid out large amounts of these Treasury notes. Indiana has generally had the best State money of any of the United States; and these Treasury notes were the best money the State ever had. They were all redeemed by the payment of taxes, as the law provided they should be."

PRESIDENT TYLER HAD A GOOD INSTINCT ABOUT FINANCE.—He said in his Message of December 7, 1841 (Vol. II., p. 1261):—In pursuance to a pledge given to you in my last Message to Congress (which pledge I urge as an apology for adventuring to present you the details of my plans), the Secretary of the Treasury will be ready to submit to you, should you require it, a plan of finance which, while it throws around the public treasure reasonable guards for its protection, and rests on powers acknowledged in practice to exist from the origin of the Government, will, at the same time, furnish to the country a sound paper medium, and afford all reasonable facilities for regulating the exchanges. When submitted, you will perceive in it a plan amendatory of the existing laws in relation to the Treasury Department—subordinate in all respects to the will of Congress directly, and the will of the people indirectly, self-sustaining, should it be found in practice to realize its promises in theory, and repealable at the pleasure of Congress.

It proposes, by effectual restraints, and by invoking the true spirit of our institutions, to separate the purse from the sword ; or, more properly to speak, denies any other control to the President over the agents who may be selected to carry it into execution, but what may be indispensably necessary to secure the fidelity of such agents ; and, by wise regulations, keep plainly apart from each other private and public funds. It contemplates the establishment of a board of control at the seat of government, with agencies at prominent commercial points, or wherever else Congress shall direct, for the safe-keeping and disbursement of the public moneys, and a substitution, at the option of the public creditor, of Treasury notes in lieu of gold and silver. It proposes to limit the issues to an amount not to exceed $15,000,000, without the express sanction of the legislative power. It also authorizes the receipt of individual depositors of gold and silver to a limited amount, and the granting of certificates of deposit, divided into such sums as may be called for by the depositors. It proceeds a step further, and authorizes the purchase and sale of domestic bills and drafts, resting on real and substantial basis, payable at sight, or having but a short time to run, and drawn on places not less than 100 miles apart ; which authority, except in so far as may be necessary for Government purposes exclusively, is only to be prohibited by the State in which the agency is situated.

I am not able to perceive that any fair and candid objection can be urged against the plan, the principal outlines of which I have thus presented. I cannot doubt but that the notes which it proposes to furnish at the voluntary option of public creditors, issued in lieu of the revenue and its certificates of deposit, will be maintained at an equality with gold and silver everywhere. They are redeemable in gold and silver on demand, at the places of issue. They are receivable everywhere in payment of Government dues. The Treasury notes are limited to an amount of one-fourth less than the estimated annual receipts of the Treasury, and in addition, they rest upon the faith of the Government for their redemption. If all these assurances are not sufficient to make them available, then the idea, as it seems to me, of furnishing a sound paper medium of exchanges, may be entirely abandoned.

THE PRESIDENT OF THE BANK OF ENGLAND.—When the

Phila. Bank of the United States failed, in 1841, that institution was largely in debt to the Bank of England. The president of the latter bank came to the United States to look after this debt. When he landed in New York, he read in the papers the Message of President Tyler, recommending that the permanent money of the country should be issued by the Government. He lost no time in visiting Washington and the White House; where and when he expressed his admiration of the monetary system advocated by President Tyler; *and stated that it should be adopted not only by the United States, but by England and every other great nation.*

1842.

THE UNITED STATES COULD NOT BORROW.—The Act of April 15, 1842, extends the time for selling the $12,000,000, of bonds one year, and provides that the loan might be made to extend any time that the Secretary and the purchaser might agree upon: not beyond twenty years. It also added $5,000,000 to the loan. The stock is allowed to be sold at less than par, if the President agreed thereto. No such thing had occurred since the close of the war of 1812. The United States did not owe $30,000,000 at that time; and they could not sell $12,000,000 of bonds at par; though taxes and duties were pledged for their payment. The Whigs were compelled to fall back upon Treasury notes. These notes were then bearing only nominal interest; but the Whigs provided, in this act, that all Treasury notes then out and those issued thereafter should bear six per cent. interest; and that they should be redeemed as soon as bonds could be sold for that purpose. These are the facts, though the Treasury notes were in good credit, and the people were satisfied with them. But a war was going on between the Whig Congress and President Tyler. The latter advocated the issuing of all the paper, as well as the metallic money by the Government; but Congress wished the paper money issued by a National bank. The President vetoed the bank bill. Congress, by way of heading him off, passed the act to make Treasury notes bear six per cent. interest, instead of being used as money.

THE ACT OF JUNE 30, 1842, provided for the issue of $5,000,000 Treasury notes to run one year, which were legal tender for all debts to the Government, and were to be paid to such public creditors and others as were willing to receive them. The creditors always preferred them. The Secretary of the Treasury is authorized to have these Treasury notes placed to his credit in banks at par and accrued interest or otherwise, to borrow money upon them. The interest upon these notes was five per cent.

THE ACT OF AUGUST 31, 1842, makes certain further provisions respecting the sale of the $17,000,000 bonds which had not yet taken place. This act provides that unless they could be sold at par, the Secretary of the Treasury should issue $6,000,000 Treasury notes. They were compelled to have recourse to what Jefferson calls the only resource of a nation. The Treasury notes authorized by this act may be reissued.

1843.

THE ACT OF MARCH 3, 1843, fixed the value in the United States of certain foreign coins. The thaler of Prussia is made 68 cents ; the milric of Portugal $1.12 ; the rex dollar of Bremen 77 cents ; the milric of Madeira $1.00 ; the milric of the Azores 83½ cents ; the mark banco of Hamburg 35 cents ; the rouble of Russia 75 cents ; the rupee of British India 44½ cents. This was Whig law.

AN ACT OF MARCH 3, 1843, authorizes the issue of new Treasury notes to supply the place of those redeemed ; and that interest should be paid upon Treasury notes after their maturity. The act provides that bonds may be issued for Treasury notes, that shall run three years.

SUMNER OF YALE EXPLAINS THINGS.—Discussing the affairs of 1843, in his " Currency ", which was not written in Bloomingdale Insane Asylum, that marvelous genius, Sumner, says : " The cases we have had to deal with hitherto have presented us with the simple phenomenon of the exportation of precious metals and increased importation of commodities, due to the repetition of the grossest error possible in currency—the attempt to use two kinds of circulating medium : one inferior to the other." Yet, in all this time—1600 to 1843,—he has never shown how our people could have got the necessary coin. He is evidently like the philosopher who replied to the man who excused some action of his by saying, " Well, I must live ! " by the very positive retort : " I

6

am not so sure of that." Sumner's icy dictum is: "Do it
or die !"

Further on, this serene sage says: "The movement of
specie would, therefore, be, if the whole world used the
metals, and regulated prices by them, without interference, as
regular, as self-controlled, and as beneficent as the movement
of the tides." The fact is that the action of the tides is controlled—like much of Sumner's cerebral action—by the
moon (*luna*).

Well, what can you expect of a man whose fetish is that
prodigious rubbish, "The British Bullion Report of 1810,"
of which he says: "So much, however, in regard to the laws
which govern paper issues, as was laid down in the Bullion
Report, is established beyond dispute. Its doctrines are the
alphabet of modern finance!" Any one who wants to read
this precious document will find it as an appendix to Sumner's book. Read it, and "learn with how little wisdom
nations are governed."

1845.

THE ACT OF MARCH 3, 1845, fixed the value of the florin
of Russia at 48 cents. This was also a Whig act, and one of
the last approved by Mr. Tyler.

In 1845 the Democrats came into power again. They
fought the Mexican War with Treasury notes.

CHAPTER X.

1846 to 1856.

1846.

THE ACT OF MAY 22, 1846, regulated the value in the United States of the following foreign coins : Of Norway, Sweden, Denmark, Prussia, Northern and Southern Germany, Austria, Belgium, Augsburg, Sardinia, Naples, Nova Scotia, and New Brunswick. Previous to this act these coins were not money in the United States. No foreign coins are money here now. They have all been demonetized.

THE ACT OF JULY 22, 1846, makes the following provisions : 1. That Treasury notes should be issued to take the place of those destroyed, to the extent of $10,000,000 only of this issue. 2. If the President saw proper he might issue stock in place of Treasury notes. 3. This act provides for the payment of $50,000 Treasury notes which had been stolen.

THE ACT OF AUGUST 6, 1846, ESTABLISHES THE INDEPENDENT TREASURY, which had been attempted in 1840, but had failed. The law of 1840 was repudiated by the people. The law of 1846 was sustained by the people, of all parties, from 1846 until 1861 ; and many of its provisions are still continued. The principal difference between the two acts was, that the law of 1840 excluded all Treasury notes as well as bank notes from the Treasury after January 1, 1843 ; but the law of 1846 made all Treasury notes issued by the United States, and gold and silver coins, equal in the payment of all debts due the Government.

This act divorced the Government from all banks, excluded all bank notes from the Treasury, and made all Treasury notes legal tender, the same as coin, in payment to the United States. It also provided that the officers of the Government, under bonds, should receive and keep all the money of the United States, and deposit the same in the Treasury, instead of in banks ; and that the money of the Government should be kept separate from that of individuals. This was one of the best laws ever enacted by the Democratic party.

1847.

MONEY FOR THE MEXICAN WAR.—The Act of January 28, 1847. The Mexican War was then in progress. The expenditures of the Government were large. An emergency existed. The remedy of which Jefferson speaks was at hand. A large issue of Treasury notes was ordered. Twenty-three millions were provided. This was a large sum for those times; more than $500,000,000 would be now. The rate of interest on this $23,000,000 Treasury notes is not provided by law. It is left to the Secretary of the Treasury, and the party to whom they were paid. These notes were intended to be used as money; and if parties would take them at one mill interest, the Secretary had a right to issue them. Many of them were so issued and used; greatly to the satisfaction of the people.

SPECULATIONS AND PANIC OF 1847.—Previous to 1847, all the banks of the United States had professed resumption. In this year, immense speculations took place in corn, wheat, flour, pork, beef, and all kinds of American productions. Large purchases were made of these commodities, which were shipped to England. Prices fell after the purchases and the arrival of the produce at its place of destination. Many failures took place in both countries, as a consequence of these speculations. Be it remembered that the money to engage in the speculations was not suspended bank paper, or the notes of the Government. On the contrary, all the money for these speculations was furnished by banks of the United States, which at that time professed to pay coin for all their liabilities.

[S. Leavitt had reason to remember this speculation; for his father was drawn into it and bankrupted by it, though he got safely through the panic of 1837.]

Nearly every witness who testified before the secret committee of the House of Commons, in 1857, agreed that gold could only be held by paralyzing the business of the country. It is estimated, by witnesses who testified before that committee, that in the panic of 1847, in Great Britain, the property of the country, by reason of the measures rendered necessary to maintain the single gold standard, was depreciated $1,500,000,000. J. W. Shuckers says that the Bank of England made untold millions out of this panic.

FRANCE HELPED THE WHOLE WORLD.—A way in which France has singularly helped the whole world is seen in her resolute maintenance of the ratio of 15½ silver to one of gold, during all this century.

This fact was described by Senator Jones, of Nevada, in his speech, in April, 1890, in the Senate, thus :

"Not only did the French law keep the metals together at that time, when the larger annual yield was of silver, but it kept them together when the larger annual yield was of gold. Had not that law been in operation during the Fifties, when a flood of gold poured from the mines of California and Australia, gold would have fallen, as in early times it more than once fell, to the ratio of 1 to 10; at which but 10 ounces of silver (instead of 15½) would buy an ounce of gold. Thus the law of one country alone—a country then of not more than one-half the population of the United States—held the metals together ; so that to whatever extent gold fell in relation to commodities, from 1848 to 1865, by reason of the large output of the mines, silver fell to the same extent ; notwithstanding the enormous decrease in its production relatively to gold, during that period."

Of course there was no logical propriety about this ; but it was fortunate—since most of the world still wishes to indulge in the luxury of commodity money—that France thus helped to prevent fluctuation in the currency.

According to the statement of Mr. Pierson, Netherlands commissioner before the International Monetary Conference of 1881, in 1803 bimetallism was established in France and continued until 1873.

From 1803 to 1820 there was a yield of four times as much silver from the mines as gold ; after that, until 1860, the yield of the metals was reversed, and the mine output was four times as much gold as silver. The coinage in France from 1820 to 1847 was nine times more silver than gold, and from 1857 to 1866 the coinage was sixty-four times more gold than silver ; and yet, in all these eighty years of fluctuation in metallic production, while her silver money averaged 69 per cent. to 31 per cent. of her gold money, the variation in the market rate between gold and silver bullion was never more than 2 per cent. !

1848.

Speculation and overtrading had not much to do with the panic of 1848. The abdication of Louis Philippe, and the Revolution in France, had most to do with it.

1849.

THE ACT OF MARCH 3, 1849, CREATED THE GOLD DOLLAR AND THE DOUBLE EAGLE.—The one was to be of the value of a dollar and the other of twenty dollars. The only dollar, that had, thus far, been created and coined was the silver dollar. This law did not make a gold dollar, but it did make a gold piece of the value of a dollar. This is the reading of the statute. There has never been in the United States a piece of gold called in the law $1, $2.50, $5, or $10. The gold pieces have been of the value of $1, of $2.50, of $5, of $10, and of $20. All of them were made, by the laws creating them, legal tender with the dollar. The dollar was the unit of value and of the money of account, by which gold was valued.

WILD CATS IN NEW ENGLAND.—There was "heaps of money" in running State banks in those days, "while the thing lasted." The extent to which these banks were enabled to loan their credit by means of the specie basis will appear from an examination of the report of the Commissioners of the banks of Connecticut, for a period of 12 years, from 1837 to 1849. The condition of Connecticut banks may be taken as an average of the banks of the country. The Connecticut report shows : Average capital, $8,688,295 ; average liabilities, $13,129,230 ; average specie, $478,719 ; average loans and discounts, $11,669,457.

1850.

GOLD DOWN. SILVER UP.—After the discovery of vast fields of gold in California and Australia, in 1849, 1850 and 1851, there was great demand for silver coin for the purchase of gold ; and the impression becoming general that these large acquisitions of gold would depreciate its value, a universal disposition was manifested among bullionists to exchange gold for silver. This caused United States, Spanish, Mexican, and Central and South American silver dollars to rise to a premium of two and three per cent. for gold, at which price the Rothschilds purchased them, not only in the United States, but in all the European markets of exchange. That the law of 1834 was not the only or principal cause of these purchases of silver, is evident from the fact that they were not confined to the United States, but existed in Europe to a greater extent than here. There the relation of 1 to 16 did not exist. But one other fact had greater influence in causing this result. About this time, commercial treaties were, for the first time, entered into between China, the United States and Great Britain. Silver dollars were the principal circulation of China. The Chinese were ignorant of the fact that, in Europe, silver was worth 15½ pounds of silver to 1 pound of gold, and in America 16 to 1. The Chinese used gold blocks for large transactions, and they valued gold at only one to 5. There a pound of gold was worth only five pounds of silver, while in Europe it was worth 15½, and in America 16 pounds of silver. Large quantities of dollars were therefore sent from all parts of Europe to purchase this gold in China. China was drained of gold and filled with silver dollars. Europe and America were drained of silver dollars and well supplied with gold. Owing to these facts Holland demonetized gold.

John Thompson said to me : "As to gold being related to silver as one to five in China, it seems like an immense speculation ; and many might suppose that Europeans made great fortunes out of it, before the Chinese discovered the trick. But I know that this was not so ; because there was so little gold in China."

1851.

Bank Notes in Australia.—In 1851 nearly all the silver of Europe was sent to Australia to be invested in gold. When Great Britain was thus drained of silver, and no more could be sent to meet this demand, the British Government authorized the establishment of a bank in Australia, the notes of which were to be paid out for gold bullion, instead of silver coin. The bank was authorized to issue three dollars or pounds sterling of notes to every dollar or pound sterling of gold bullion held by the bank ; and said notes were made by the law creating the bank legal tender the same as coin. The result was that all the bullion and coin went into the bank, and the notes of the bank circulated among the people in the business of the country, though

they were the notes of a bank only, not those of a nation.
Thus England always protects her own interests and her
own (rich) people, at least, while the Congress of the United
States legislates for the benefit of England.

The following is the *Journal des Économistes'* table of the
production of gold and silver from 1852 to 1876 :

Date.	Gold, millions.	Silver, millions.	Total.
1852	182½	40½	223
1853	155	40½	195½
1854	127	40½	167½
1855	135	40½	175½
1856	147½	40½	188
1857	133	40½	173½
1858	124½	40½	165
1859	124½	40½	165
1860	119	40½	159½
1861	114	42½	156½
1862	107½	45	152½
1863	107	49	156
1864	113	51½	164½
1865	120	52	172
1866	121	50½	171½
1867	116	54	170
1868	120	50	170
1869	121	47½	168½
1870	116	51½	167½
1871	116½	61	177½
1872	101½	65	166½
1873	103½	70	173½
1874	90½	71½	162
1875	97½	62	159½

1853.

THE ACT OF FEBRUARY 26, 1853, CREATED THE FIRST
LIMITED LEGAL-TENDER coin in the United States. Previously all United States gold, silver, and copper coins had
been full legal tender. The rich and the poor had the
same money. Now, and since 1853, we have one money for
the rich, and another money for the poor, as the nations of
Europe have. Under this law halves, quarters, and dimes
were made over seven per cent. light, and lawful money for

$5 only. They were as good as the silver dollar, or gold, up to $5. Above that sum they were not money, but light bullion. Two half dollars have, under this law, 384 grains standard silver—28½ less than the dollar. This act was among the last approved by a Whig President. It should be repealed.

THE CLEARING-HOUSE, which had been suggested by Albert Gallatin, in 1841, was finally established in 1853, on the plan of Mr. George Curtis.

CHAPTER XI.

1856 to 1861.

1857.

THE PANIC OF 1857.—Here we enter another great financial epoch. Proposing to give several explanations from reliable authorities of the causes of the terrible panic of 1857, we begin with a short one from an unknown writer—which seems to touch bottom as to the cause that "lay nearest to it." Here it is :—

The immediate cause is not generally known. It was this : In the latter part of 1857, when the Bank of England was struggling to maintain specie payments, it came into the New York market and sold about seven million dollars worth of American securities ; and took the gold from the banks of that city. Knowing the condition of that huge bank, and that it had plenty of American securities, the New York banks became exceedingly alarmed, and began to contract and call on the country banks for gold.

" *Hinc illæ lachrymæ !*"

Here is one of the deep causes :

THE ACT OF FEBRUARY 21, 1857, DEMONETIZED ALL FOREIGN COINS in the United States. It was done by the Democratic party. It was a strange act for those who favor hard money, and insist that the law does not make metallic money ; but that the metal is money without authority of law and without the stamp of the nation, as a few *ignorant* Democrats now do. Since February 21, 1857, no foreign coin has been money in the United States, because the laws of 1857 and 1873 say it shall not be. The law makes and unmakes money. The law of 1873 was a Republican act. The law of 1857 also created a new cent and three-cent piece, composed of 88 parts copper and 12 parts nickel, which were made full legal tender, and were to be used to redeem the old heavy cents. This law introduces a new metal into our coinage. We refer to nickel. It had never before been used. It is not named in the Constitution. Have the

Democrats violated the Constitution by using this metal? We think not. The signing of this act was one of the last acts of Mr. Pierce. It was in favor of the bullion brokers. So long as all foreign coins were money they could not buy and sell them at a profit.

Now for Stephen Colwell.

The panic of 1837 roused that great and noble New York merchant, Kellogg, to write his "New Monetary System." The panic of 1857 roused that equally great and noble Philadelphia merchant, Stephen Colwell, to write his "Ways and Means of Payment." Here is some of his talk about the immediate effect of the latter panic:—The late panic has inflicted, in all its bearings and ramifications, a loss upon the country which may be variously estimated from $500,000,000 to $1,000,000,000. No doubt the ill-effects of the panic were much enhanced by the previous abuse of credit, and that a considerable portion of this devastation should be set down to that account. With every allowance in that respect we shall have a vast sum of loss to charge to the panic. And whether this sum be $400,000,000 or $800,000,000 matters not, to our view. The loss was to a great extent *unnecessary, cruel, terrible,*—a loss which has carried privation, distress and ruin to a million of homes. For a time, at least, not yet passed, it reduced hundreds of thousands of the best people to a state of entire dependence, if not beggary.

What was the occasion of these dire calamities? The banks of the United States had a reserve of specie for several years previous to 1857—and during the first half of that year —amounting to somewhat over $50,000,000; and of this the banks in the city of New York held a little more than one-fifth. To save this amount of specie [from going to England.—S. L.] the banks contracted the currency one-half; denied the usual facilities upon their books; put up the rate of interest to from 12 to 36 per cent.; put down exchange upon England to nine or ten per cent. below par; reduced the revenue from customs to less than half the usual amount; drew a surplus of $20,000,000 of gold out of the public Treasury; drove the Government to an issue of paper promises to pay its current expenses; deprived hundreds of thousands, perhaps millions, of their customary employment; caused some 5,000 or 6,000 failures among men of business; and, finally, inflicted a loss on the country, in the depreciation of securities, in the reduction of prices, and by insolvency, of several hundred millions. Not to save this sum of $50,-000,000 from being lost, sunk in the ocean, or thrown away, were all these evils encountered ; but merely to prevent it from passing into circulation among the people ; or, at the worst, to prevent it from being exported in payment of debts due in foreign countries. Nine-tenths of the debts of the country are paid, as we have seen, by the agency of discounts and deposits ; with some aid from the circulation of the banks: But the banks have been placed under such heavy penalties to pay all their liabilities on demand, that when they are threatened with a panic, a commercial revulsion, or a heavy export of specie to foreign countries, they are compelled—like Samson in the temple of the Philistines—to pull down the whole fabric of credit, public and private, about the ears of the people; to disturb and check the progress of industry in all its departments ; to make bankrupts of their customers ; and to sow pauperism broadcast in the field of labor. .

This compelled policy of the banks, under the stringency of the laws which govern them, has been called " paying specie." But with how little propriety. Instead of paying their liabilities with commercial promptness, and the faithfulness of those who are discharging a legal and moral obligation, they resist it with all the power and weapons they can command. In the struggles incident to this resistance, they strike down friends as well as enemies ; and deprive the public of an amount of currency, necessary to business, ten times greater than the specie they are unwilling to pay out. And this is the convertibility so long aimed at. and to secure which so much legislation and so much thought has been expended !

This is the triumph of banks which pass through a season of panic and revulsion without suspension [like Chemical Bank of New York.—S. L.]—a triumph like the victory which leaves 100,000 dead bodies on the field of battle; which makes 10,000 widows, 50,000 orphans and 200,000 paupers.

————

Remember, in reading the above, that Stephen Colwell was a rich, prosperous merchant, not upset by that panic or any other.

Here is what the always profound and reliable Judge War-

wick Martin says, in a chapter in which he refutes the idea
that American panics have been caused by speculation :—

The suspension of 1857 was not caused by speculation.
The causes were: 1. The attempt to enforce specie basis.
2. In 1853 Congress demonetized all silver halves, quarters
and dimes in sums over $5. Much of the reserves of the
banks were in these fractional silver coins, which were full
legal tender, and in gold and silver coins of the United
States and of other countries. The silver dollars of Spain,
Mexico, South America, and the United States were worth
a premium over gold, and were purchased by the Rothschilds
and sent out of the country. The banks did not, therefore,
hold them as reserves. The demonetization of these fractional silver coins deprived the banks of a large portion of
their reserves, and of paying their circulation therein, these
coins under the law of 1853 being legal tender for $5 only.
3. Up to February, 1857, all foreign gold coins and the silver
coins of most nations were, in the United States, full legal
tender with our coins, at the values fixed by our laws ; and
gold being, since 1834, over-valued in the United States,
immense quantities of these gold coins came to the United
States and remained. They were also held by the banks as
reserves in large quantities. But on the 21st of February,
1857, Congress demonetized all foreign coins of both gold
and silver. These coins held by the banks as reserves were,
after the passage of this law, no longer legal tender in payment of debts, and the banks could not use them at par to
meet their liabilities. They were compelled to sell them at
their home value instead of at the value fixed upon them by
the former laws of the United States. They were, therefore,
sold and sent out of the country in large quantities, never
again to return. It will be seen that the laws of 1853 and
of 1857 greatly diminished the full legal-tender gold and silver coins of the United States, reducing the reserves of the
banks, and rendering them incapable of standing runs upon
them for coin. 4. The law of 1846 divorced the Government from all banks and excluded all bank-notes from the
Treasury, confining the receipts therein to gold, silver, and
Treasury notes. This law was intended to weaken confidence in banks and in their circulation, and it had that
effect. It was in force in 1857 and up to 1861. These four
causes combined prepared all the banks for suspension as

soon as any disturbing influence arose in the banking or the commercial world. 5. This disturbing influence made its appearance in the failure of the Ohio Life Insurance and Trust Company in the fall of 1857. This bank had a capital of $2,000,000 and unbounded credit. The banks of the West kept large deposits with the New York agency. The entire solvency of the bank had not been suspected. Its credit had never, up to the day of its failure, been doubted. Its failure fell upon Wall Street like a clap of thunder in a cloudless sky. It destroyed confidence in banks. A run at once commenced for coin which the banks could not meet. The banks of New York and New England suspended, as banks always do under such circumstances, and those of the West and South followed.

[Mr. Martin does not seem to know that a principal cause was a strong pull on gold from the Bank of England.—S. L.]

TREASURY NOTES AGAIN.—The winter session of Congress raised the courage to issue Treasury notes. The Act of December 23, 1857, provides for the issue of $20,000.000 Treasury notes, to take the place of coin; the banks having suspended with the coin in their vaults. The rate of interest was not fixed by the law. It was left to be fixed by the Secretary of the Treasury and the persons receiving the notes. These notes were intended to be circulated as money, though Congress had not the boldness to make them such in plain words. They were made legal tender in all payments to the United States, and were willingly received by the people. Many of them were outstanding in 1861.

THE FALL OF GOLD.—B. S. Heath says:—In 1857, in his work "The Fall of Gold," Chevalier said : " The quantity of gold annually thrown on the general market approaches, in round numbers, a milliard of francs ($200,000,000). For a long series of years, California and Australia must produce such quantities as to render a marked decline in its value inevitable. It is absolutely certain that a production so vast should be accompanied with a great reduction in its value. In no direction can a new outlet be seen, sufficiently large to absorb the extraordinary production of gold, so as to prevent a fall in its value. Unless, then, we possess a very robust faith in the immobility of human affairs, we must regard the fall in the value of gold as an event for which we should prepare, without loss of time."

Under this and similar appeals, from different parts of Europe, by the money and creditor class (who saw, in the near future, their coin and their securities depreciating in value, relatively as the poor man's labor and the producer's wealth increased, through the increased volume of money), Germany, Austria and several other countries demonetized gold.

On this subject, our Congressional monetary commission says : " The movement in Europe for the general demonetization of gold would have become general, but for the resistance of France. It was changed, in 1865, into a movement for the demonetization of silver. But this change from demonetizing gold to demonetizing silver, was more of form than of substance. The object aimed at by both was a disuse of one of the money metals—to protect the creditor classes, and those having fixed incomes against a fall in the value of money, and arise in general prices of labor and property. This is the pith and the marrow of the monetary discussions of the past twenty years. In all the European discussions, after 1848, and prior to the German demonetization of silver and its consequences, the point made was not that either metal had depreciated relatively to the other, but that, by reason of extraordinary supplies of gold from California and Australia about 1865, and by new supplies of silver from Nevada, both metals had depreciated relatively to commodities, and that kings, princes and office-holders, having fixed incomes, and the creditor class, having fixed annuities, were being injured by a rise in the price of labor and commodities."

The labor and producing classes were getting the better of the idle, non-taxed and non-producing classes. So long as the double standard existed, a new supply of either metal was an addition to and only affected the general mass of money, and not the relative value of the metals. The " fall in gold," which Chevalier lamented in 1857, was its fall in relation to property. In order, therefore, to protect the " income classes," it was claimed to be necessary to demonetize one of the metals, and gold—being the metal which then promised the most abundant yield—was selected for that purpose.

1860.

THE WAR PANIC.—The panic and crash of 1860, during which over 6,000 business failures took place, was caused by the loss and contraction of nearly all our Western currency, by failure of banks based upon Southern State stocks. After the Greenback era of 1862, the number of failures diminished, with the increasing of the currency; and when contraction began in 1866, the failures began to increase again, and kept even pace with such contraction.

The State bank money had been a great nuisance. Besides its inherent weakness, it was terribly counterfeited. Some idea of the extent of the evil may be gained by examining the following table, taken from Shuckers' "Life of Salmon P. Chase." It shows the monetary condition of the United States in 1862 and six years previous:

	1856.	1862.
Whole number of banks	1,409	1,500
Number whose notes were not counterfeited	463	253
Number of kinds of imitations	1,462	1,861
Number of kinds of alterations	1,119	3,039
Number of kinds of spurious	224	1,685

THE PATIENT PACK-MULE—the burden-bearer—the Treasury note—is now trotted out again, and is destined during the war to do greater service than any Government money ever did before. The Act of December 17, 1860, provides for the issue of $10,000,000 Treasury notes—to run one year, and bear six per cent. interest. The interest was to run, and the notes to remain out, until sixty days after notice was given by the Secretary of the Treasury that he was ready to redeem them. They were to be paid at par to the public creditors, and were to be legal tender for all debts due the United States. Some of these notes were to be used in replacing those which had been redeemed and destroyed, as provided for in the Act of June 22, 1860.

Stephen Colwell, of Philadelphia, spoke thus in his "Ways and Means of Payment," in 1860:—The common phrase that our bank circulation is based on gold and silver is absolutely untrue. If our paper currency had no other basis than this very uncertain, insecure and ultimately impossible convertibility, it could not be upheld for a week, nor even a day.

The real basis of our paper currency—that which does sustain it through extraordinary emergencies—is the individual promissory notes and other evidences of debt, in exchange for which it is issued. These must all be paid, or the debtor must fail or suspend. * * * The real strength of the banks is in this,—that their business is founded on the trade and industry of the country. And all the business men, with all the commodities of daily consumption in their hands, are under the strongest inducements to offer these commodities for the notes and deposits of the bank. * * * The obligation to pay specie on demand can be nothing more than a check on the abuse of banking, or a security to the public; and as such only should it be regarded and discussed. If it be indispensable, it is upon the ground that no other adequate security is attainable. We do not believe this; and regard this attempt to place the credit system on the back of our coinage system, as partaking of that caution and wisdom *which should place a locomotive for its best service upon a one-horse cart.*

———

As we are approaching the time of war bonds and currency, when we were dosed with 15 kinds of money, while the plain Treasury note, receivable for all public and private debts, would have been infinitely preferable, I will give a brief advance synopsis of the issues; as they are calculated to puzzle the most acute, and were intended to. Let it be remembered that the acts mentioned simply " authorized " certain issues. In many cases but a small portion of that authorized was issued.

Act of February 8, 1861. A six per cent. 20 year loan of $20,000,000.

Act of March 2, 1861. A six per cent. issue of $35,000,000 Treasury notes, payable in three years.

Act of July 17, 1861. For $250,000,000 seven per cent. 20 year bonds. Any part could be issued in three year Treasury notes at 7.30 interest; or non-interest Demand notes, or one year Treasury notes at 3.65 interest, exchangeable for 7.30 notes. All demand notes not to exceed $50,000,000.

Act of August 5, 1861. Issue of six per cent. 20 year bonds, to exchange for one year and three year notes at any time.

5

Act of February 25, 1862. For $500,000,000 six per cent. bonds; the 5,20s. Also $150,000,000 Treasury notes, $50,-000,000 of them in place of the Demand notes of July 17, 1861; to which $10,000.000 was added by Act of February 12, 1862.

Act of July 11, 1862. For $150,000,000 more Treasury notes, and of March 3, 1863, $150,000,000 more, making $450,000,000 in all.

Act of February 25, 1862. For $25,000,000 "deposits" at five per cent. This was raised to $50,000,000 by the Act of March 17, 1862, and to $100,000,000 by the Act of July 11, 1863 (January 30, 1864, $50,000,000 added at 6 per cent.). All this called "temporary loans" was to be repaid on ten days' notice. Was mostly funded in 1865, 1866.

Act of March 1, 1862. For one year debt certificates to creditors at six per cent. These were issued for army supplies, to the amount of $561,753,241, and all but $4.000 was funded or replaced otherwise in 1863, 1864 and 1865.

Act of July 17, 1862, made postage legal tender in sums less than $5.00.

Act of March 3, 1863, confirmed June 30, 1864, gave $50,000,000, fractional currency. $46,000,000 was out January 1, 1873.

Act of March 3, 1863. For a $900,000,000 loan at six per cent. for 10 to 40 years, *principal and interest payable in coin.* This was the first issue of anything payable in coin since the Demand notes. That the people generally were not bothering about coin is shown by the fact that only $75,000,000 was issued, and the law was repealed June 30, 1864. The few long-headed, long-nosed men who bought them paid, however, a premium of 3½ to 4 per cent. The "orthodox" historians say: "A preference was given because of a possible distinction existing adverse to the payment of the 5-20s in coin."

The same act authorized $400,000,000 of one, two and three year Treasury notes, at not over six per cent.—principal and interest payable, as usual, in lawful money. There was an over-issue of these—in all they were $477,595,440, mostly at five per cent.

The same act authorized the issue of new Treasury notes for any of these issues outstanding at any time and badly worn, and provided for $150,000,000 more of non-interest notes to facilitate the exchange. Treasury notes were all the vogue in 1863.

Act of March 2, 1864. A loan of $200,000,000 at five or six per cent. *principal and interest in coin.* These 10-40s of 1864 nearly all went at five per cent. and brought from one to seven per cent. premium.

Act of June 30, 1864. The 5-20s of 1864 drew six per cent. interest, and were payable in lawful money. The issue was $125,561,300.

The same act authorized $200,000,000, 7-30 Treasury notes to run three years (Act of March 3, 1865 extended this to $600,000,000). Of these 7.30 interest-bearing Treasury notes $829,992,500 were issued. All were funded before July 15, 1868."

Act of March 3, 1865. For $600,000,000 six per cent. bonds to fund Treasury notes and other obligations. July 1, 1865, of this $322,998,950 was issued, and November 1, $203,327, 250. In all $526,326,200.

By authority of the same act as construed by the Act of April 12, 1866, a further issue was made in July, 1867, of $379,616,050 and of $42,539,350 on July 1, 1868—making $943,481,600 under this act. They are called " consols of 1865. 1867 and 1868."

Act of March 2, 1867, $50,000,000 three per cent. temporary loan certificates of deposit were authorized to redeem compound-interest notes.

Act of July 25, 1868, authorized $25,000,000 more. Under these Acts $85,150,000 was issued.

The Act of July 14, 1870, provided a billion and a half refunding bonds, viz.: $200,000,000 five per cents. $300,000,000 four and a half per cents. and $1,000,000,000 four per cents.

They were 30 year bonds, and the " Credit Strengthening Act " having paved the way, with infernal ingenuity, were payable, principal and interest, in coin. As silver was still at three per cent. premium there was no discussion then about gold. But 1871 was to see the beginning of the plot in Europe to break silver down.

The Act of Jan. 20, 1871, increased the five per cents. by $300,000,000, interest payable quarterly.

Act of July 12, 1882, produced $254,808,650 three per cents.

CHAPTER XII.

1861 to 1866.

WAR.

1861.

THE ACT OF FEBRUARY 8, 1861, authorized the issue of Treasury notes, or a loan of $25,000,000, to take up Treasury notes. One of those acts that leave all discretion to the Treasurer.

THE ACT OF MARCH 2, 1861, provides for a loan of $10,000,000 to take up Treasury notes and for the expenses of the Government. If the bonds could not be sold, then the Treasury notes were to be issued and relied upon. As Jefferson says, they are always a safe reliance. The revenues of the Government, excepting those required to support the Government, are pledged for the payment of the bonds and the Treasury notes. If bonds were sold, they are to be redeemable in ten and payable in twenty years.

THE YALE HEN IS " ON ! "—The great Civil War was now begun, and the nation entered upon what Sumner of Yale (for once) properly describes as a series of temporary financial make-shifts. This weak way of meeting the emergency was caused by the interference of such men as Sumner with the wise and energetic plans of such true leaders as Thaddeus Stevens and Henry Wilson, in Congress. If Sumner had lived 1,000 years ago, he could have found some justification of his position. He even doubted the need of paper-issues during the war. Positively, the only place in his " Currency " that I notice, in which this " guardedly conservative " oracle admits the possibility of paper money is this at page 196: " The economy of convertible [mind you, not inconvertible.—S. L.] paper issues is assumed and repeated by many persons who have never taken the pains to analyze that economy ; to see wherein it consists, and how great it is. *I am not prepared to take total abstinence ground against* paper issues, because I believe that they can be made useful, and economical; though we have not yet learned to do it." Whenever the Yale pundit has hatched out this egg, we will doubtless hear him cackle. Until then, no more paper issues! Let the world stop and speak in whispers; and say, with bated breath, "Whist! The Yale hen is on!"

IMMENSE ISSUES OF MONEY.—In the summer of 1861, the war money begins to assume enormous proportions. The Act of July 17, 1861, authorizes a loan of $250,000,000, or the issue of Treasury notes bearing 7-30 interest; or if bonds are issued they are to be at seven per cent., redeemable in twenty years, at the pleasure of the Government. This act is also first to provide for the issue of Demand notes, payable in coin, of a denomination of not less than $10. All notes of larger denomination than $50 were to bear interest. The law provides that these notes might be paid to Government employees and officials: but they were *not then made legal tender for duties.* The banks not having yet suspended, these notes were forced by the banks and brokers to a discount, though they were payable and paid in coin, when coin was demanded. These notes were receivable for bonds. The bonds were redeemable in ten years, and payable in twenty years.

SEVEN-THIRTIES AND DEMAND NOTES.—The Act of August 5, 1861, provides for the investment of 7-30 notes, which were not, under these acts, legal tender, in six per cent. bonds, not redeemable until 20 years. This also provides for the issue of Demand notes in denominations of not less than $5, to the extent of $50,000,000. They are made receivable for "public dues", but what dues are not stated. The first authority to issue them, as we have shown, did not specify for what particular payments they were to be received. This is more definite, but not full. But as the law suspends the Act of 1846, so as to allow deposits to be made by the Secretary of the Treasury in banks, it was construed to exclude these Demand notes from the custom-house, the same as bank notes. They, therefore, went to a discount. But when the Secretary of the Treasury ordered them *received for duties,* they immediately went to par with gold, though they were not by law legal tender at that time.

The above suspension of the Act of 1846 was engineered by the banks for their special benefit.

Warwick Martin says : " Shylock's conspiracy, during the war, began when the banks, in 1861, tried to compel the retirement of the Demand notes."

The New York banks suspended Dec. 31, 1861.

Wm. A. Birkey, in his valuable book " The Money Question," says of the Demand notes :—

These notes were receivable for all public dues, duties on imports included, and were subsequently made a legal tender for private debts , and the result was that they commanded the same premium over the ordinary Greenback that gold did ; and went up with gold, step by step, to the enormous premium of 285 ! Could any better evidence than this be required, to prove that a Greenback, made a full legal tender, would circulate at par, or nearly so, with gold ? The Demand notes were, of course, very obnoxious to the bullionists : because they gave the lie to all their theories about paper money : and accordingly they were got out of the way at the earliest moment possible,—all except about $75,000, which are probably lost ; and, if such is the case, constitute a gain of that amount to the people at large.

It is ever memorable that these notes were not at par because they were payable in coin ; but for the reason that they were receivable for duties on imports, and all other debts due the Government. So long as they were not so receivable, they were at a discount, though. payable in coin.

1862.

LEGAL TENDERS NOW FIRST REPUDIATED BY GOVERNMENT.—Never until 1862 was the power of the Government to make its own paper money, or that of the banks, legal tender for all payments to the United States. denied. The evil consequences of this denial and prevention have been hideous.

In January, 1862, Edward Bates, U. S. District Attorney, delivered this opinion :—The Constitution contains restrictions upon States. * * * No State can make anything but gold and silver coin a tender in payment of debts. This applies to a State only, and not to the nation ; and thus it

has always been understood with regard to the next preceding clause in the same section—no State shall " emit bills of
credit." The prohibition to emit bills of credit is quite as
strong as the prohibition to make anything but gold and
silver a legal tender; yet nobody doubts—Congress does not
doubt its power to issue bills of credit. Treasury notes are
bills of credit; and I think the one is just as much prohibited
as the other—neither is forbidden to Congress.

In January, 1862, the banks of New York, Boston and
Philadelphia combined to prevent the passage of the Legal
Tender Act, and sent delegates to Washington for that pur-
pose.

Debates were hot and heavy in Congress on the money
question, early in this year. Wm. Fessenden was a specimen " Conservative."

After arguing that the war would be over by the end of the
year, he proceeds to say, in a special argument in favor of
paying the interest of the U. S. bonds in gold : " We shall
have a heavy capital of debt, but all that is necessary is to
secure the payment of the interest. A public creditor looks
not for the principal. * * * He wants to know what his interest
will be. The example of England proves this abundantly.
Nobody supposes that England will ever pay her debts;
nobody has supposed it for years; and yet her stocks are
always sound, and are sought for even at a very low rate of
interest."

This is the high-toned repudiator who was afterwards called
to be Secretary of the Treasury.

For a time, patriotism prevailed. A full legal-tender
bill passed the House February 6, 1862. The vote was 93
to 59.

The full legal-tender bill passed the Senate February 12,
1862. The vote was 30 to 7.

THE ACT OF FEBRUARY 12, 1862, provides $10,000,000
additional Demand notes, in the same form as the $50,000,000
of August 5, 1861. Secretary Chase was terribly in want of
money, and was getting behind in his payments. We learn,
from Spaulding's " Financial History of the War," that

Chase was sending pitiful appeals to Congress, to hurry **up** some sort of a big issue of Treasury notes.

The struggle was terrific. On February 20, 1862, Thaddeus Stevens—the leader of the money reformers—uttered "a great and bitter cry." He said of the Senate amendment, that struck out the legal-tender clause of the House bill : "I have a melancholy foreboding that we are about to consummate a cunningly-devised scheme, which will carry great injury and great loss to all classes of people throughout this Union. * * * There was a doleful sound came up from the caverns of the bullion brokers, and from the saloons of the associated banks. * * * It now creates money ; and by its very terms declares it a depreciated currency. It makes two classes of money—one for banks and brokers—another for the people."

On his deathbed the "Great Commoner" said: "Yes, we had to yield. The Senate was stubborn. We did not yield, however, until we found that the country must be lost or the bankers gratified ; and we have sought to save the country, in spite of the cupidity of its wealthier citizens." Again (he died before the panic of 1873): "When, a few years hence, the people shall have been brought to general bankruptcy, I shall have the satisfaction of knowing that I attempted to prevent it."

Senator Henry Wilson of Massachusetts said : "I venture to express the opinion that 99 out of every 100 of the loyal people of the United States are for the legal-tender clause. I do not believe that there are 1,000 people in the State I represent who are not in favor of it. The entire business community, with hardly a single exception,—men who have trusted out in the country, in commercial transactions, their tens and hundreds of millions,—are for the bill with the legal-tender clause. Yes, sir, the people in sentiment approach unanimity on this question. * * * I believe that no measure that can be passed by Congress, unless it be a bill to provide revenue to support the Government, will be received with so much joy as the passage of this bill, with the legal-tender clause. In my judgment, if you strike out *the legal-tender clause*, you will have every *curbstone broker* in the country, the bulls and bears of the Stock Exchange, and all that class of men who fatten on public calamity and the

wants and necessities of the people, using all their influence
to depreciate the credit of this Government, and break down
the value of the Demand notes. * * * I have received several letters from my own State on the subject,—one, a day or
two ago, signed by several large commercial houses, representing millions of capital,—and from others; and they say
to me that they do not know a merchant in the city of Boston,
engaged in active business, who is not in favor of the legal-
tender clause."

That extraordinary man, E. G. Spaulding, was like John
Sherman, a true Greenbacker at first. Indeed, he originated
the Greenback and the five-twenty. But he was seduced, or
rather overborne, by the money-power. Like many another,
he saw, after a hard fight for true money, that he would have
to give it up, or retire from public life, and the prospect of
wealth. So he went with the tide—heroes and martyrs are
scarce now. He said at this time in Congress :—

Congress may decide whether it will authorize the Secretary of the Treasury to issue demand Treasury notes,—and
make them a legal-tender in payment of debts,—or whether it
will put its six or seven per cent. bond on the market, at ruinous rates of discount, and raise the money at any sacrifice the
money-lender may require, to meet the pressing demands
upon the Treasury. In the one case, the Government will
be able to pay its debts at fair rates of interest ; in the other
it must go into the streets shinning for the means, like an
individual in failing circumstances ; and sure of being used
up, in the end, by the avarice of those who exact unreason-
able terms. But, sir, knowing the power of money, and the
disposition there is among men to use it for the acquisition
of greater gain, I am unwilling that this Government, with
all its immense power and resources, should be left in the
hands of any class of men, bankers or money-lenders, however respectable and patriotic they may be. The Government is much stronger than any of them. Its capital is much
greater. It has control of all the bankers' money, and all
the brokers' money, and all the property of the 30 millions
of people under its jurisdiction. Why, then, should it go
into Wall Street, State Street, Chestnut Street, or any other
street, begging for money? Their money is not as secure
as Government money. All the gold they possess would not
carry on the Government for 90 days. They issue only prom-

ises to pay, which, if Congress does its duty, are not half as secure as United States Treasury notes, based on adequate taxation upon all the property of the country.

After his back-down, Spaulding sang a different song. He saw that if he remained an honest reformer, and did not swing with the tide, he must " have nothing and be nothing."

So he went with the tide !

And said that the Greenback must go !

What a change occurs ! He eulogizes the legal tender; but revels in the prospect that the Greenbacks will soon be withdrawn, and their places taken by the National bank circulation ; argues the superiority of the latter over the former because, while the Greenbacks were only backed by the responsibility of the nation, the National bank notes will have the additional guarantee of the banks ! ·

With the most charming *naïveté* he says : " Legal tender notes issued direct from the Treasury constitute a loan to the Government, without interest. Bank notes, under this bill, would be loaned to the Government and the people at six and seven per cent. interest. We give to the banking associations the interest on the National currency (354 million) issued by them, as an inducement for them to form associations, and be liable for its redemption."

THE MUTILATED LEGAL-TENDER ACT WAS FINALLY PASSED, FEBRUARY 25, 1862.—This is the first legal-tender act. It provides for the issue of $150,000.000 legal-tender notes, $50,000,000 of which were to be used to redeem $50,000,000 Demand notes, which were then at a discount. The issues under this act were *made legal tender* to the Government and the people for everything "*excepting* duties on imports and interest on the public debt." Had they been made legal tender for everything, they would never have been at a discount. This would have saved $1,000,000,000 to the public. . These notes, under this law, were made receivable for " *bonds the same as coin.*" The bonds issued under this act were to be 5-20 bonds—redeemable in five and payable in 20 years, in *lawful money*, meaning legal-tender notes. This act also provided that the Government shall receive deposits of sums of $100 and over ; and shall give convertible receipts or certificates for this money. And after ten days' notice the holders of the certificates could receive this money, principal and interest. The amount to be thus received on deposit was $25,000,000 only, under this act. The limit was soon full. The certificates were as good as money when held by the people; and the Government had the use of the money in time of need. The rate of interest should have been only three per cent., instead of five. Duties on imports were to be paid in coin and Demand notes, as provided in this act. The coin was to pay interest on bonds or on interest notes, and used to reduce the bonded debt one per cent. per annum. The balance was to be carried into the Treasury.

February 25th, 1862, was a very important day for the United States. We give here an allegorical description of some of the results of that day's botched work.

B. S. Heath, the author of "The Labor and Finance Revolution," who was editor of the Chicago *Express*, at the time of his death, had a very lively and spicy style. Several extracts from his book will be found in this work. The following specimen will illustrate his peculiar style :— .

THE GREAT NATIONAL BEAR :—It is related that in the Canton of Berne, in Switzerland, it had been customary, from time immemorial, to keep a bear at public expense; and the people had been taught to believe that if they had not a bear on hand they would be undone, and the country would go to wreck and ruin. So they endured the bear, notwithstanding the expense, and the fatal injury that he inflicted upon pigs and children that happened to step over the line of his jurisdiction. It happened one day that bruin sickened and died, too suddenly to have his place immediately supplied with another. During the interval, the people were amazed and delighted to see that the sun continued to shine, the corn to grow, and the vintage to flourish; and everything went on the same as before—saving the danger and expense of the bear. So they came to the sensible conclusion not to keep any more bears.

With no more sense, and at much greater expense, the civilized world has been harboring and keeping a bear for the last 2,000 years. Every civilized nation has had its bear. Our Revolutionary fathers repulsed the British lion, but accepted the embrace of the English bear—specie-basis. It has been an expensive and dangerous beast to keep. In 1809, its depredations occasioned great public distress; and in several instances involved the entire country in bankruptcy and ruin, from which it took years to recover. In 1814, 1819, 1825, and at other periods, the beast got on his periodical rampage producing the most terrible and disastrous results. But the bear must be kept, or we, like the peasants of Berne, would be undone. He was the idol of civilization. To him society offered up its sacrifices, with the same devotion that the Hindoo mothers yield up their babes to the crocodiles of the Ganges.

One day he sickened and died. It was on February 25, 1862. Devout worshipers from Boston, New York and Philadelphia flocked to Washington, to weep and howl over his untimely death. They were frantic and inconsolable. They feared the sun would cease to shine, the crops to grow, or the tide to ebb and flow. But time passed on. The sun kept its course. The seasons came and went, just as of old. People prospered, as they never had before. Men grew rich. Labor was fully employed, well-paid and not molested. Civilization extended, and the wilderness disappeared. The rose blossomed where the tangle-bush had grown. Railroads spanned the unknown waste. The march of improvement kept time to the music of machinery and the hum of industry. There was no bear to molest or make afraid. Still, idolatry, like the old man of the sea, clung to the public mind. Men could not believe that prosperity without gold could be real. They prayed for the return of their idol, and warned society that for all its seeming prosperity, and delusive dreams of wealth, corresponding sacrifices must be made to their idol, or the country would be a howling bedlam of madmen and fanatics.

So, on April 12, 1866, keeper McCulloch was ordered to begin negotiations for a bear. Immense sacrifices of men and property followed. The next year 2,000 men fell, and over $80,000,000 were lost. Each succeeding year the number of human sacrifices increased, and the amount of pecuniary loss augmented, until the reinstatement of the beast in 1879 ; 10,000 men and firms having fallen and $300,000,000 of wealth being sacrificed in the previous year. Now we have our blood-thirsty god reinstated, and John Sherman as high priest. [He should have added that the victims were numbered by millions, and the losses by annual billions, through the general stoppage of industries.—S. L.]

"THE ORIGIN AND HISTORY OF FIVE-TWENTY BONDS," Act February 25, 1862, is given at length by John G. Drew, in his "Money Muss." He shows how, after Mr. Spaulding had, on January 7, 1862, reported a bill for $100,000,000 full legal-tender Greenbacks; and Attorney General Bates had en dorsed their constitutionality, the money monopolists "felt the same solicitude as to the profits resulting from 'measures of value' as you would for your monopoly of the pint-pot, if you owned the only one existing; and you learned that it was the intention of Government to multiply such measures to such extent as the requirements of the community might indicate." He describes the delegation of bankers, and how they seduced Mr. Chase, and shows how the Com- mittee of Ways and Means—E. G. Spaulding, Samuel Hooper and Erastus Corning—opposed them, and re- ported the original bill 240, for the issuance of Greenbacks and funding them in 5-20s. A large quotation from Mr. Drew's book will be found at the date when Grant signed the bill that made the 5-20s. payable in coin.

Spaulding's History [1869] thus describes the certificates authorized February 25, 1862: "They were to be issued to creditors, in sums under $1,000, payable in one year at six per cent. And, by Act of March 17, this power was en- larged, so as to embrace checks drawn in favor of creditors by disbursing officers, upon sums placed to their credit in the books of the Treasury. The power thus conferred upon the Secretary of the Treasury, to issue certificates, was broad and unlimited.

"The certificates issued under these acts were in the simili- tude of bank-notes, fitted for circulation as money, and did circulate to a considerable extent as currency, until there was such an accumulation of interest upon them as to make it an object for capitalists to hold them as an investment.

"The Secretary began issuing certificates simultaneously with the issue of Greenbacks, and continued to issue them, in large amounts, during the progress of the war. This was advantageous to the Government, but was, at the same time, another fruitful source of inflation, and operated directly against any considerable funding in the long 5-20 bonds."

LOAN CERTIFICATES.—The Act of March 12, 1862, pro- vides for the issue of $50,000,000 additional temporary loan certificates, which would be redeemed in legal-tender notes

upon ten days' notice. Why not issue the legal-tender notes
in place of the certificates, and save the interest? If these
certificates were not presented for one year, they were to
bear six per cent. interest. They were to be paid out to
public creditors. Why not pay out the legal-tender notes to
said creditors? Well, the American public was being thus
gradually, painfully and expensively educated by fifteen
kinds of paper money up to an understanding and appreciation of fiat money. The process is slow. A majority
believe in it now; but they have not the spunk to vote
for it.

DEMAND NOTES FULL LEGAL TENDER.—An Act of March
17, 1862, made the Demand notes legal tender for everything—which they had never previously been. The Secretary of the Treasury was ordered to reissue Demand and
legal-tender notes upon their coming into the Treasury. He
was to exchange new for old and defaced notes. The old
ones were to be destroyed.

THE HAZZARD CIRCULAR.—An apparently authentic circular of the summer of 1862 has long been kept in print and
"in stock" by the labor and money reform papers. It is
called "The Hazzard Circular," and is thus described: In
the summer of 1862 the money monopolists of London saw
an opportunity to extend their system to this country, and
accordingly embodied their scheme in a "confidential" circular, and commissioned one Hazzard, a London banker, to
propagate it among the American bankers, with a view to
having the finance legislation of Congress pave the way for
its final adoption as the settled policy of the nation. Here
it is: "Slavery is likely to be abolished by the war power,
and chattel slavery to be destroyed. This, I and my European friends are in favor of. For slavery is but the owning
of labor, and carries with it the care for the laborer, while
our plan is for capital to control labor by controlling wages.
This can only be done by controlling the money.

"The great debt that capital will see to it is made out of
this war, must be used as the means to control the volume
of money. To accomplish this, the debt must be bonded,
and the bonds must be used as the banking basis.

"We are now waiting to get the Secretary of the Treasury
to make the recommendation to Congress. It will not do to
allow the Greenbacks to circulate as money for any length of

time; for we cannot control them, but we can control the bonds, and through them the bank issues."

July 1, 1862, B. S. Heath, in "Labor and Finance," gives as already issued of Seven-thirties, $123,000,000, and of Green-backs, $151,000,000, and of temporary ten-day loans and one-year certificates of indebtedness, $108,000,000.

POSTAGE LEGAL TENDER.—The Act of July 17, 1862, makes postage stamps legal-tender money for $5, and re-deemable in legal-tender notes, in sums of $3 and upward. They were to be sold by Government officials for legal-tender notes at par. This act also provides that after August 1, 1862, no bank, corporation or individual should issue any note to circulate as money under one dollar, upon pain of fine or imprisonment.

LARGE AND SMALL GREENBACKS.—Several writers give the issue of $150,000,000 legal-tender notes as under an Act of July 11. Martin gives it thus :—

Act of August 5, 1862 (Statutes 12, p. 532). This law authorized the issue of $150,000,000 legal-tender notes, of the same character as the first issue, which were to be received for bonds ; and also authorized the issue of bonds which were payable in legal tenders. This issue added to the first made $300,000,000. Had these notes been made full legal tender, and issued up to $1,000,000,000, they would have been always at par with coin, and our debt would have been small.

$35,000,000 of this issue was in small notes—a very im-portant and desirable act.

And now gold was going up. In October it reached $1.33.

WHO BOUGHT THE FIVE-TWENTIES.—W. A. Birkey, in his "Money Question," gives this testimony about Hugh Mc-Culloch and the 5-20s. :—

McCulloch bears testimony as to what class of people took the 5-20 bonds. In a letter to the *N. Y. Tribune*, dated at London, in September, 1875, he said : " I recollect the time when subscribers for U. S. bonds were regarded as patriots ; and I happen to know to what class they belonged. With rare exceptions, they were not capitalists.* * * The purchasers of our bonds were the patriotic men and women of all parties : chiefly men of moderate means ; who were resolved that the

Union should be saved, no matter at what cost of money or blood."

It may be interesting to state that McCulloch was not one of those who were resolved that the Union should be saved, no matter at what cost, etc. At that time he was a country banker, "of moderate means," somewhere in the State of Indiana ; and was solicited, we believe by the Sub-Treasurer of the United States, Mr. Cisco, to have his bank take and dispose of some of " our bonds." He treated the request with contempt. This matter was so well known at the time of his appointment, as Secretary of the Treasury, as to be talked of on the streets of Washington ; and was hushed up by his friends, only with great difficulty.

The following item, as to a later date, throws a lurid light upon Mac's patriotism : " Judge Strong's decision in the case of the United States against Edwin R. Lewis, trustee for the creditors of Jay Cooke & Co., draws attention afresh to the transactions between Secor Robeson and McCulloch. The London house of Jay Cooke, McCulloch & Co. appears to have been set up on public funds advanced by Robeson ; and is admitted to have depended for its continuance on additional deposits by him, amounting to at least $1,200,000 ; against which iron rails worth about half that amount were hypothecated."

1863.

Spaulding says that up to January 12, 1863, only $25,000,-000 Five-twenties had been sold ; because Greenbacks were still scarce, and the people did not want to part with them.

NATIONAL BANKS AUTHORIZED.—The Act of February 2?, 1863, authorizes the National banking system now in existence. The bill was introduced by Senator Sherman, who assigns reasons why the notes of these banks should take the place of legal tender notes. He said that the latter should and would be all destroyed. His reasoning was fallacious, and time has shown his conclusions false.

The status of the National bank note is shown by its inscriptions. At the top is this : " This note is secured by bonds of the United States deposited with the U. S. Treasurer at Washington." At the center is this : " First N. bank of   will pay   dollars to bearer on demand." On the back is : " This note is receivable at par in all parts of

the United States in payment of all taxes and excises and
other dues to the United States, except duties on imports.
And also for all salaries and other debts and demands owing
by the United States to individuals, corporations and associations within the United States, except interest on the public
debt."

Here are Sherman's words in the Senate when introducing
the National Bank bill:

"Another objection is, that they can only be used during
the war. The very moment that peace comes, all this circulation that now fills the channels of commercial operations
will be at once banished ; they will be converted into bonds;
and then the contraction of prices will be as rapid as the inflation has been. The issue of Government notes can only
be a temporary measure, and is only intended as a temporary measure to provide for a national exigency. * * * But
it is asked, why look at all to the interests of the banks ; why
not directly issue the notes of the Government, and thus save
the people the interest on the debt represented by the notes
in circulation ? The only answer to this question is that history teaches us that the public faith of the nation alone is
not sufficient to maintain a paper currency. There must be
a combination between the interests of private individuals
and the Government." Which is all false.

THE LAW ALLOWING THE INTERIOR BANKS TO KEEP LARGE
AMOUNTS OF THEIR RESERVES IN SO-CALLED REDEMPTION
BANKS, OR BANKS IN MONEY CENTERS.—The National banks
in money centers are under great obligations to Mr. Sherman
for putting this provision in the National Bank Act, as it
afforded these banks the means of using larger sums of money
which did not belong to them. It was used in making call
loans to speculators in bonds, gold, and stocks. The country banks are also under obligation to Mr. Sherman for allowing these banks in the money centers to pay them interest for
the money thus kept by them. But the people of the interior
had a right to complain that the money kept by their banks
with banks in the money centers was thus withdrawn from
the locality where it was needed in business : and kept where
it was not needed, and could not be used to benefit the
country ; but where it was used for speculative transactions
only, to the derangement and injury of business generally.
This law was wholly in the interest of banks and bankers,

8

and against the interests of the people generally. What wonder that now, in 1890, the South is clamoring for State banks.
The poorer money the notes of these banks are the surer
they are to stay at home ! Any money is better than none.

Spaulding gives the vote on the National Bank bill thus :
Senate, yeas 23, nays 21 ; House, yeas 78, nays 64. A close
shave.

THE TEN-FORTIES, FRACTIONAL CURRENCY, ETC.—Spaulding gives this synopsis of the Ten-forty Act of March 3, 1863 :
The first section authorized a loan of $300,000,000 for the
then current year ; and $600,000,000 for the then next fiscal
year ; and to issue bonds therefor, at not less than ten nor more
than forty years, at not exceeding six per cent. in coin : not
exceeding, in all, $900,000,000. 2. By sec. 2, of the same
act, the Secretary, in lieu of an equal amount of said bonds,
was authorized to issue $400,000,000 of Treasury notes, bear-
ing interest not exceeding six per cent. payable in lawful
money ; which notes, payable in periods expressed on their
face, *might be made a legal tender at their face value.* 3. By
the third section $150,000,000 in amount of U. S. notes, made
a legal tender, might be issued. The restriction in the sale
of bonds to market value was repealed. And the holders of
U. S. notes, under former acts, shall present the same for the
purpose of exchanging them for bonds as therein provided,
on or before July 1, 1863 ; and thereafter the right to exchange the same shall cease and determine. 7. This section
imposed a tax of one per cent. each half year, on a graduated
scale of State bank circulation ; according to the capital stock
of each bank.

I give this statement from Spaulding (who had become at
the time of writing an enemy of Greenbacks and a friend of
bank issues and bonds) as a preface to what certain friends
of Greenbacks say.

Judge Warwick Martin says :—

The Act of March 3, 1863, is dated six days after the first
National Bank Act was approved. It was intended to carry
out Sherman's intention to retire the legal tenders. To do
this the following points had to be covered : (1) Six per
cent. bonds must be supplied in such excess as would make
them dull and cheap for bank investment. So 900 million
10-40s were issued, purchasable with legal tenders—bonds
and interest payable in coin. Interest on these above $100

payable semi-annually—under that annually; thus giving preference to big buyers. (2) State bank and legal tenders and Demand notes must be squelched. So (a) State bank notes were taxed ten per cent. per annum, which drove them to turn to Nationals. (b) Legal tenders were to be refused for bonds after July 1, 1863. This rushed the legal tenders into the Treasury—the people fearing their repudiation. They were not so received again until 1865. This hit them hard, and they went down to $2.85 to $1 gold. But money was needed to pay the soldiers, at the end of the war; and they demanded Greenbacks. So the law was repealed—that bonds might be bought with Greenbacks to supply means of payment. This was one of the darkest acts of our history. Wall Street made fortunes out of it, by purchasing the legal-tender notes and holding them; and investing in bonds at $40 in the $100 for gold, as soon as they were again receivable. (c) Fearing the people would still not buy the bonds, Sherman provided in the act for 400 million three-years six per cent. notes, payable in legal tenders and themselves full legal tenders. If these were issued only 500 million bonds were to come out. The latter would give a basis for National banks—the former would redeem the legal tenders, and then be funded. A cunning scheme; but it failed. The people clung to the legal-tender Greenbacks. Sherman showed his crafty hand in the section of the act demonetizing the legal tenders,—just as he did later, in the act demonetizing silver. In both cases, it takes a Philadelphia lawyer to see the trick.

To insure the reception of the three-years notes, they were made convertible into legal tenders; and to cover this scheme, the act authorizes 150 million more legal tenders to redeem three-years notes when presented; but not to be issued for any other purpose.

The act also provides, on a large scale, for the issue of interest certificates for temporary loans. All the laws passed at this time sought to convert the non-interest debt of the nation—which was used as money—into an interest-bearing debt. So the suffering people were loaded up.

One redeeming feature of the act gave us 50 million fractional currency. But the same crafty hand pulled that in, January, 1875; and substituted silver, at an annual cost of

$2,500,000 ; to the disgust of the people, and the profit of the five per cent. bondholders.

TRICKS THAT WERE NOT VAIN.—A very brief and pointed epitome of the financial scull-duggery of this year is given in this extract from John Sherman's report as chairman of the Senate Finance Committee. This· is written " as with lead in the rock forever," in the minds of all true money reformers : " *It became necessary to depreciate the notes in order to create a market for the Bonds. The limit of the notes was trebled and the right to convert them taken away.*"

Yet, in spite of all these tricks, it was hard to get the legal tenders away from the people. No nation, before or since, ever had a sufficiency of good money. The consequent prosperity was enormous. For once, our people were, like France, doing business with money, instead of the usual vast preponderance of promissory notes and checks, in the English style.

At the time of this writing, the city of New York enjoys, for the first time in many years, a full supply of water ; enough to reach all the top floors of four-story houses. Such was the condition of this country as to currency in 1864 and 1865. For once, the outlying rural districts had money enough to do business with.

But, as usual, the dealers in money and securities made the big rake. Those who had money, and knew that after the close of the war the law would be repealed, purchased the legal tenders at the heavy discount—they costing them not more than $40 on the $100, in coin—and invested them in six per-cent. bonds, under the management of Secretary McCulloch. There is nothing in the financial history of the United States of which the people had, and have, greater cause to complain than this law and its effects, and none for which the bondholders, capitalists, and national bankers had, and have, more cause to feel grateful. The passage of this Act of March, 1863, was the most effectual plan that could have been adopted to carry out the policy of crushing the legal-tender notes—first introduced in favor of National banks in the speech of Mr. Sherman, in February, 1863. But this, as well as all other efforts, failed. The people still confided in legal-tender notes, as the best money they could have, notwithstanding these combined efforts to destroy them.

All branches of business flourished in a healthy way; every one was paying off old debts and mortgages. The condition and prospect was disgusting only to money-lenders.

The scheme for getting out the five-twenties at last began to work, by help of Jay Cooke & Co. Spaulding gives July 1, 1863, $168,880,250 of 5-20s sold; October 1, $278,511,500; and January 21, 1864, $500,000,000, and $11,000,000 over.

By the Act of July 11, 1863, the ten days loans, that were raised from $25,000,000 on February 25, 1862, to $50,000,000 on March 17, 1862, are raised to $100,000,000. Such were the temporary makeshifts during the great war.

B. S. Heath gives the paper currency outstanding July 1, 1863, as follows: Old Demand and Treasury notes of the time before the war (I give only millions) one million: ten-days loans and certificates, 259 millions; seven-thirties, 140 millions; non-interest, demand and legal-tender notes, 382 millions; fractional currency 20 millions; and State bank notes 239 millions; or about 1,041 millions in all.

The same writer gives this list of State bank money from 1854 to 1863: 1854, 205 millions; 1855, 187; 1856, 196; 1857, 215; 1858, 155; 1859, 193; 1860, 207; 1861, 202; 1862, 184; and 1863, 239 millions.

In October, 1863, gold reached 1.50.

SARSAPARILLA TOWNSEND'S WISDOM.—One of the most remarkable cases of early illumination upon the money question was that of Dr. S. P. Townsend. This noted man made a fortune and did a public service by popularizing sarsaparilla. Clear back in 1863, he knew nearly all that we do now about this question. Many will remember the "palace" he built on Fifth Avenue, New York, where that of A. T. Stewart now stands. It was one of the joys of Stewart's life to pull it down and build a finer one on the same spot.

As to Townsend's career, he shall speak for himself. His able and well-informed brother, Tappen, first indoctrinated me in "currency reform", and has fought a good fight in the cause, even unto death.

In a speech before the Union League of New Providence,

N. J., November 9, 1863, Dr. Townsend went over the question very thoroughly. Here are some of his points : He said that when the first Sumter gun was fired, he was building fifty large houses on Murray Hill, New York. His venture was prostrated as by a tornado. But a new tariff and a new currency set business a-going again. Capitalists who do not think that the country is safe unless money is tight and merchants in distress, and dealers in cotton that is marketed in England like to have money scarce in America.

Already he saw Mr. Chase shivering in terror, like Frankenstein, before the mighty genii, the Greenbacks and Demand notes, that he had created. But he informed the Secretary that the time was passed for this country to be ruled with a rod of gold " more powerful, more cruel than a rod of iron." He was wise about the price of gold, and said :—The high premium on gold has indisputably been of incalculable value to the country; it has certainly prevented excessive importations of foreign goods; and enabled our people to export hundreds of millions of dollars in value of the products of the country, which, with gold at par, would have remained at home. Sir, while men are eager to sell marble stores in Broadway and Wall Street for a less price (and take pay in Greenbacks) than the same property would have sold for before the suspension of specie payments, I cannot be made to believe that this money is depreciated. The same is true of Brooklyn property, and of farms in any direction within fifty miles of the great metropolis. * * * The owners of coal-fields and the stock-holders of the railroads and canals leading to the mines form a combination, taking advantage of the requirements of the Government and people, and ask an enormous price for coal. Is it the Greenbacks or the extortioners that should be censured ? Monopolists can increase the price of any article, including gold, at pleasure. * * * It is curious but true, that it requires as much nerve and courage for a statesman to advocate the use of Treasury notes in Congress as it formerly did to oppose the encroachments of the slave power. The money kings flourish and use their thongs with all the audacity that the slave lords, in olden time, used their slave-whips. That staunch, practical, common-sense man and true patriot, Thaddeus Stevens, was ridiculed, last winter, in and out of Congress, for proposing to use Treasury notes not bearing interest, in

preference to those that did. Old Thad, as he was called,
never was cowed by the slave-holding aristocrats. May he
as successfully fight the bullionists.

1864.

TEN-DAY LOANS.—The Act of Jan. 30, 1864, added 50
Million dollars to the Ten-Day Loans—making 150 millions.
Spaulding makes this significant admission: "The certificates were circulated to some extent in the clearing-houses,
and among individuals; thereby aiding the general inflation
that began with the passage of the Legal-tender Act."

ACT OF MARCH 2, 1864. A loan of $200,000,000, five or
six per cent. 10-40s.

GOVERNMENT SELLING GOLD.—The Act of March 17, 1864,
gives the Secretary of the Treasury power to sell gold, and
to pay interest upon bonds, one year in advance of when it
became due: with or without rebate.

Here is this precious joint resolution of Congress of March ·
17, 1864—a fair specimen of the more infamous and bare-
faced steals in which that body connived with the usurers.
It read: "That the Secretary of the Treasury be authorized
to anticipate the interest on the public debt, by any period
not exceeding one year, from time to time, *either with or without rebate of interest upon the coupons*, as to him may seem ex-
pedient; and he is hereby authorized to dispose of any gold
in the Treasury of the United States not necessary for the
payment of interest on the public debt."

Thus did the rogues in and out of Congress suck the life-
blood of the people during the most terrible exigencies of
the war.

S. M. Brice of Mound City, Kansas, in his able "Financial
Catechism," printed in 1882, speaks in the following spirited
way of this sweet-scented transaction:—

No scruples were entertained with regard to the means to
be used, so that the robbery could be accomplished under
cover of law. The laws under which the bonds were issued
called for paying the usury in coin semi-annually. Coin
was now at a premium of 2.85. The opportunity must not
be lost. A law must be passed in order that this advantage
could be realized to its fullest extent. Accordingly, on March
17, 1864, an act was passed authorizing the Secretary of the
Treasury to pay the usury one year in advance, without

rebate. Here was an opportunity for a nice financial transaction: The money-dealer has invested $35,100 in coin in $100,000 legal-tender notes; he steps into the United States Treasury and pays these notes for a bond of $100,000, bearing usury at the rate of six per cent. per annum. He now draws usury from the Government on nearly three times as many dollars as he has invested in gold. But still not satisfied he says: " Mr. Secretary, I believe since the passage of the late Act of Congress, you are permitted to pay the usury on these bonds one year in advance, without rebate. Would it be convenient for you to pay me the first installment on this bond this morning?"

Certainly. And the accommodating Secretary counts him out $6,000 in gold for the first year's usury on his bond. He steps across the street and sells his gold to an importer for $2.85 in currency for a dollar in gold, giving him $17,100, with which he returns to the Treasury and invests in another six per cent. bond of that amount. He now has, on account of the vicious legislation of the Congress of the United States, six per cent. bonds to the amount of $117,100 for an outlay of $35,100—more than three dollars for each one invested. He might have demanded, under the law, the usury on this bond also, for a year in advance. But extreme modesty compelled him to forbear encroachments on the time of the gentlemanly officials, in order to give opportunity for others of the bondholding fraternity to avail themselves of the special privilege created for them by law to rob the Treasury of the United States.

Hereby hangs a long tale.

During the forty-fifth Congress Representative J. B. Weaver introduced into the House the following resolution: " *Resolved*, That the Secretary of the Treasury be, and is hereby directed to report to this House whether he has at any time anticipated the payment of interest on the public debt: if so, how much has been paid in advance, and to whom."

This resolution was referred to the Committee on Ways and Means, of which Fernando Wood was chairman. Mr. Wood sent the resolution to Secretary Sherman, with a request to state when he would report. Mr. Sherman replied that " *There was no public document that would give the information required.*" But he added, " *The Department has been in the habit for five years* [he knew well it was 16 years] *of*

paying the interest in advance without charging anything."
When we recollect that the act permitting this outrage was
passed March 17, 1864. when gold was at a premium, which
made it a big object to obtain the usury in advance ; and this
resolution of inquiry was sent to the Secretary in 1880, 16
years after, when gold commanded no premium, and he states
that it has been the custom for the last five years to pay the
interest on the bonds one year in advance without charging
anything—connected with the other statement, that there
was no public document in his office which would show how
much money had been so paid, and to whom paid, we are
driven to the conclusion that it has been the practice since
the passage of the act ; and that the Secretaries of the Treasury have conspired with the money-dealers to rob the Government through all this period, and keep no [public] record of
the fact, by which the amount of the robbery could be ascer-
tained.

Judge Warwick Martin says :—The laws of 1862 and 1863
authorized the Secretary of the Treasury to purchase bonds
for legal-tender notes, but did not authorize him to sell gold
for legal-tender notes, and to purchase bonds with the proceeds. The Act of March 17, 1864, authorized the sale of
gold. Gold had accumulated, and was accumulating so fast
in the Treasury that from one hundred to one hundred and
fifty millions of dollars were constantly in the Treasury.
This act authorized it to be sold for legal-tender notes. Mr.
Fessenden, and even Mr. McCulloch, sold this gold without
giving notice of the time when, and the place where the sales
would take place. This had a salutary influence upon Wall
Street. The gold gamblers could not tell when and where
the blow would fall. But, nevertheless, the sales of gold
were not wisely made. These Secretaries of the Treasury
should have urged, in all their communications to Congress,
the absolute necessity of making the legal-tender notes receivable for duties on imports ; which alone would at once
have brought them to par with gold, and made them more
desirable than gold. But they did not see proper to do this.
In the absence of such a law, they should—with the large
amount of gold in their possession—have forced legal-tender
notes to par with coin, by selling, and continuing to sell,
$5,000,000 per day. Instead of this, small sales only were
made. The object seemed to be to make a profit upon the

sale of gold; instead of reducing the discount upon the legal-tender notes. There never was a time when the forcing of $10,000,000 or $20,000,000 of gold upon the market would not have broken down the Wall Street combination to keep it up. On "Black Friday," in 1869, the sale of $5,000,000 reduced gold from 60 per cent. premium to 30 per cent. The sale of another $5,000,000 would have brought it to 20 per cent. To have continued these sales every day for a week would have brought legal tenders to par, without the sale of more than $30,000,000 coin. The coin would have come back into the Treasury immediately, in payment of duties on imports, or for certificates of deposits. The business demand for gold was small: the speculative demand was large. In this way, the Secretary of the Treasury could and should have broken up the gold sales. But from the days of Chase and Fessenden, there was a combination between Wall Street and the Treasury, to increase, instead of reducing, the premium on gold for legal-tender notes; the object being to drive them from circulation, and fill their places with National bank notes.

INTEREST-BEARING NOTES MADE LEGAL TENDER.—The Act of June 3, 1864, Revised Statutes, section 3476, specially provides: "Treasury notes, bearing interest, may be paid to any creditor of the United States at their face value, excluding interest; or to any creditor willing to receive them at par, *including* interest."

Here is the famous section of that same act on which is based the true statement that the National banks borrow from the Government at one per cent.: "And in lieu of all existing taxes, every association shall pay to the Treasurer of the United States, in the months of January and July, a duty of one-half of one per centum each half year, from and after the first day of January, 1864, *upon the average amount of its notes in circulation.*"

Upon this subject, the late John G. Drew sent me the following letter when I was editing in Chicago:

JOHN G. DREW, Journalist.

ELIZABETH, N. J., Aug. 14, 1891.

Friend L.:—Do you notice a statement current in the papers that John Sherman has recently said that he never knew that the Government ever loaned money at one per cent. interest (and called it tax). If he would kindly refer to his Revised Statutes of the United States, section 5157 *et ultra*, or section 39 *et ultra* of the National Bank Laws, chap. 3, headed, " Obtaining and issuing circulating notes," he can refresh his memory muchly. He should not rise from that interesting and exhilarating study without especially noting and digesting section 5214 Revised Statutes, and section 90 National Bank Laws, where, with an insolence worthy of a Nero or a Caligula, it rules on the superincumbent filth in part as follows :

[Mr. Drew then quotes the law as given above, and adds :] But, dearly beloved, don't publish it in the *Sentinel* of Gath, and keep it from the *Express* of Askelon ; or the distributors of hayseed may abandon their claim for two per cent. money, and adopt the time-honored plan, never forgotten by John Sherman, of lending money on good security for nothing, except the privilege of taxing the loan one per cent. per year " in lieu of all existing taxes."

NATIONAL BANKS FIXED FOR GAMBLING.—The Act of June 13, 1864, repeals the Act of February 25, 1863, and provides more fully and extensively for the issue of the National bank circulation. One provision is that banks in cities, or money centers, shall always keep, as reserves, 25 per cent. of their circulation and deposits in lawful money, or legal-tender notes ; and that banks not in money centers should keep 15 per cent. of the circulation and deposits in lawful money. A neglect to comply with this clause in the law subjects banks to the forfeiture of their charters. These banks had fully secured their circulation by bonds of the United States to the extent of 10 per cent. over the amount issued upon them. The legal-tender notes were not, therefore, required to make the circulation secure. The object of this section of the law was to reduce the amount of legal-tender notes in circulation, and to fill their places with National bank notes ; and also to concentrate money in New York and other money centers, for speculative purposes. This act required these banks, before they could lift their bonds deposited in the Treasury as security for circulation, to return their notes to the Treasury. This was just and proper ; but we will see, further on, how the law was changed in the interest of the banks and bondholders. The notes of these banks were made legal tender to the Government, and to the banks, for everything except duties on imports, and interest on the public debt; but they were not legal tender to the people, or receivable in redemption of legal-tender Treasury notes. The former were redeemable in the latter, but the latter were not redeemable in the former.

Judge Warwick Martin says :—The most ruinous provision in the act provides for selecting banks in redemption cities, to redeem the notes of National banks; and that one-half the reserve of said banks thus selected may be in these redemption banks. This section in the law took the money of the bank from the place where the bank was located, and transferred it to New York and other places where it was not needed for business, and where it was used for stock and gold gambling, to the injury of the country. The notes of the banks needed no redemption by other banks. They were par everywhere. The notes of one bank were as good as those of another. No redemption of said notes took place. The whole provision was intended to place the funds of National banks in New York, so that the money market could be controlled by New York at any time. We all remember the disastrous results of said law in the fall of 1873, when the New York banks suspended currency payments owing to their gambling operations.

GOLD FUTURES STOPPED AND UNSTOPPED.—The Act of June 17, 1864, provided, under penalty, that neither gold nor sterling exchange should be sold for future delivery; which was intended to put a stop to gold gambling. While it remained in force, this law had the desired effect; the gold sold and purchased was demanded by the laws of commerce. Had this law not been repealed, it would have proved of immense advantage to the United States. But it would have closed the gold board; and that Wall Street could not permit. The brokers marshaled their forces to battle with Congress once more. They went to Washington, "terrible as an army with banners," and demanded the repeal of the above law. Congress at once complied with the demand; the law was repealed on July 2. It lived just fifteen days. It is ever thus with Congress, "when they would do good evil is present with them." The tax imposed by this Act of July 2, 1864, was never collected. The result was that Wall Street, as usual, triumphed over Congress.

Spaulding shows that only 73 millions of ten-forties had

been sold by June 21, 1864; for the reason that the interest had been reduced from six to five per cent.

CHASE FRIGHTENED OUT.—June 30, 1864, was an important date. Secretary Chase, frightened at the rise of gold to 2.50, resigned; and Fessenden, taking his place, promptly put it up to 2.85.

Spaulding gives this from Fessenden's report on taking hold—as representing the total currency issues outstanding at that date:

U. S. notes, Greenbacks	$431,178,670.84
Postal currency	22,894,877.25
Interest-bearing legal-tender Treasury notes..	168,571,450.00
Certificates of indebtedness	160,720,000.00
National bank notes	25,825,695.00
State banks not less than	135,000,000.00

$944,190,693.09

Seven-thirty Treasury notes.	$109,356,150.00	
Temp. deposit certificates..	72,330,191.44	
		181,686,341.44

Total currency and used as currency.....$1,125,877,034.53

SIX PER CENT. BOND.—An Act of June 30, 1864, provides for the issue of $400,000,000 six per cent. bonds, redeemable in five or payable in 30 or 40 years. The Secretary is authorized to sell these bonds in Europe or America, "for coin or other lawful money;" or certificates of indebtedness; or any other obligations of the Government, excepting the bonded debts, whether bearing interest or not. The bonds are to be exempt from taxation of all kinds. It will be seen that for these bonds the legal-tender notes were to be received; but this did not authorize their reception for any other bonds. This act also provides for the issue of $200,000,-000 7-30 notes, in sums of not less than $10; redeemable in three years, and payable in "lawful money." Such of these notes as made the principal and interest payable at their maturity only were made legal tender,—the same as the legal-tender notes,—for their face value. To creditors of the Government they were to be paid at par, including interest. They were convertible into bonds, at the will of the holder, or the discretion of the Secretary of the Treasury. This act also provides for the issue of $150,000,000 temporary loan interest certificates. Out of the $450,000,000 legal-tender notes authorized, $50,000,000 were to be retained at all times in the Treasury, to redeem certificates when presented.

B. S. Heath gives 15 million compound interest notes as outstanding July 1, 1864.

Secretary Fessenden, in his report in December, 1864, makes the following admissions that seem singular in view of the conspicuous part played by him in mutilating the Greenback, etc. He said : " The experience of the past few months cannot have failed to convince the most careless observer that, whatever may be the effect of a redundant circulation upon prices of coin, other causes have exercised a greater and more deleterious influence. In the course of a few days, the price of this article rose from $1.50 to $2.85 in paper for $1.00 in specie ; and subsequently fell, in as short a period, to $1.87 ; and then again rose as rapidly to $2.50 ; and all without any assignable cause, traceable to an increase or decrease in circulation of paper money, or an expansion or contraction of credit, or other similar influence on the market tending to occasion a fluctuation so violent. It is quite apparent that the solution of the problem may be found in the unpatriotic and criminal efforts of speculators —and probably of secret enemies—to raise the price of coin, regardless of the injury inflicted upon the country,—or desiring to inflict it." No man living, except John Sherman of Ohio, was better able to explain how, and through whose instrumentality, these rascally speculators were enabled to prosecute their "unpatriotic and criminal efforts," than Mr. Fessenden himself. Under the circumstances, Mr. Fessenden did not find the position of Secretary of the Treasury a very comfortable one, and at the beginning of Mr. Lincoln's second term he surrendered it with feelings of great relief.

In 1864 new cent and two-cent pieces were created, the cent containing only 48 grains of copper, tin and zinc. One dollar or one hundred of these contain only 4,800 grains, instead of 26,000, as under the law of 1792. A pound of this metal costs only 20 cents. It coins 160 one-cent pieces. The commercial value of the metal is only 20 cents. The legal value of the money is $1.60. The law here makes a clear gain of $1.40.

It will be observed that two new metals, tin and zinc, not named in the Constitution, were thus introduced as money metals.

PLAYING INK-FISH.—An impartial review of the financial history of these war years seems to lead to the conclusion that our leading politicians were trying to play ink-fish; and so blacken the waters, that no ordinary honest mortal could, at any future time, see through all the ins and outs of their fifteen different kinds of currency (when the plain Greenback was all that was necessary); and detect the one fact running through it all—that the main object was to play into the hands of the usurers.

1865.

CAREY ON McCULLOCH.—Noble Henry C. Carey said, in 1875: "At the close of the war, Mr. McCulloch was seated in the Treasury chair, there placed by Mr. Lincoln, in the full belief that he was a decided protectionist, and as decided an opponent of contraction. That he was so in May, a few weeks later, I know from personal intercourse with him. Nevertheless, but three months later—and without the slightest explanation of the cause of change—he presented himself, in correspondence with his agent then in England, in a totally different character. That change was to be followed in October by his Fort Wayne decree—as discreditable a paper, in my belief, as was ever issued from the treasury of any civilized country whatever. By it, all who were so unfortunate as to be in debt, were cautioned that they must sell off and pay their debts; all who could command the use of money being simultaneously cautioned not to purchase; the prices of labor, materials, houses and lands being all too high, and it being the determination of the Treasury to bring them all down to " hard pan "; thus restoring to us that admirable system which had existed before the war, when each successive British crisis brought ruin to half the households of the country; and so effectually prevented the growth of public confidence that the prices paid as interest ranged between six and 200 per cent., whenever not so high as 500 per cent. Shortly thereafter, the Controller of the Currency made a report, by which it was clearly shown that the total amount of bank-notes, **Green-backs** and interest-bearing legal tenders, in actual use, as money, among our people, was but $460,000,000 ; being but $80,000,000 more than the notes of and under 20 dollars, now in use among the people of France ; and less by above $100,000,000 than the total notes in use among a people who, more than almost any other, had been accustomed to regard the precious metals as the only description of money on which they could place reliance. Add to the notes the metallic money in actual use in the country, and it will be found that the currency in actual use exceeds by fully fifty per cent. that which then here existed, whose extraordinary abundance was denounced by a gentleman who, a few months before, had accepted office as an anti-contractionist. * * * The Treasury was converted into a great manufactory of bonds for exportation ; and to the end that a foreign market might be created, Congress was repeatedly urged to put the country on a par with Spain, Turkey, Egypt, and other semi-civilized countries ; by providing that the interest should be made payable on the London Exchange ; these extraordinary and expensive operations being intended, as we were assured, as a means of reaching that early resumption of specie payments, with its attendant advantages to the already rich, from which Mr. Secretary McCulloch had so utterly revolted, throughout the first few weeks of his administration.

THE ACT OF JANUARY 25, 1865, provides for the issue of non-interest-bearing Treasury notes, in lieu of any balance of the loan of June 30, 1864; provided that this issue shall not extend the amount to over $400,000,000.

February 4, 1865,　gold was 2.00.

SEVEN-THIRTIES.—An Act of March 3, 1865, provides for the issue of $600,000,000 bonds or Treasury notes, the bonds to bear six per cent. interest, and to run four years ; none of which were to be for less than $50. They are payable at any time within forty years. If these bonds are paid in other lawful money, they were to bear 7.30 per cent. per annum. Authority is given to sell the bonds in the United States and in Europe, for coin or for Treasury notes, or legal-tender notes, or any obligations of the Government, bearing or not bearing interest ; excepting bonds of the United States. This act was passed at the request of McCulloch, and was intended to cause all forms of legal-tender money issued by the United States to be funded into bonds. This act positively prohibits the issue of any more legal-tender notes. The plan was to retire and destroy all of said notes; so that the National banks might have an open field for circulation. The war then was—as all saw—about to end. The monied men were buying legal-tender notes at a heavy discount, intending to invest them in bonds, which they did.

ANOTHER ACT OF MARCH 3, 1865, provides that National banks shall be granted 90 per cent. circulation upon bonds up to $500,000, but less than 90 per cent. when the bonds exceed that sum. This appears to have been passed to prevent banks in large cities from taking up all the circulation. This law is, however, repealed by the Act of January 14, 1875.

STATE BANKS TAXED TO DEATH.—Another Act of March 3, 1865, imposed a heavy tax upon all State-bank circulation, to take effect after July 1, 1866. After the banks suspended in December, 1861, they greatly increased their circulation, and used their means to injure the legal-tender notes. All their strength was combined to compel the Government to abandon the legal tenders, and to use their suspended notes. If the bank-notes lived, the Government notes must die. This tax was imposed to put an end to State-bank circulation. It had the desired effect. The act was justifiable. The Government had the same right to suppress this hostile circulation that it had to put down any other public enemy.

THE FREEDMEN'S BANK.—Another Act of March 3, 1865, established the Freedmen's Bank, authorizing loans to be made upon Government bonds only. After certain sharks in Washington obtained control of the bank, they induced Congress to change the charter, allowing investments made in bonds and mortgages, and loans to be made upon collaterals. This ruined the bank. Had the institution been confined to its original charter, all would have been right. The bank would have been a blessing to the colored race. But the politician ruined it and them.

In April gold was 1.50.

McCULLOCH'S TREACHERY.—Henry C. Carey thus reports upon McCulloch's treachery :—

9

In May, 1865, very shortly after his accession to the post of Secretary, I had a conversation with him, in the course of which he declared himself a disciple of Mr. Clay, and thorough believer in his protective doctrines. Regarding him as sincere in this expression of opinion, I said that, in view of the great changes now to be met—millions of men, North and South, returning from the field and needing to seek employment, at a time when the Government must not only cease to be a purchaser, but must, on the contrary, become a seller of commodities it had already purchased—it was most desirable that all our measures should tend in the direction of stimulating production and making demand for labor; and that, if I had my will, gold should be at 2.00 for the next seven years; as the premium afforded a protection that even false invoices would not enable the foreigner to avoid.

Fully coinciding in the view thus suggested, the Secretary answered: "That is too much; but I would gladly see it at 1.75." Three months later, he was instructing his representatives abroad, to give assurance that we should have resumed specie payments before the first 7-30s became due. Two months yet later, came the destructive Fort Wayne decree; and from that hour did the Secretary persist in the absurd and injurious course of policy therein announced. But few months later, he presented himself as an opponent of these doctrines of Mr. Clay, of which he had been before the advocate. What is the value to be attached to his present opinions, may be judged from this exhibit, now for the first time, put on paper; although fully authorized by him on the day succeeding the conversation above described. He is, as I believe, the only one of our finance ministers who has ever retired with the reputation of a large fortune, accumulated during his term of office.

B. S. Heath makes the amount of National bank notes, July 1, 1865, to be 67 millions.

McCulloch began to retire Greenbacks, August, 1865. Had 70 millions retired by July, 1868.

Sept. 1, 1865, 830 millions of 7-30 notes were outstanding. This was the highest figure. They were redeemable Aug.

15, 1867; June 15, and July 15, 1868. $195,800 were outstanding June 3, 1875.

RETIRING LEGAL TENDERS.—The Act of Sept. 12, 1865. The legal-tender notes did not come in to be invested in bonds as fast as the Secretary of the Treasury had hoped for. An additional law was enacted at the above time. The war was now ended. The soldiers and sailors had to be paid off. They did not want bonds; they desired lawful money. The law of March 3, 1865, had prohibited any further issues of legal-tender notes. But legal tenders were the only money which the soldiers were willing to receive, notwithstanding the heavy discounts which the law had made upon them. This law of Sept. 12, 1865, provided that the legal tenders might be received for bonds to the extent of $10,000,000 in the next six months, and $4,000,000 per month after that time. This was continued until an order came from Congress to stop the reduction. This is styled an act to retire the legal-tender notes.

In October, 1865, McCulloch issued his Fort Wayne decree, announcing his determination to contract the currency.

THE TOTAL DEBT.—W. A. Birkey gives the following as the total debt and currency of the country on Oct. 31, 1865, National bank notes not included:

Total bonds (which he enumerates)........$1,163,769,611.39

CURRENCY.

Compound interest notes, due in 1867, 1868......	173,012,141.00	
7-30 Treasury notes, due in 1867, 1868...............	830,000,000.00	
Temporary loans, ten-days' notice................	99,107,745.46	
Certificates of indebtedness, due in 1866............	55,905,000.00	
Treasury notes, five per cent., 1865.............	32,536,901.00	
U. S. Notes..............	428,160,569.00	
Fractional currency........	26,057,469.20	
		1,644,779,825.66

Total debt............. ...$2,808,549,437.05

Two Billions of Currency.—As to the fact that there was near two billions of currency in 1865 and 1866, Judge Wm. D. Kelley spoke in Congress in February, 1879. Quoting McCulloch's admission in his report of December, 1865, that " 30 millions of the compound interest notes are in circulation as currency, and many of the small denominations of the 7-30s are also circulating, and *all of them tend in some measure to swell the inflation,*" the Judge says: "The $143,000,000 compound interest notes were outstanding, and were legal tender for their face value; and if the $830,000,000 of 7-30 Treasury notes were not so, the people who accepted and used them as such were deluded by the phraseology of the law under which they were issued. If they were not legal tender the proviso which declared that they should not 'be legal tender in payment or redemption of any notes issued by any bank, banking association or banker calculated or intended to circulate as money' was worse than useless verbiage; inasmuch as it was calculated to deceive, as to the character of the security they were to receive, those to whom the Government was, under the provisions of the act, to appeal for a loan of more than $800,000,000. If they were not intended to be a legal tender for all other purposes, *why was it necessary to thus specifically prohibit banks from paying their notes with them, as they were required to do with the non-interest-bearing legal-tender notes, known as Greenbacks ?"*

This from Logan comes in well here: "The circulating medium has been contracted $1,018,167,784.—John A. Logan in Congressional Record, page 139, Appendix for 1874."

There is abundant evidence all through this book that we had near two billions of money in 1865. Here are some items not given elsewhere:

Mr. Hotchkiss, of New York, July 25, 1866, in a debate in the House, said : "We have now in circulation about $1,000,-000,000 of paper currency, exclusive of the $800,000,000 of 7-30s, which pass from hand to hand as a circulating medium to a great extent."

Mr. Morrill, of Maine, stated in a speech in the House, March 16, 1866 : "That the banks held immense sums of interest-bearing notes during the maturity of interest, and were disposed to flood the country with them after interest had been realized."

Hon. W. Loughridge, of Iowa, April 9, 1874, in the

House, said: "During the war the volume of currency was largely increased from time to time, until at its close the amount in circulation, including the 7-30s and all the different issues which served the use of currency, was about $1,700,000,000, and this amount had been up to the close of the war confined to the States not in rebellion."

J. J. Knox, late Controller of the Currency, said in the Bankers' convention, Oct. 12 and 13, 1887 : "About four years after the war had commenced, in August, 1865, the public debt amounted to $2,845,907,426 ; and included in this huge mountain of indebtedness, there were 1,540,000,000 of Treasury notes either payable on demand or bearing interest, of which more than $1,500,000,000 was a legal tender. If temporary loans, payable in thirty days, and certificates of indebtedness, payable one year after date, should be included with Treasury notes, the whole would amount to considerable more than three-fifths of the $2,846,000,000 of the debt of the country."—Proceedings of the Convention, pages 20-21.

Senators Beck, Ferry and others, besides hundreds of Congressmen and business men, have stated that the interest-bearing notes were used as money, and pointed out the distress which followed their being withdrawn from circulation

McCULLOCH'S MAD POLICY.—In his report of Dec. 4, 1865, McCulloch said to Congress: "The issue of United States notes as lawful money was a measure of expediency, doubtless, and necessary in the great emergency in which it was adopted. But this emergency no longer exists ; and however satisfactory these notes may be as a circulating medium, and however desirable may be the saving of interest, these considerations will not satisfy a departure from that construction of the Constitution which is essential to the equal and harmonious working of our peculiar institutions."

Reformers sneeringly ask, "What peculiar institutions?"

Again he says :—

"The rapidity with which the Government notes can be withdrawn will depend upon the ability of the secretaries to dispose of the securities. The Secretary, therefore, respectfully but most earnestly recommends : *First*, That Congress declare that the compound interest notes shall cease to be a legal tender : *Second*, that the Secretary be authorized to sell bonds of the United States, bearing interest at a rate not exceeding six per cent., for the purpose of retiring not only compound interest notes, but the United States notes. **The** first thing to be done is to establish a policy of contraction.

Heath says : "This Congress, established by resolution on Dec. 18, 1865. How many of the eleven millions of producers, toiling in their shops and factories, delving in the subterranean storehouses of the earth, or bending their backs to the harvest sun, petitioned Mr. McCulloch to make these suggestions to Congress on its meeting? How many of these millions asked that the thing for which they were all toiling might be made more scarce and difficult to obtain? How many of them prayed that, instead of receiving Greenbacks for their products, they might be made to pay a semi-annual gold bonus to have them destroyed? How many of them voluntarily consented to have the value of their property depreciated one-half, and the value of their products reduced? How many of them consented to be turned into the streets, their families into the poorhouse, a hundred thousand bankrupted—and the most fortunate among them taxed beyond their ability to pay—simply to conform to a system of contraction, for the benefit of——whom ? "

For some facts about McCulloch and Robeson's "peculiar institution," in London, in 1865, see item about McCulloch's London Bank in " 1862."

JUDGE KELLEY PLEADS IGNORANCE.—As to the stupid vote for Resumption in Congress, Dec. 18, 1865, Judge Wm. D. Kelley said, in his speech on " Financial Mismanagement," Feb. 14, 1879 :—

I regret to say that my vote on that resolution was, with the overwhelming majority, in its favor ; there having been but six members of the House who appear to have foreseen the terrible results such a measure must produce, and voted against it. The resolution was adopted Dec. 18, 1865, and read as follows : " *Resolved*, that this House cordially concurs in the views of the Secretary of the Treasury, in relation to the necessity of a contraction of the currency ; with a view to as early a resumption of specie payments as the business interests of the country will permit ; and we hereby pledge co-operative action to this end as speedily as practicable."

My vote attracted the attention of many of the most enlightened business men of Philadelphia ; from whom I received earnest protests against the initiation of a policy so destructive as that of attempting resumption by contracting a volume of currency that was legitimately and profitably employed ; and the retirement of which, by its conversion into interest-bearing bonds, would inevitably impoverish the American people, and transfer our debt from them to the syndicates and bankers of Europe.   The Christmas vacation was at hand, and on my return to Philadelphia my venerable friends Henry C. Carey and the late Stephen Colwell, whose work entitled "Ways and Means of Payment" is, in my opinion, the most valuable contribution ever made by one man to the financial literature of the world, each honored me with protracted interviews ; during which they approved the judgment of the business men who had censured my vote ; and so instructed me in the laws of trade and finance, as to enable me to act with an enlightened judgment, on such financial questions as might thereafter come before Congress.

CHAPTER XIII.

1866 to 1873.

CONTRACTION.

1866.

THE Contraction Act was passed April 12, 1866. Previous to the passage of this act the Secretary, under the law of 1865, had been permitted to reduce the legal-tender notes $10,000,000. This Act of 1866 gave him authority to receive for bonds $4,000,000 legal-tender notes per month. Under this law he went on reducing the legal tenders until February, 1868. He would have continued the investment of the whole of them in six per cent. bonds had not Congress, owing to the solicitations of the people, compelled him to stop, of which he complained. These acts are disgraceful to the Secretary of the Treasury, having been enacted at his request, and they are by no means flattering to Congress. Under this act $1,300,000,000 of actual currency was turned into bonds.

———

Judge Warwick Martin says of THE FINANCIAL DIFFICULTIES OF ENGLAND IN 1866 :—We have shown that the financial difficulties of the United States, in 1866 and 1867, were not produced by speculation, but by a ruinous contraction of the circulating medium. In England, in 1866, there were much greater financial embarrassments than in the United States in 1866 or 1867, all of which were caused by immense speculations in railroad and other stocks. The consequences of these speculations were, in England, most disastrous. Twenty-seven banks and bankers failed in London in one day. Hundreds of old, hitherto substantial business houses failed. Among these were Overend, Gurney & Co., and Sir Morton Peto, of world-wide fame. The monetary condition of England was such that the Bank was compelled to raise the rate of interest to the point where the law of 1844 allowed the Bank to suspend coin payments. What the Bank then

did was equivalent to the suspension of specie payments.
All these results were caused by wild speculations. The
money to carry on said speculations was not suspended bank
paper, or the irredeemable issues of any nation, or irredeemable paper money of any kind. It was the notes and credits
of the great Bank of England, and of the joint-stock banks
of the kingdom; all, at the time they made the advances,
professing to pay coin for their liabilities. .

H. H. Bryant, after showing how England organized ruin
here by "calling" our gold in 1857, says :—Now, in 1866, the
Bank of England was in trouble again, and failed, as she was
obliged to do in 1857. But we were not on a specie basis in
1866; and she could have no more effect on our monetary
system than a drop of water would have when it falls into the
ocean—nor so much, for it could have none whatever. Nor
·could the failure of every bank and banker in all Europe have
caused a single ripple on the surface of our monetary system. Then the industries of the country could not be
knocked down, as with a bludgeon, and plundered, at ease,
by any one who had the *power* or the need to demand a little
gold of us.

H. C. Carey says :—The extreme importance of the
view here presented, to wit, the necessity for avoiding
" entangling alliances " in reference to a matter so important
as the monetary machinery of exchange, was made clearly
obvious when, in 1866, like a clap of thunder in the clearest
sky, the great crisis of that year, greater than any by which
it had been preceded, brought ruin to hundreds of what had
been considered the greatest British houses, and made demand on all the world for aid, if the Bank of England itself
were to be enabled to avoid suspension. The crash was terrific, yet it never affected our domestic operations for even a
single hour. Our monetary independence had been established. Our machinery of exchange being a non-exportable
one, we had no use for gold; and if it were needed abroad,
we could say, " Let it go ! " Accordingly, no less than $30,-
000,000 were at once dispatched; the Bank was saved, and
injury was thus avoided, to an extent that would scarcely be
exaggerated, were it counted by hundreds of millions of
pounds. And thus did Britain benefit by the fact that the
currencies of the two countries were different. Had we
been using gold, where should we then have found ourselves ?

In the midst of a crisis greater than the country had ever known.

THE ACT OF JULY 26, 1866, provided that bonds issued to the Pacific Railroad, to the amount of $64,000,000, might be made in sums greater than $1,000, if so required. These bonds are all payable in currency.

CASH PAYMENTS.— Judge W. D. Kelley thus describes the blessings of "Cash Payments" in 1865 and 1866:—

We had, in round numbers, about $2,000,000,000 of circulating medium and reserve. The American people then held the greater part of the debt of the country. One-fourth of our national debt was held by our National banks; one-half of the discounts and loans made by the banks were to the Government,—the evidences of whose indebtedness they were glad to hold. Business men did not want discounts. All could get money for whatever they had to sell. The old-fashioned credit system of 18 months, or 12 months, or six months, or even three months, had disappeared. Cash payments were the order of the day; and from ten to thirty days was the longest credit asked in ordinary transactions.

1867.

THREE PER CENT. CERTIFICATES.—The Act of March 2, 1867, provides for the issue of $50,000,000 three per cent. interest certificates to pay compound-interest notes. These certificates were to be held by National banks as reserves, instead of legal-tender notes, which were then so used. This relieved the money pressure to that extent. Why were not $50,000,000 new legal-tender notes issued in place of $50,000,000 three per cent. certificates? This could have been done almost without cost, and it would have saved $1,500,000 a year. Why were not the $44,000,000, redeemed and lying idle in the Treasury, paid out? Anything rather than save interest to the people. These $44,000,000 remained in the Treasury undisturbed, until the New York banks, in 1873, demanded them to save themselves from failure; when $26,000,000 were paid out. The people could not get them. The banks could, and did. The people amount to little with the Republican party. The banks are everything.

"ADDITION, DIVISION AND SILENCE."—March 20, 1867, was

the date of the long famous "Addition, Division and Silence" letter of W. H. Kemble; to which the *New York Sun* was still thus referring in 1880 :—

Does the State of Pennsylvania and the city of Philadelphia still keep public funds on deposit in the People's Bank of Philadelphia? It may not be generally known in Pennsylvania, but the president and principal owner of that institution is now a convict and a fugitive from justice, dodging from State to State. He is the same man, who, while himself State Treasurer, wrote the following statement of his principles :

TREASURY DEPARTMENT OF PENNSYLVANIA,
HARRISBURG, March 20, 1867.

MY DEAR TITIAN,—Allow me to introduce to you my particular friend, Mr. George O. Evans. He has a claim of some magnitude that he wishes you to help him in. Put him through as you would me. *He understands addition, division and silence.*

Yours,

W. H. KEMBLE.

To Titian J. Coffey, Esq., Washington, D. C.

It would be interesting to know how many millions of public money this man has had in his hands, by virtue of deposits from State and city treasurers, say during the last five years, and how many millions his bank still holds.

VANDERBILT WATERS NEW YORK CENTRAL.—In 1867 and 1868 Cornelius Vanderbilt watered the stock of the New York Central and Hudson River Railroad 47 million dollars. Upon this eight per cent. dividends were regularly paid. These dividends upon that water, compounded annually, for thirteen years [1880], amounted to over 75 million dollars. The most of our "great" men, in other industries, have done the same—according to opportunity.

1868.

SHERMAN'S ENTERING WEDGE.—In January, 1868, John Sherman, being then chairman of the Committee on Finance in the Senate, introduced a bill to change the gold coins of the United States, so as to make them correspond with the French five-franc piece; and to make the silver half-dollar correspond, in weight, to two and a half silver francs; and *dropping the dollar entirely*. This was the cunningly-applied entering wedge, that was to ultimately split "the dollar of the Fathers" off from our currency.

A SHORT STOP.—The Act of February 3, 1868, ordered the reduction and destruction of the legal-tender notes to be stopped. They had been reduced from $450,000,000 to $356,000,000—reduction amounting to $94,000,000—and six per cent. bonds given therefor. The politicians did not order the cancellation of these notes to cease because they loved the notes, but because the people compelled them so to do. Even Mr. Sherman made a great speech in favor of this measure; not from the love of legal-tender notes, but because he feared the people. Why did not Congress, at this time, add a few hundred millions to the legal-tender notes, instead of increasing the National bank circulation at large cost to the people?

The Act of February 10, 1868, authorizes the National bank shares to be taxed under State authority as much as those of other banks were, but not more.

CHECK TO ROTHSCHILDS.—It is alleged that the Rothschilds were in possession of several hundred millions of 5–20 bonds, at this time, purchased at about 60 cents on the dollar, or less; and were particularly interested, therefore, in our politics. That their agent, August Belmont, who secured the position of chairman of the Democratic National Committee, was instructed by Baron James Rothschild, as early as March 13, 1868, that unless the Democratic Party went in for paying the 5-20 bonds in gold, *it must be defeated.* The first step was to have the National Convention held in New York City.

July 4, 1868, the Democratic Convention met in New York, according to programme. Belmont and his satellites were unable to control the convention—at least in the matter of the platform—and it declared that all obligations against the Government not expressly payable in coin should be paid in lawful money of the United States. [See Oct. 15.]

"The Great Commoner," Thaddeus Stevens, was still around, and able to lift his voice. In his speech of July 17, 1868, he said: "If I knew that any party in this country would go for paying in coin that which is payable in [lawful] money, thus enhancing it one-half,—if I knew there was

such a party platform, and such a determination, this day,
on the part of any political party, I would vote for the other
side, Frank Blair and all; I would vote for no such speculation in favor of the large bondholders, the millionaires, who
took advantage of our folly in granting them coin payment
of interest."

A "HOWLING SUCCESS."—As a specimen of how the
National banks were " getting there " all this time, take the
following from the speech of S. S. Marshall of Illinois, in
Congress, July 21, 1868:—

I will report what a gentleman on this floor states as having
occurred in an Eastern State within his own observation :
" An association of gentlemen raised $300,000 in currency.
They went to the office of the Register of the Treasury,
and exchanged their currency for $300,000 in six per cent.
gold-bearing bonds. They then went to the office of the
Comptroller of the Currency, in the same building, organized
a National bank, deposited their $300,000 in bonds, and re-
ceived for their bank $270,000 of National currency. They
had let the Government have $30,000 in currency more than
they received for banking purposes ; and had on deposit
$300,000 on which they received from the Government
$18,000 a year in gold (exempt from taxation). That was
pretty good financiering for these bankers to receive $18,000
in gold on the $30,000 in currency which they had thus
loaned to the Government.

" But this was not the whole story. They had their bank
made a public depository. They soon discovered that there
was scarcely ever less than $1,000,000 of Government money
deposited within their vaults. They did not like to see this
vast sum lie idle. They therefore took a million of this
Government money and bought a million of 5-20 bonds with
it. In other words, they loaned a million of the Government's own money to the Government, and deposited the
bonds received in the vaults of their bank, on which they
received from the same Government $60,000 in gold annually,
as interest.

" Thus, for the $30,000 in currency which they originally
loaned the Government, they were receiving annually in
gold (and exempt from taxation at that) $78,000. And all
this was under the regular operation of your banking laws."

THE ACT OF JULY 25, 1868, provides for the issue of

$25,000,000 more three per cent. interest certificates, **of** the same character and for the same purpose as the $50,000,000 provided for in the Act of March 2, 1867. They also were to be held by banks as reserves, for which legal-tender notes were then held; so that the legal-tender notes might circulate. Why not issue new legal-tender notes in place of the certificates and save the interest? But this was not the policy of Mr. Sherman and of Wall Street.

ROTHSCHILDS WIN, SEYMOUR BEATEN.—August Belmont owned a large interest in the N. Y. *World*, the leading Democratic paper of the country, which on Oct. 15, 1868, came out in a double-leaded editorial denouncing Seymour as unavailable, and unfit for President of the United States; and *advised his withdrawal.* This so demoralized the Democracy that Grant had an easy walk-over, on the course. The platform on which Seymour ran called for quick payment of the debt; and in paper when coin was not stipulated in the bond; taxation of Government bonds; one currency for the people, the bondholder, office-holder, etc. Of course, our Boss Rothschild would not stand any such nonsense as that; and so Belmont was ordered to order Manton Marble to play Benedict Arnold with his always-for-sale *World* just before election—just on the eve of a great battle; and Seymour was shelved. It is an interesting fact that Marble, who, not long before, had been a reporter on the *Evening Post* (and who had run the *World*, at a loss, for various masters), now suddenly acquired a fine brown-stone mansion on Fifth Avenue, and all that that implies. Residing at present in Paris, he occasionally instructs the American public, by Orphic oracles, concerning "the money question:" to which nobody who at all understands it, pays any attention.

Before this time, Sherman, Morton and other leading Republican Senators had opposed coin payment of the bonds. They were bought and silenced by Grant's election. Then, as we shall see, came "The Strengthening Act." Save the mark!

The great economist Wolowski of Paris made this truthful prophecy in 1868, when the subject of demonetization of silver was discussed. He said that if that were done: The decline in prices will compel nations internationally indebted to depart, more and more, from the principles of free trade towards a policy of protection.

The nations of the world will be divided into two groups
—the one trading in gold, the other in silver—and this condition will render commerce precarious and unsafe.

Throughout the world a decline in prices will follow, injurious alike to owners of real property and the laboring
classes, and advantageous only—and unjustly so—to the
holders of State bonds and similar securities.

One of the principal difficulties in this period of general
depression will be that the people will look for its causes in
all possible directions.

The advocates of the gold standard will offer all possible
groundless and fantastic excuses or reasons of a secondary
nature only, and the real cause, the demonetization of silver,
will be overlooked.

THERE'S MILLIONS IN IT.—The speculators of the gold
exchange for years kept gold up that they might buy Greenbacks cheap ; to invest in bonds at par ; and below is the
result, showing the year, the amount of Greenbacks exchanged
for bonds, and the amount in gold, for which the Greenbacks
were purchased from 1862 to 1868 :

Year.	Bonds.	Cost in gold.
1862	$ 60,982,450	$ 44,030,649
1863	160,987,550	101,890,850
1864	381,292,250	189,697,636
1865	279,646,150	208,214.090
1866	124,914,400	88,591.773
1867	421,469.550	303.215.303
1868	425,443,800	312,826,323
	$1,854,736,150	$1,248,466,624
Here is a net profit of........		606,269,526
Add interest to 1880........		1,430,000,000
		$2,036,269,526

The above figures are taken from the public record, and
may be relied upon.

The bondholders have received back more than twice the
value they loaned, and still [1880] hold the bonds to draw
more every year, until they mature ; when they expect to receive their face in gold, or keep the blister drawing until it is
paid.

1869.

CHECKS ON BANKS.—The Act of February 19, 1869, provides that National banks shall not loan money on their own notes; as it would tend to create a scarcity in the money market by locking money up. Quite a patriotic effort on the part of our rulers!

March 3, 1869, Congress passed an act against over-certification by banks. The banks were equal to the occasion, as usual; as will be seen.

THE CREDIT STRENGTHENING ACT.—President Grant, in his Inaugural of March 4, 1869, notified the public that he would regard all who did not favor the payment of the 5-20 bonds in gold as repudiators, who need not expect any favors from his administration.

March 11, 1869, when the Credit Strengthening Act was coming up, Governor O. P. Morton gave this last gasp against the gold bondage: " I am anxious to have the bonds paid in gold or its equivalent, and that will be the result when we return to specie payments, as I hope we soon shall. But when I am asked to say that it is the original law of the contract creating some of the bonds, I cannot do it, without changing my convictions as to the construction of the statutes, which I have entertained from the first."

The Act of March 18, 1869, called "The Credit Strengthening Act," demonetized the legal-tender notes, and provided—contrary to the laws and the facts—that both legal-tender notes and 5-20 bonds were payable in coin, and should be so paid. By this act, the people lost and the capitalists gained $500,000,000. Large books have been written on the 5-20s, which were so largely affected by this evil legislation. John G. Drew wrote of their "Origin and History." He opens thus: "On the 12th of March, Mr. Schenck, of Ohio [better known afterward as Poker Schenck.—S. L.], introduced a bill into the House which, after the customary game of battledore and shuttlecock with the Senate, was passed. The same bill had before passed Congress, and been sent to the President (Johnson); but he—whether advised that Congress was exceeding its province in invading the functions of the Supreme Court by construing law, or whether he considered it as a sort of town-meeting resolution, we don't know—took no notice of it ; and thus the previous action lapsed by his default."

Here is the Act of 1869, as approved by Grant :—

An Act to Strengthen the Public Credit of the United States :

Be it enacted, etc. : That, in order to remove any doubt as to the purpose of the Government to discharge all its obligations to the public creditors, and to settle conflicting questions and interpretations of the law, by virtue of which such obligations have been contracted, it is hereby provided and declared that the faith of the United States is solemnly pledged to the payment in coin, or its equivalent, of all the obligations of the United States not bearing interest known as United States notes, and of all the interest-bearing obligations, except in cases where the law authorizing the issue of any such obligations has expressly provided that the same may be paid in lawful money, or in other currency than gold and silver ; but none of the said interest-bearing obligations not already due shall be redeemed or paid before maturity, unless at such times as United States notes shall be convertible into coin at the option of the holder, or unless at such time bonds of the United States, bearing a lower rate of interest than the bonds to be redeemed can be sold at par in coin. And the United States also solemnly pledges its faith to make provision for the redemption of the United States notes in coin.

U. S. GRANT.

Approved March 18, 1869.

It is proof positive that Europe did not consider the 5-20s coin bonds, that on Nov. 30, 1867, they were sold in London at 70⅜ cents ; while New Brunswick and Cape of Good Hope six per cents sold at 105 ; Russian five per cents at 85, and Brazilian five per cents at 75.

B. S. Heath said of this act :—In 1869, when the Credit Strengthening Act was passed, changing the payment of • the bonds from Greenbacks to coin, there was outstanding $1,500,000,000 of 5-20 bonds ; all to become due and payable within the next twelve years. At that time, the coin resources of the Government were no more than sufficient to enable it to meet its current interest obligations. Nevertheless, Congress obligated it to pay $1,500,000,000 of gold and silver. This was an apparent impossibility. *It was*

10

intended to be such. The Act was for the express purpose of *immortalizing* the public debt ; that it might never be paid.

But when Nevada opened her rich vaults of silver,—and made it possible to pay the debt in accordance with the new terms imposed,—that metal was demonetized, and payment limited to gold. It may seem strange to some that the bondholders should desire such legislation as would absolutely defeat payment to them. But they regarded the bonds as the best-paying investment into which they could put their money.

To say that our bonds were issued and sold to raise money to carry on the war is absurd and false. It was a year and a half after they were authorized before they were put upon the market; and when they were offered it was not because the Government needed the money.

BLACK FRIDAY.—Warwick Martin says :—The running up of gold from 25 to 62½ on Black Friday, in Sept., 1869, and the crisis of 1873, were immediately caused by the banking law allowing banks at money centers to draw interest on the deposits of country banks. The money is loaned on call to speculators, who cannot respond when a scare comes. Secretary Richardson tried to have a law passed preventing this. But Wall Street prevailed.

Up to 1869, the sales of gold had been made by the Secretaries of the Treasury secretly ; but, in 1869, when General Grant became President and Mr. Boutwell Secretary of the Treasury, Congress were induced to authorize notice to be given of the time when gold would be sold, and bonds would be purchased. This was done by Mr. Boutwell, Mr. Richardson, Mr. Bristow, and Mr. Morrill, Secretaries of the Treasury. Nothing could have promoted the interest of Wall Street better than this law and the practice under it. As soon as notice was given each month, the gold brokers commenced reducing the premium upon gold until the day when the sales were to take place. On that day gold always ruled low. The Secretary received the lowest price for this gold sold. On the day following his sales the premium on gold, instead of going down, owning to said sales, always went up. The brokers sold what they had purchased from the Secretary of the Treasury, making a good profit thereon. In this way and by these means the Secretary enabled Wall Street brokers to make fortunes.

One thing more and we close. In Sept., 1869, when no unusual demand for gold existed, it in some way became known that the Secretary of the Treasury did not intend to sell gold that month. The brokers of Wall Street thought it a proper time to get up a corner on gold, as though some great demand therefor existed. From day to day and week to week the, rate went up from 25 per cent. until it reached 60 per cent. premium. The sales by the Treasury of even one or two millions would have prevented the advance of the premium ; but no sales were made until the premium went up to 60; then $5,000,000 were sold, and in one hour the premium went down to 30. Had $10,000,000, instead of $5,000,000 been sold, the premium would have gone much lower. The notes could easily have been made par.

We do not accuse Mr. Boutwell of any combination with Wall Street to produce this state of things, but there is no doubt that some one very high in position was in that combination, expecting to participate in the profits. This combination prevented sales of gold from taking place on a certain day. The matter should have been fully investigated.

1870.

The Act of July 2, 1870, increases the circulation of National banks to $354,000,000; which was to be divided among the States, according to population. The Act of 1864 had limited them to $300,000,000.

THE LAW OF 1870, PROVIDING THAT NATIONAL BANKS MIGHT SURRENDER THEIR CIRCULATION AND LIFT AND SELL THEIR BONDS.—The previous legislation relating to bonds and National banks had raised the price of bonds, which cost not more than $40 coin to the $100, to $120 and $125. It was a most favorable time to sell 5-20 bonds, before many of those issued under the funding laws of 1870 and 1871 could be sold and the 5-20s called in. Consequently Sherman, who had charge of the National banks in the Senate, placed a section in the Act of 1870, which provided that by placing the despised legal-tender notes in the Treasury to the amount of the circulation of the banks, they could lift and sell their bonds, and the Government would redeem the bank notes. Two objects were accomplished by this provision in this act. The National banks, thus surrendering circulation, sold their 5-20 bonds,—which they would soon have been compelled to surrender under the law of 1870,—at a premium of 20 or 25 per cent., and were prepared, after making a large sum, to supply their places with five per cent. bonds at par. For this act the National banks should feel grateful, and no doubt they do. Another object of this provision of the act was, to lock up the legal-tender notes in the Treasury, and to keep the National-bank notes out; and thus reduce the circulation of the country, and especially of the legal tenders. Another legal device to contract the currency—and especially the legal-tender notes—was to provide that when National banks failed, and their bonds were sold by the Government, the money (not in coin for which the bonds were sold, but in legal-tender notes) should be deposited in the Treasury, to redeem the notes of the failed banks. This reduced the quantity of legal-tender notes out in the business of the country, but kept the National-bank notes out among the people, until the Government saw proper to pay out the legal tenders deposited for their redemption. It will be seen that every move made tended to the carrying out of the original intention of Mr. Sherman,—as stated in his speech of February, 1863,—to retire the legal-tender notes, and to substitute National-bank notes in their place.

In 1870 and 1871, the six per cents were worth 20 per cent. premium in Greenbacks; which were 11 per cent. below coin. Under the above act, the banks sold about $300,000,000 of 5-20 bonds,—they having at the time $400,000,000; including some at five per cent. interest. 20 per cent. on $300,000,000 is $60,000,000—a neat profit.

THE GREAT REFUNDING ACT.—The Act of July 14, 1870, authorized the issue and sale of $1,500,000,000 United States bonds, to refund the 5-20s: 200 million at five per cent.; 300 million at four and a half per cent., and 1,000 million at four per cent., interest and principal in " coin." This loan was intended to be raised in Europe,—especially among the English, who had been so hostile to us during the war; and then bought Confederate bonds at a premium, while refusing ours. We did not need to borrow—the Government having an annual income of 300 million. We could have borrowed any amount at home, at five per cent. The country was tolerably prosperous. The 5-20s were not due. Large quantities of them were in 50s and 100s; which were distributed among the people of small means ; and were to them the same as money ;—bearing interest when they did not need money, and always salable at par, or above par for legal tenders. It was a great hardship for the people to surrender these bonds for the benefit of native and foreign capitalists. We got no foreign coin for them : England took care to prevent that.

THE SUPREME COURT AND THE LEGAL TENDER.—In 1870 the Supreme Court decided—by a vote of five to three —that Congress had no constitutional power to make its notes legal tender in the payment of pre-existing debts. A change in the composition of the court resulted, in 1871, in a reversal of this decision by a majority of one. In 1884, unenlightened public opinion was only represented, as will be seen, in this court by Judge Field of California.

"GOD-MADE" MONEY.—For the purpose of setting some thoughtless people right on the question of intrinsic value in money, we quote from the famous case of Knox *vs.* Lee, in the United States Supreme Court in 1871. After deciding that Congress had full constitutional right to authorize the issue of legal tender money, the court said :—

Here we might stop ; but we will notice briefly an argument presented in support of the position that the unit of money value must possess intrinsic value. The argument is derived from assimilating the constitutional provision respecting a standard of weights and measures to that conferring the power to coin money and regulate its value. It is said there can be no uniform standard of weights without weight, or of measure without length or space, and we are asked how anything can be made a standard of value which has itself no value. It is hardly correct to speak of a standard of value. The Constitution does not speak of it. It contemplates a standard for that which has gravity or extension, but value is an ideal thing. The coinage acts fix its unit as a dollar, but the gold or silver thing we call a dollar is in no sense a standard of a dollar. It is a representative of it. There might never have been a piece of money of the denomination of a dollar. There never was a pound sterling coined until 1815, if we except a few coins struck in the reign of Henry VII., almost immediately debased, yet it has been the unit of British currency for many generations.

The court further said :—

The States can no longer declare what shall be money or regulate its value. Whatever power there is over the currency is vested in Congress. If the power to declare what is money is not in Congress, it is annihilated. * * * The Constitution does not ordain what metals shall be coined, or prescribe that the legal value of the metals, when coined, shall correspond at all with their intrinsic value on the market. Nor does it even affirm that Congress may declare anything to be a legal tender for the payment of debts. Confessedly the power to regulate the value of money coined, and of foreign coins, is not exhausted by the first regulation. More than once in our history has the regulation been changed without any denial of the power of Congress to change it, and it seems to have been left to Congress to determine alike what shall be coined, its purity, and how far its statutory value as money, shall correspond, from time to time, with the market value of the same metal as bullion. * * *

No one ever doubted that a debt of $1,000, contracted before 1834, could be paid by 100 eagles coined after that year, though they contained no more gold than 94 eagles such as were coined when the contract was made, and this, not because of the intrinsic value of the coin, but because of its legal value. The eagles coined after 1834 were not money until they were authorized by law, and had they been coined before without a law fixing their legal value, they could have no more paid a debt than uncoined bullion or cotton or wheat.

[In view of the fact that a full bench of the Supreme Court in 1884 reaffirmed this decision, one would think that intrinsic-value people would be afraid to go before the public with such foolish statements as "God made money."]

REPEAL OF THE INCOME TAX (Statutes 16, p. 256) occurred in 1870. So long as this tax existed, it compensated, to some extent, for the failure to tax bonds. The bond-holders were taxed upon the income derived from the interest on their bonds. This was the most just and equitable tax ever imposed : but as it came from the rich and not from the poor, Congress, ever careful of such, kindly repealed the law applying to incomes, legacies and successions in 1870— to take effect in 1872. This tax was upon railroads, banks, bondholders, capitalists and corporations. But this was repealed, and those upon the industries left standing.

MORE WEALTH IN TEN YEARS THAN IN 250 PREVIOUS.— The wealth of this country had greatly increased by 1870; in spite of all drawbacks. The *Rural World* said, soon after that date, quoting the census :—In round numbers, the entire net wealth of the nation—produced by all the labor expended from the day the Pilgrims landed upon Plymouth Rock to the year 1860—was 15 billions. The combined wealth in 1870 was 30 billions. More wealth was created from 1860 to 1870, during the Greenback reign, than during the entire history of the country before that ; when we were hobbying along upon a gold basis theory. The estimates in 1860 include the millions in human chattels which were extinguished before 1870 ; and during the decade from 1860 to 1870 we had a destructive war, in which hundreds of thousands of men were engaged in destroying wealth instead of producing it.

1871.

The Act of January 20, 1871, made interest on the five per cents. payable quarterly [See July, 1870] and added $300,000,000 to them.

THE THREE-SIXTY-FIVE BONDS.—November 9, 1871, Horace Greeley gave, in the New York *Tribune*, an exposition of the famous 3-65 bond plan, which is considered a very good statement. As the plan is now obsolete, it need not be rehearsed. If the grand old man were now alive, he would be with the vanguard of reform—trying to cut down " interest, rent, and speculative profit," to the lowest possible point.

Most people think that Greeley's nomination to the Presidency in 1872 was a mistake. But here is what Bishop J. W. Hood said of it in 1884 : " The nomination of Greeley *took the poison out of Southern sentiment;* and a fearless, upright man can now win the respect of the people and work his way without difficulty."

CARPET-BAG DEBTS.—The following from the New York *World* of 1879, gives a dark picture of carpet-bag debts in the South, in 1871 :—Now that we have heard so much about Southern State debts, suppose we cite a few figures which were in circulation seven or eight years ago, and then provoked not a little comment. They showed the debt and contingent liabilities of the States in 1861 before, and again in

1871 after they had experienced the blessings of civil war, reconstruction and carpet-bag government. Inasmuch as these States were compelled to repudiate such indebtedness as they had incurred for the purposes of war, the increase was exclusively due to the Republican carpet-baggers, who were not satisfied with stealing all that had been left to the people after four years of war, but undertook to appropriate in advance the earnings of the South for the next generation.

DEBTS AND LIABILITIES.

State	Old.	New.	Increase.
Alabama.........	$7,945,000	$52,761,917	$44,816,917
Arkansas........	2,084,179	19,398,000	17,313,821
Florida..........	370,617	15,797,587	15,426,970
Georgia.........	2,670,750	42,560,500	39,889,750
Louisiana.......	11,000,000	40,021,734	29,021,734
Mississippi......	None	1,697,431	1,697,431
North Carolina..	12,689,245	34,387,464	22,198,219
South Carolina..	4,407,958	22,480,516	18,072,556
Texas...........	2,000,000	14,930,000	12,930,000
Virginia.........	33,248,141	47,090,866	13,842,725
	$76,415,890	$291,626,015	$215,210,125

It seems to us but yesterday that Mr. Schurz, who was then a Reformer, was grieving over the spectacle of these down-trodden and scientifically plundered States; and that even the *Tribune* had to shake its head at Spencer. And now!

FRENCH PAPER MONEY.—In the "Cyclopedia of Money and Finance" I have partly shown that France's great victory over Germany in the payment of three-quarters of the billion dollar indemnity by German bills of exchange, was principally due to the fact that the French rulers, right after the war, flooded the country with paper money, and thus pushed all the industries, and made French goods cheaper than German. The writer of the following, Ivan C. Michels, gets a glimpse of this in the italic part. His figures are an interesting corroboration of the great claim we Greenbackers have always made for French financiering :—

The indemnity from France to Germany after the war of

1870-71, including interest at five per cent. per annum,
amounted to $1,060,209,015. After crediting France with the
value of certain railroads in Alsace and Lorraine, the amount
of indemnity due Germany was $998,172.069. or 4.990,860,-
349 francs, which was paid by the French Government
through the Bank of France. At my request, the Bank of
France furnished to me several years ago the following
statement as to the mode of having paid said indemnity :

	Francs.
In bank-notes of the Bank of France........	125,000,000
In French gold coins......................	273,003,050
In French silver coins	239,291,875
In German bank-notes......................	105,039,045
Bills of exchange drawn in thalers...........	2,485,513,729
Bills drawn on Frankfurt in florins..........	235,128,152
Bills drawn on Hamburg in marksbancs......	265,216,990
Bills drawn on Berlin in reichsmarks........	79,072,309
Bills drawn on Amsterdam in florins.........	250,540,821
Bills drawn on Antwerp and Brussels in francs...............................	295,704,546
Bills drawn on London in pounds sterling....	637,349,832
Total francs.........................	4.990,860,349

Equal to $998,172,069, the dollars reckoned at five francs.

The patriotic people of France raised the vast sum by a
loan in less than six months from the time the Government
appealed to them. Germany expected to receive for years
to come 5 per cent. per annum on the indemnity bond ; but
the Bank of France, through the French bankers, drew on
Germany, England, Scotland and Belgium, and in four
months time the whole indemnity was paid. Never in the
history of the world has this financial transaction been
equaled, and I doubt that any other banking institution could
have succeeded so well as the Bank of France. Germany
expected the payment in gold coin or bullion, having previously and purposely demonetized silver ; but the fact remains that actually in gold only 273,003,050 francs, equal to
$54,600,610, were paid by the Bank of France, and that sum
only left France, was remelted in Germany and coined into
reichs-marks. England, with her gold standard, had to part
with her gold to the amount of 637,349,832 francs, equal to

$127,469,964. Bills of exchange on the German bankers throughout the German empire, especially on Hamburg, Berlin and Frankfurt, amounted to 3,064,931,180 francs, equal to $612,986,236, nigh on two-thirds of the whole amount of the indemnity. This magnificent stroke of finance on the part of the Bank of France and the French bankers came near ruining the leading German bankers, and forty-one banking houses throughout the German Empire had to suspend temporarily, not being able to honor the drafts made upon them. *The extravagance of the German people during the war of 1870–71 brought them into debt to France for luxuries, wines, etc.,* to an enormous extent, and when the Bank of France purchased bills of exchange from the French bankers, who drew on their German correspondents, a panic ensued, and the Germans suffered far more than it is generally believed.

CREDIT MOBILIER AND TWEED RING.—In 1871, the Credit Mobilier at Washington, and the Tweed Ring at New York, were exposed.

1872.

EARNINGS IN PRODUCTION AND IN BANKING.—John G. Drew gives the following comparison of American earnings in production and in banking in 1872:—

The average increase of our earnings is three and a half per cent. The Comptroller of the Currency, in his report of December, 1872, shows the net earnings of National banks to be 10 and a third per cent. Add to this rent, salaries, etc., it would be 15 per cent. Street rates are doubtless 20 per cent. Net earnings of banks, for year ending Aug. 31, 1872, are : Milwaukee, 17.93 ; Iowa, 17.70 ; Minnesota, 14.36 ; Missouri, 18.14 ; Kansas, 15.89 ; Nebraska, 14.02 ; Oregon 36.10 ; Utah, 49.36 ; Idaho, 38.87 ; Montana, 24.30.

With three per cent. earnings and 20 per cent. taken by the money-lenders, it follow that the people who are borrower sink 17 per cent. a year. This would bring the cleaning-out panic once in six years. As all do not borrow, the panic comes about once in ten years.

PREPARING FOR THE PANIC.—The N. Y. *Tribune,* in 1875, shows how bravely we were preparing for the panic in 1872 : —From October, 1865 to Oct. 1872, the following changes took place in the principal items of the balance sheets of the National banks :

	1865	1872
Private Loans and Discounts.	$487,170,000	$877,198,000
United States Bonds........	427,731,000	409,669,000
Loans to Banks and Brokers,	107,372,000	128,181,000
Stocks....................	19,049,000	23,533,000
Paper Money and Specie.....	224,308,000	147,140,000
Circulation................	171,322,000	333,495,000
Individual Deposits.........	500,911,000	613,290,000
United States Deposits......	48,170,000	12,418,000
Due to Banks..............	174,200,000	144,836,000
Capital Paid in............	393,157,000	679,929,000

The above table shows that *the banks took up the business of inflation when the Government dropped it;* that they increased their loans and discounts 80 per cent., at the same time diminishing their cash reserve more than one-third: and also diminishing their United States bonds, while increasing their liabilities to depositors, and nearly doubling their circulation.

APOTHEOSIS OF JAY GOULD.—About twenty years ago, Jay Gould was the N. Y. *Sun's* "master thief." In those days it could not chide in sufficiently strenuous terms, Reid of the *Tribune* as "Jay Gould's boy." Long after the big *Tribune* building was erected, the little *Sun* hung like a hornet upon its flank. But times change. The *Sun* now has excuses for and praise of Gould, as a "great man." And Dana has long been on fraternal terms with Reid. As the *Sun's* condemnation of Gould is still fresh in the average memory, I go back still further, and present the *Tribune's* diatribes upon him, years before he became the owner of that paper,—as a fitting and *touching* contrast to the *Sun's* present defence [1889], and its terrible fulminations against young Ives—as the real "master thief" of the age. Here is an abstract of what I find in the N. Y. *Tribune*, Nov. 26, 1872. It is given as "a story worth repeating," so I repeat it. It tells how Gould persuaded Daniel Drew to join him in a raid on Erie, and unloaded on Drew—as that worthy had often served his confederates. The *Tribune* editorial says: "We can watch with composure the robbing of Mr. Drew by Mr. Gould ; and we shall look on with equal composure when Mr. Drew gets his turn. * * * But the outside innocents are ground to powder. * * Poor clerks who had staked a few spare hundreds on the great lottery, in the hope of adding something to their scanty salaries; tradesmen who had risked their savings; professional men who had expected to win enough in Wall Street to buy Christmas presents for wife and children, or to pay the New Year's bills,—were the victims. * * Mr. Gould was merciful. He took all they had, and excused them from paying the rest."

Another editorial from the same paper, just after Stokes shot Fisk. Describing the course of the Fisk and Gould ring, the *Tribune* said :—They taught the world that before their money, their effrontery and their ingenuity, courts were powerless and law was a mockery. Almost every step in their career was upon a broken statute. They subsidized judges of the Supreme Court to assist them in the illegal over-issue of stock by which they first got a standing in the market. They used the writ of injunction in so scandalous a manner, in protecting this over-issue, that men began to believe it would be better for the public if *ex-parte* proceedings in equity were abolished altogether. When the officers of the railway company were enjoined from issuing the disputed certificates, Mr. Fisk stole them, and threw them on the market. When attachments issued for this gross contempt, the whole board of directors ran to Jersey City with their money and their concubines. From across the ferry they shouted defiance at judges and laws; and organized gangs of mercenaries to keep guard about the tavern which they called their fort. They maintained this attitude for weeks; and when they were ready to divide their plunder with the speculators on this side of the river, they made their bargain, came over in broad daylight, and laughed at the Supreme Court. We have more than once told the history of this shameful proceeding; by which the road was first robbed of $9,000,000, and then handed over to Fisk and Gould as their personal property. And what became of the order of arrest? Why, Judge Barnard put it in his pocket, and entered the service of the men against whom it had been issued.

The degradation of the bench was now complete. At Fisk's call, Barnard left his mother's death-bed, in Pough-keepsie, to sign outrageous *ex-parte* orders (if, indeed, his signature was not fraudulently affixed afterward) in the apart-ments of Fisk's mistress. At Fisk's order, the telegraph

was used to serve writs in Albany, purporting to be issued in
New York. At Fisk's demand, when the great gold conspiracy broke down, 28 injunctions were sued out to save the
conspirators from the consequences of their ruined enterprise; and men whom they had swindled were forbidden to
appear in court, except in the character of criminals. At
Fisk's behest, when the English attempted to save their
depreciating property, Barnard seized 60,000 shares of stock,
and placed them virtually in Fisk's hands, to be voted with
and canceled. At Fisk's order, the Supreme Court became
a tool of the Erie Company, in its raid upon the Albany and
Susquehanna road; and persecuted Ramsey with injunctions
and fraudulent actions; which have only been dropped since
the death of their prime mover. And as corruption on the
bench spreads downward, and destroys, in time, the moral
· dignity and purity of the bar, so it was possible for these
vulgar rogues to use as the instruments of their misdeeds a
distinguished advocate whose sense of honor had been described as Quixotic.

GERMANY KICKS.—840 business associations of Germany,
largely agricultural, petitioned that Government, in 1872, to
return to the silver standard.

A WARNING SILVER PROPHET.*—Gen. A. J. Warner, in 1879,
quoted in Congress the following, as the utterance of Ernest
Seyd, the English economist, in 1872. This shows what
strong warnings the world had about silver:—The demonetization of silver, abstracting say 40 per cent. from mediums
of exchange,—or rather the violation of the contract basis
upon which these relations now rest,—will be tantamount to
a gratuitous addition to the power of invested capital and
fixed income; while labor and property will fall in value.
Whether the result takes place suddenly or gradually (as
the advocates of the gold valuation put in for an excuse), the
principle involved remains the same. The wrong remains

---

* A mystery still unexplained in 1893 hangs over the man Ernest
Seyd. He appears as a sort of Dr. Jekyll and Mr. Hyde in our finances.
I have sometimes thought the names Seyd and Loyd have been
mixed in somebody's manuscript. Here now we have Ernest Seyd as a
very wise bi-metalist, and again we have an Ernest Seyd appearing with
a half million of dollars to buy up our Congress and get silver demonetized in 1873.

Will somebody explain? Did the Shylock-Sherman combine seduce
him?

paramount. Thus the value of all State debts (in themselves immoral) would increase greatly; the burden of taxation would become the heavier in proportion; and labor would become more enslaved than ever. There are persons who allege that the additional supply of gold might soon make up the difference. The folly of this assertion equals that of a man who wantonly scuttles his ship, in the hope and expectation that he might get another to replace it.

ENGLAND'S FIVE BILLIONS OF CREDIT MONEY.—The credit money of England was reckoned at five billion dollars in 1872, as follows :—An English writer quoted by Henry Carey Baird gives these figures in dollars :

Gold and silver in Great Britain.......... ... $339,500,000
Circulation of Bank of England notes........   166,500,000
Other bank-notes in Great Britain in 1872......   85,425,000
                                              ─────────────
                                               $591,425,000

R. H. I. Palgrave says that the deposits of the British banks were, in 1871,—$ 2,900,000,000. He estimates from sales of stamps for bills payable, their average amount at any one time as $1,200,000,000. He estimates the private or other debts,—for which no bills are given by nobility and gentry,—at the same figures. So we have

Bank deposits........................... $2,900,000,000
Bills of exchange   1,200,000,000
Private debts...........................   1,200,000,000
                                          ─────────────
                                           $5,300,000,000

All this is payable on demand by the less than 600 million of money.

CHAPTER XIV.

1873 to 1880.

SEVEN YEARS OF FAMINE IN A LAND OF PLENTY.

1873.

THE DEMONETIZATION OF SILVER.—The first great financial event of 1873, is one that should make those who caused it feel very small—namely—the demonetization of silver on February 12.

The recent utterance of the able Peoria, Ill., *Journal*, makes a good opening on this question. It said, in substance :—

On December 16, 1872, a bill relating to mints, assay offices and coinage was reported to the House from the Senate by Sherman. It had been prepared two years before, by the agent of the foreign bankers, the New York Chamber of Commerce and John J. Knox,—who was then Comptroller of the Currency. It provided for a thorough change in our silver coinage ; on a plea of equalizing it with that of France. The real object was to drop the silver dollar. Sherman said the bill had passed the Senate, at its last session ; and he proposed to modify only a single section. He wished the Senate to pass it without reading. Senator Casserly of California opposed the bill. It was ordered printed and read. When it was put upon its passage in the Senate, January 17, 1873, Sherman added 17 amendments to it instead of one. The House disagreed with his amendments ; and then he made his favorite movement for a conference committee, with himself at its head. When he had convinced the committee that they did not know anything about the coinage system of the United States, he introduced the following amendment, which was passed : "That any owner of silver bullion may deposit the same at any mint, to be formed into bars or into dollars of 420 grains troy, designated as trade dollars, *and no deposit of silver for other coinage shall be received.*" These are the few lines that abolished the coinage of the old 412½ grain silver dollar. Mr. Sherman was anxious to have free coinage for the Chinese, but not a single dollar for the people of this country; although they were involved in a debt of over $2,000,000,000 occasioned by the war of the Rebellion; to say nothing of municipal, township, county and State indebtedness. At the time that silver was degraded there was, all told, according to the reports of the different Secretaries of the Treasury, less than $2,000,000 of silver in the Treasury, and only about $5,000,000 in private and National banks, and in the hands of private individuals.

Senator Jones of Nevada said in 1890:—And again in 1873, when all bonds provided for by the Refunding Act of 1870 had been sold, and had passed out of the hands of the Government, another act was passed, intended by the money-lenders again to strengthen the public credit; and again to the disadvantage of the people, and to the exclusive and enormous advantage of the bond-holders. It bore the innocent title of " an act revising and amending the laws relative to the mints, assay offices and coinage of the United States." This act, bearing on its face no suggestion of any change more serious than that of regulating the petty details of mint management,—has proved to be an act of momentous consequence to the people of this country. This is the act that demonetized the silver dollar; which it did by *merely omitting that coin from the enumeration of the coins of the United States.*

Ernest Seyd.—Another writer says: The English capitalists raised $500,000 and sent one Ernest Seyd to America to have silver demonetized. He came. In the bill was skillfully inserted the clause demonetizing silver. Before the bill passed a member of the committee which had it in charge stated that :

" Ernest Seyd of London, a distinguished writer and bullionist, who is now here, has given great attention to the subject of mint coinage. After having examined the first draft of this bill, he has made various sensible suggestions which the committee ADOPTED and EMBODIED in the bill. Congressional Record, April 9, 1872."

The money kings of the world knew what they were about. They had determined to control and enslave labor by means of their control of the world's money. They had determined not only to preserve the barbaric idolatry for metal money, but concentrate that idolatry on gold alone. Gold was brilliant and fascinating in color, it was heavy, but not bulky. It could be easily transported or hoarded. Silver should be stricken down, and half the money metal of the world be made a mere commodity like iron.

Gen. Warner said in 1879:—Mr. Sherman, in January, 1868, being then Chairman of the Committee on Finance in the Senate, introduced a bill to change the gold coins of the United States, so as to make them correspond with the French 25 franc piece; and to make the silver half-dollar correspond in weight to two and a half silver francs, *and dropping the dollar entirely*. The bill as introduced in the House, however, contained a dollar piece. This piece was afterward dropped, and the trade dollar substituted. The words now incorporated in section 3511, making the gold dollar the sole unit of value, were embraced in the bill as first introduced by Mr. Hooper. Who suggested this provision, or whose hand framed it, does not appear; and no one has had the courage to own it. Suffice it to say that no heavier hand was ever lifted against this country.

While the bill was under consideration in the House, except a mere allusion by Mr. Hooper and Mr. Potter, there is not a single word in the discussion that took place, then or afterward, in the House or in the Senate, indicating that anybody understood that a change was to be made in the standard of value in the United States; or that this was part of a concerted movement to drop silver from the money of the world. From the discussion that took place,—which pertained altogether to other matters; such as minor coins, and whether the eagle should be retained on fractional silver pieces or not,—it was evident that nobody contemplated any such thing, or knew that a provision was in the bill making such a change in our monetary standard.

If further evidence of these facts were needed, we have it in the vote taken in this House in April, 1874,—more than a year after the passage of Mr. Hooper's bill,—on a resolution by a distinguished member from Massachusetts (Mr. Hoar) * * * A distinguished senator from New York [Conkling] a few days later, asked, apparently in astonishment, if it was true that there was by law no American dollar. Not an intimation was given to the country by the public press any-

11

where that such a change was contemplated. You will
search in vain the journals of the country to find anywhere a hint of such a thing. Doubtless there were those
who understood it. The money-dealers of Wall Street, of
Lombard Street, of the Bourse of Paris and of Hamburg
understood it. They knew Ricardo by heart: they knew
the history of such changes in other times ; and they knew
the history of resumption in England ; and they knew very
well what would be the effect of such an alteration in the
standard,—with national debts aggregating $25,000,000,000.
The cunning knavery concealed under the impenetrable disguise thrown around the bill, at the time of its passage, has
come finally to be the most marked feature of the whole
measure. I repeat that the bill passed through the Senate,
without even being read through, and without one single
word in the debate upon it there to indicate any change in
the metallic standard. But we have evidence from another
source that no such thing was in the minds of the chief
officers of the Government. The President, who signed the
bill, evidently was not aware of the covert provisions it
contained.

Nobody need believe that John Sherman did not know all
those years what he was doing : though he pretends that
he did not. It is evident that he got into the conspiracy
soon after Germany demonetized silver.

More candid was Dr. Linderman, director of the mint,
who, in his testimony before the United States monetary
commission of 1876, said : " Within thirty days after the
policy of Germany had been determined upon, of course
everybody saw and everybody knew, that to carry out that
policy, Germany must get rid of two-thirds of her silver and
put an equal amount of gold in stock. That would make an
immediate draft on gold stocks in the market, and brokers
commenced to charge a difference and the decline of silver
commenced immediately."

Warwick Martin said in 1880 : "That Mr. Richardson,
Secretary of the Treasury, in the fall of 1873, did not know
of or understand the law, is evident from the fact that,
months after its passage, he recommended immediate resumption of specie payments in silver, and made a vain attempt to carry out his recommendation. That the President,
though he had signed the bill, did not understand its effect,

is evident from the fact that he afterward wrote a letter advocating the payment of silver; and stating that we ought to have $300,000,000 of silver coin in circulation."

The allegation that the Mint of the United States in 1873 had ceased to coin silver dollars, has no foundation in truth; for in 1870, 1871, 1872 and three months in 1873, there were coined a larger amount of silver dollars than ever before in the same period, as follows: In 1870, $588,308; in 1871, $659,929; in 1872, $1,112,961; in 1873 (three months), $977,150. These seem small, unimportant figures, but an IMMENSE fact is deducible from them. The long heads saw that since silver had got as cheap as gold, and was likely to be cheaper, a *vast amount of it would be coined, and this would destroy their scheme for a universal gold basis, unless silver should be demonetized.* This idea I have not seen elsewhere stated.

Senator Teller said in 1890:—Mr. President, the Act of 1873 was equivalent, as I have said before, to adding to every debt in the land, private and public, if to be paid to-day, from 30 to 33 per cent. more than the party contracted to pay. Suppose the attempt had been made by the creditor class by law to add to their holdings 30 per cent., to compel the debtor to give them 30 per cent. more of money or products, the whole country would have been in arms; there would have been revolution and war, and rightfully, too.

Warwick Martin says:—Under the law of 1873, the trade dollar was created. It contained 420 grains standard silver, and was made legal tender for $5 only. In 1876 this dollar was declared legal tender for nothing. In 1878 the dollar of 412½ grains was again monetized. The trade dollar, for want of legal value, was worth only 90 cents. The dollar of 412½ grains was and is 100 cents; because legal tender to any amount. The commercial value of the metal in the trade dollar is 7½ grains greater than in the other dollar. But the one has legal value and the other has none. This makes the difference. The only good that was ever derived from this dollar is the complete proof of our proposition. The law makes and unmakes the money.

Here is the wording of the bill after Mr. Hooper's tinkering: "That the silver coins of the United States shall be a dollar, a half dollar, or 50-cent piece; a quarter dollar, or 25-

cent piece; a dime, or 10-cent piece. The weight of the dollar shall be 384; the half dollar, the quarter dollar and dime shall be, respectively, one-half, one-quarter and one-tenth of the weight of said dollar. Which coins shall be a legal tender, at their nominal value, for any amount not exceeding five dollars in one payment."

This section was stricken out by the Senate Committee, and the following inserted: "That the silver coins of the United States shall be a trade dollar; a half dollar, or 50-cent piece; a quarter dollar, or 25-cent piece; a dime, or 10-cent piece. The weight of the trade dollar shall be 420 grains troy, the weight of the half dollar shall be 12½ grammes, the quarter dollar and the dime shall be, respectively, one-half and one-fifth of the weight of the said half dollar. Said coins shall be a legal tender at their nominal value in any sum not exceeding five dollars in any one payment."

Observe the cunning trick of leaving off "grains troy" after the "384" and the use of "grammes" instead of the usual number of grains in the second version.

To substantiate the greatness of the great fraud of 1873, the following points are added from the records:—

John Sherman seeks to create the impression that the demonetization of silver was well understood by the senators and representatives at the time they voted for it. He justifies his vote for it, and yet at the same time seems quite anxious to divide the responsibility with others.

Hon. W. D. Kelley, Chairman of the Coinage Committee of the House, did not know that the bill demonetized silver, though he reported the bill. Garfield did not know it; Blaine did not know it. They were both then members of the House. Conkling did not know it. So these gentlemen asserted, and they were certainly as truthful as Old Sherman.

Sherman, in his opening speech of the late campaign, delivered at Paulding, Ohio. August 27, 1891, in regard to the bill of 1873 demonetizing silver, said: "The Act of 1873 was not an act of the party then in power, but it was an act of all parties. It was voted for by Democrats and Republicans alike, after full consideration for three years in Congress. It was voted for by every representative from the silver States."

Now, we want to prove Sherman a prevaricator. From

the history of the Act of 1873 and the Act of 1878, we copy the following :—Judge Kelley, of Pennsylvania, was Chairman of the Committee on Coinage, Weights and Measures in 1872, when the bill originally passed the House. This is what he said on the floor of the House March 9, 1878 :— In connection with the charge that I advocated the bill which demonetized the standard silver dollar, I say that, though the Chairman of the Committee on Coinage, I was as ignorant of the fact that it would demonetize the silver dollar, or of its dropping the silver dollar from our system of coins, as were those distinguished senators, Messrs. Blaine and Voorhees, who were then members of the House, and each of whom, a few days since, interrogated the other : " Did you know it was dropped when the bill was passed ? " " No," said Mr. Blaine ; " did you ? " " No," said Mr. Voorhees. I do not think that there were three members in the House that knew it. I doubt whether Mr. Hooper, who, in my absence from the Committee on Coinage and attendance on the Committee of Ways and Means, managed the bill, knew it. I say this in justice to him.—(Congressional Record, volume 7, part 2, Forty-fifth Congress, second session, page 1605.)

Mr. Holman, in a speech delivered in the House of Representatives July 13, 1876, said :—I have before me the record of the proceedings of this House on the passage of that measure, a record which no man can read without being convinced that the measure and the method of its passage through this House was a " colossal swindle." I assert that the measure never had the sanction of this House, and it did not possess the moral force of law.—(Congressional Record, volume 4, part 6, Forty-fourth Congress, first session, appendix, page 193.)

Again, on August 5, 1876, he said :—The original bill was simply a bill to organize a bureau of mines and coinage. The bill which finally passed the House and ultimately became a law, was certainly not read in this House. * * * * It was never considered before the House as it was passed. Up to the time the bill came before this House for final passage, the measure had simply been one to establish a bureau of mines ; I believe I use the term correctly now. It came from the Committee on Coinage, Weights and Measures. The substitute which finally became a law, was never read.

and is subject to the charge made against it by the gentle-man from Missouri (Mr. Bland), that it was passed by the House without a knowledge of its provisions, especially upon that of coinage.

I, myself, asked the question of Mr. Hooper, who stood near where I am now standing, whether it changed the law in regard to coinage. And the answer of Mr. Hooper cer-tainly left the impression upon the whole House that the sub-ject of the coinage was not affected by that bill.—(Congres-sional Record, vol. 4, part 6, Forty-fourth Congress, first ses-sion, page 5237).

Mr. Cannon, of Illinois, in a speech made in the House on July 13, 1876, said :—This legislation was had in the Forty-second Congress, February 12, 1873, by a bill to regulate the mints of the United States, and practically abolished silver as money, by failing to provide for the coinage of the silver dollar. It was not discussed, as shown by the Record, and neither members of Congress nor the people understood the scope of the legislation.—(Ibid., appendix, page 197).

Senator Conkling, in the Senate, March 30, 1876, during the remarks of Senator Bogy on the bill (S. 264) to amend the laws relating to the legal tender of silver coin, in surprise, inquired :—Will the Senator allow me to ask him or some other senator a question ? Is it true that there is now by law no American dollar ? And, if so, is it true that the effect of this bill is to be to make half dollars and quarter dollars the only silver coin which can be used as a legal tender ?

Mr. Bright, of Tennessee, said of the law :—It passed by fraud in the House, never having been printed in advance, being a substitute for the printed bill ; never having been read at the clerk's desk, the reading having been dispensed with by an impression that the bill made no material altera-tion in the coinage laws ; it was passed without discussion, debate being cut off by operation of the previous question. It was passed, to my certain information, under such circum-stances that the fraud escaped the attention of some of the most watchful as well as the ablest statesmen in Congress at the time.* * * Ay, sir, it was a fraud that smells to heaven. It was a fraud that will stink in the nose of posterity, and for which some person must give account in the day of retribu-tion.—(Record, vol. 7, part 1, second session, Forty-fifth Congress, page 584.)

General Garfield, in a speech made at Springfield, Ohio, during the fall of 1877, said:—Perhaps I ought to be ashamed to say so, but it is the truth to say that, at that time being chairman of the Committee on Appropriations, and having my hands overfull during all that time with work, I never read the bill. I took it upon the faith of a prominent Democrat and a prominent Republican, and I do not know that I voted at all. There was no call for the yeas and nays, and nobody opposed that bill that I know of. It was put through as dozens of bills are, as my friend and I know, in Congress, on the faith of the report of the chairman of the committee; therefore I tell you, because it is the truth, that I have no knowledge about it.

Senator Allison, on February 15, 1878, when the bill (H. R. 1093) to authorize the free coinage of the silver dollar was under consideration said : " But when the secret history of this bill of 1873 comes to be told, it will disclose the fact that the House of Representatives intended to coin both gold and silver, and intended to place both metals upon the French relation instead of on our own, which was the true scientific position with reference to this subject in 1873, but that the bill afterward was doctored, if I must use the term, and I use it in no offensive sense, of course——"

Mr. Sargent interrupted him and asked him what he meant by the word " doctored."

Mr. Allison said : " I said I used the word in no offensive sense. It was changed after discussion, and the dollar of 420 grains was substituted for it."—(Congressional Record, volume 7, part 2, Forty-fifth Congress, second session, page 1058.)

On February 15, 1878, during the consideration of the bill above referred to, the following colloquy between Senator Blaine and Senator Voorhees took place :

Mr. Voorhees.—I want to ask my friend from Maine, whom I am glad to designate in that way, whether I may call him as one more witness to the fact that it was not generally known whether silver was demonetized. Did he know, as Speaker of the House, presiding at that time, that the silver dollar was demonetized in the bill to which he alludes?

Mr. Blaine.—I did not know anything that was in the bill at all. As I have before said, little was known or cared on the subject. [Laughter.] And now I should like to exchange questions with the Senator from Indiana, who was then on the floor, and whose business it was, far more than mine, to know, because by the designation of the House I was to put questions; the Senator from Indiana, then on the floor of the House, with his power as a debater, was to unfold them to the House. Did he know?

MR. VOORHEES.—I very frankly say that I did not.—(Ibid., page 1063.)

Senator Beck, in a speech made in the Senate, January 10, 1878, said :—It [the bill demonetizing silver] never was understood by either House of Congress. I say that with full knowledge of the facts. No newspaper reporter—and they are the most vigilant men I ever saw in obtaining information—discovered that it had been done.—(Congressional Record, volume 7, part 1, Forty-fifth Congress, second session, page 260.)

Mr. Thurman said :—" I cannot say what took place in the House, but I know, when the bill was pending in the Senate, we thought it was simply a bill to reform the mint, regulate coinage, and fix up one thing and another , and there is not a single man in the Senate, I think, unless a member of the committee from which the bill came, who had the slightest idea that it was even a squint toward demonetization."

On January 14, 1875, the same date that he signed the Resumption Act, President Grant sent a special message to Congress, advising the establishment of two or more mints at Chicago, St. Louis and Omaha to coin silver dollars to provide for resumption.

In this message General Grant said : " With the present facilities for coinage it would take a period probably beyond that fixed by law for final specie resumption to coin the silver necessary to transact the business of the country." [My understanding has been that Sherman in the Senate and Hooper in the House understood and passed the bill. —S. L.]

THE SECRETARY OF N. Y. CHAMBER OF COMMERCE.—This man, John Austin Stevens Jr., who, 30 years before, was a neighbor and boy companion of the writer, put a piece in the N. Y. Times in 1873 that was much used at the time by J. G. Drew and other writers. He said :—The country at large has felt the pressure of the screw, but they have not been able to discover precisely from what quarter the pinch comes, because the currency contraction was mostly confined to those Treasury notes which, though not currency in the strict sense of the term, *were used as such in the larger transactions of trade and financial exchange.*

THE GREAT PANIC OF 1873.—Judge Kelley gives this valuable sketch of the way in which the thunderbolt fell in 1873 :—In 1865–6, as I have shown, business was on a cash basis. Few business men were borrowing money for any purpose ; the rate of interest was low ; and there was employment, at liberal wages, for everybody who could and would work. My venerable friend, Henry C. Carey, and I, during the month of August, 1873, visited the Northwest. In the course of our travels, we noticed the fact that savings-banks in Pittsburg were publicly offering seven per cent. for deposits, and we were assured, by reputable business men connected with some of these institutions, that they were privately paying higher rates. We had already learned that eight per cent. was being offered by such institutions in Chicago, and had heard that higher rates were paid. We did not hesitate to predict a speedily coming financial crisis ; and a prominent banker of Chicago, in response to our predictions, asked why we had come among them as prophets of evil, in the midst of such abounding evidences of present and prospective prosperity. To which, Mr. Carey replied by asking, " At what rates of interest savings-banks must be lending money, when they could undertake to pay eight or ten per cent. for deposits ? " That conversation occurred on August 18, in one of the parlors of the Grand Hotel. When we returned to Philadelphia, we found that the acceptances of merchants of excellent standing, and of the leading transportation companies whose offices were in the city, were being hawked upon the market at the rate of 12, 15 and 18 per cent. per annum ; and that much paper was paying at the rate of 24 per cent. As the money of the country had been withdrawn, men who were engaged in enterprises must borrow credit, and in desperate efforts to struggle against fate, —after our contraction policy had decreed their ruin,— were, in the hope of making a fortunate turn ; and seeing bankruptcy before them if they could not make such a turn, borrowed at any rate.

Precisely one month from the interview referred to, on

September 18, the great house of Jay Cooke & Co. suspended ; and in a few days thereafter the National banks of New York city also closed their doors against their depositors, whose checks they were unable to pay, either in Greenbacks or their own notes ; instead of which they issued certificates of deposit, which rapidly depreciated to 94 or 95 per cent. in Greenbacks.

John E. Williams, President of New York Metropolitan Bank, and a famous Greenbacker, said in 1875 :—In my letter to Senator Sherman, (under head 5), I discussed this point at some length. A close examination of the panic of 1873 sheds additional light, however, on the question. Then the aggregate quantity of circulation was set down at 800 millions—about equally divided between legal-tender and National bank notes. It is now quite evident, from the record of the operations of September and October, 1873, that 800 millions were not only not too much, but certainly too little for the emergency. As proof of this, early in September, gold was at a premium of 16 per cent.; between that time and October 11, it fell to 8¼ per cent., about one-half ! While currency,—the well-abused, scandalous currency [Greenbacks],—during that six weeks, rose in the market, and sold at from 103½ to 104—four per cent. above nominal par ! If this does not show that more paper rather than more gold was wanted to relieve the extraordinary pressure, then figures go for nothing ! Mills stopped for want of currency, in cases where owners were worth millions ; railroads, coal-mines, and all sorts of manufactories found it difficult to get currency to pay their hands. Later, it is true, the scarcity alarmed persons who had notes to pay, and they locked up in their safes currency to meet their indebtedness. But the overwhelming demand was from the West. Sight drafts on this city against grain shipped, amounted, at one time, to a million dollars a day. The crop was large, foreign demand good, farmers anxious to realize, Europe ready to buy, at full prices ; and hence the heavy shipments, with unprecedented drafts. At the rate of a million a day, a single month would take out of the city 25 millions.

True, the cheap money of the preceding summer, to this amount, or more, had been loaned to brokers and others, on call ; but when the call came, the currency had been sent away, the debtors could not pay,—the bank vaults were emptied of the currency they relied upon.

The panic of 1873 occurred under somewhat remarkable circumstances. Our foreign trade was thought to be in our favor. We were importing specie at that time; but that afforded no relief; in fact, was regarded, even by bullionists, with disfavor. What the public hungered and thirsted for was *Greenbacks,*—or even bank bills. But no more of these could be had ;—they had emigrated—gone West !

Judge Martin says :—The running up of gold from 25 premium to 60, terminating in " Black Friday " in 1869, and the terrible crisis of September, 1873, were caused [immediately. —S.L.] by the provision of the banking law, which allows banks in money centers to pay interest on the deposits of country banks. To make the interest they are compelled to use the money in some way. They cannot discount paper upon these deposits, as they are liable to be drawn for at any moment. They dare not loan this money to merchants or manufacturers, or for business of any kind. They, therefore, loan it on call to stock gamblers. This was extensively done in the fall of 1873. The Western and Southern banks and bankers needed their money thus deposited in New York, and drew for it. It could not be paid by the New York banks. The banks called on the stock gamblers for payment. They could not respond. There was no sale for stocks. The stock board was closed for two weeks. Several large banking-houses and two or three banks failed. All the National banks in the city suspended currency payments, and issued $30,000,000 Clearing-house certificates, which passed as money between the banks. These banks would have failed, and been put into the hands of receivers, but for the fact that the Secretary of the Treasury advanced these National banks $26,000,000 legal-tender notes. These banks received on deposit all the money they could get ; but they marked checks " good," and did not pay them at that time. * * * The President of the Gallatin National Bank, and other bank officers, attributed this crisis to this one cause, and labored to break up the practice; but they were unsuccessful. Mr. Richardson, Secretary of the Treasury, laid the matter before Congress, and insisted upon the passage of a law prohibiting National banks from paying interest on deposits. But Wall Street, as usual, was too strong for Congress.

THE BANK INFLATION—Is well illustrated in the following extract from the report of the nine presidents of Associated Banks of New York, who had been appointed to report a revision of the Clearing-house system after the panic of 1873:—Deposits which are derived from strictly commercial operations cannot fluctuate so widely, from time to time, as to produce disturbance in the community: and banks which confine their business to them, as they naturally arise, are always reliable and regular in the treatment of their dealers; and can be conducted with ease and comfort to their managers, and safety to the public. On the contrary, deposits which are purchased by payment of interest, or otherwise; and which must, therefore, of necessity, be largely loaned "on demand", are the cause of continual agitation and solicitude, to those who hold them in charge. They are certain to be withdrawn at the season of the year and at the moment most inconvenient to the banks, and to their dealers. This fact is best illustrated by the following figures :

The average deposits of the 60 Clearing-house banks for 10 weeks, from July 5 to Sept. 6, were....................................	$232,228,000
The lowest amount reached since the panic was....................................	143,170,000
Showing a total reduction of..............	$89,058,000

Of the above amount during the
10 weeks, 12 interest-paying
banks held................ $111,585,000
The lowest total reached by them
since the panic.............. $52.609.000

Showing a loss in 12 banks of..............	$58,916,000
And in the other 48 banks of..............	$30,142,000

And were it not for the fact that several of the 48 banks are more or less involved in the same practice, this disparity would be still more apparent.

On the other hand, see THE LEGAL-TENDER CONTRACTION :—The following statement was taken from the books

of the Treasury Department by Moses W. Field. It exhibits the contraction of the circulating medium, from September 1, 1865, to December 1, 1873, exclusive of coin :

CURRENCY, SEPTEMBER 1, 1865.

U. S. Notes...................................	$433,160,569
Fractional Currency...................	26,344,742
National Bank-notes.....................	185,000,000
Compound Interest Legal-tender Notes....	217,024,160
Treasury 5 per cent Legal-tender..........	32,536,991
Temporary Loan Certificates 10—d—d....	107,148,713
Certificates of Indebtedness..............	85,093,000
Treasury Notes past due Legal- tender and not presented	1,503,020
State Bank Notes........................	78,867,575
Three-Year Treasury-notes...............	830,000,000
	$1,996,678,770

CIRCULATING MEDIUM, EXCLUSIVE OF COIN, DEC. 1, 1873 :

U. S. Notes..........................	$367,001,685
Fractional Currency.......................	48,000,000
Certificates of Indebtedness bearing interest..	678,000
National Bank Currency.................	350,000,000
Total Dec. 1, 1873......................	$765,679,685

$$1,996,678,770$$
$$765,679,685$$

Contraction $1,230,999,085.

That deep-thinking merchant W. H. Winder, in explaining
the panic of 1873—before a Congress committee in 1878—
made excess of imports (one of the results of contraction) a
prominent cause. He said : " Imports in panicky '73, were
642 millions, or 300 millions more than in 1868, or six times
those of 1833 (101 millions). For five years prior to 1873,
the imports were 579 millions more than the exports ; and
for ten years they were 1,127 millions—facts not before
noted."

Now hear a pompous " conservative," David A. Wells,
talk about, without even attempting to explain, our panic.
He sagely enumerates " phenomena antecedent." This

poor creature, who was one of a half a dozen men most responsible for the " Hard Times," sneaks away from the facts as follows, in 1887 :—David A. Wells in *Popular Science Monthly* for July : The period of economic disturbance, which commenced in 1873, appears to have first manifested itself, almost simultaneously, in Germany and the United States, in the latter half of that year. [?] In the former country, the great and successful results of the war with France had stimulated every department of thought and action among its people into intense activity. The war indemnity, which had been exacted of France, had been used in part, to pay off the debt obligations of the Government ; and ready capital became so abundant that banking institutions of note almost begged for opportunity to place loans at rates as low as one per cent., with manufacturers, for the purpose of enlarging their establishments. As a legitimate result, the whole country projected and engaged in all manner of new industrial and financial undertakings. In Prussia alone, 687 new joint-stock companies were founded during the year 1872, and the first six months of 1873 ; with an aggregate capital of $481,045,000. Such a state of things, as is now obvious, was most unnatural [?], and could not continue ; and the reaction and disaster came with great suddenness, as has been already stated, in the fall of 1873 ; but without anticipation on the part of the multitude. Great fortunes melted rapidly away ; industry became paralyzed ; and the whole of Germany passed, at once, from a condition of apparently great prosperity to a great depth of financial, industrial and commercial depression that had never been equaled. [Mark —no cause at all given for this.—S. L.]

In the United States, the phenomena antecedent to the crisis were enumerated at the time to be—" a rise of prices, great prosperity, large profits, high wages and strikes for higher, large importations, a railway mania, expanded credit, overtrading, overbuilding and high living." [Mostly bosh, as to 1873].

The crisis began on September 17, by the failure of a comparatively unimportant railway company—the New York and Oswego Midland. On the 18th the banking house of Jay Cooke & Co. failed. On the 19th, 19 other banking-houses failed. Then followed a succession of bankruptcies, until, in four years, the mercantile failures had aggregated $775,865,-

000; and on January 1, 1875, the amount of American railway bonds in default amounted to $789,367,655.

How luminous is Sir Oracle, in the above! All through this book the real causes of the hard times are found. He says nothing of the great fact that silver demonetization was a chief cause in both Germany and the United States. His statement that Germany went heavily into manufactures, and failed at it, is very interesting in view of the fact that France, the conquered country—that did not demonetize silver, but flooded itself with paper—rushed its industries—its manufactures, with such success that it paid Germany three-quarters of the milliard indemnity in goods and *German securities!* and killed all those German factories!

THE BROKEN BANKS AND TRUST COMPANIES.—On October 23, 1873, a nine-column article by Samuel Leavitt was printed in the N. Y. *World*, which gave a full review of the New York bank suspension since the Tweed epidemic of 1871-2 ; the condition of the broken banks, and the prospects of their depositors.

The State banks discussed were the Stuyvesant, Davis Collamore, Prest., which failed Oct. 13, 1871 ; the Bull's Head, Richard Williamson, Prest., failed March 20, 1873.

The National banks were : The Ocean, Columbus S. Stevenson, Prest., failed Dec. 1871 ; The Union Square, Henry Beekman, Prest., failed Dec. 13, 1871 ; The Eighth National, Union Adams, Prest., failed Dec. 13, 1871 ; The Atlantic, J. F. Southworth, Prest., failed April 26, 1873 ; The Commonwealth, George Ellis, Prest., failed Sept. 20, 1873.

The savings banks that failed then and afterwards included all those on Third Avenue. Naturally enough, their bank buildings were all turned into drinking-saloons ;—discouraged depositors concluding to spend their own money, in a way that would give a definite and immediate pleasurable result. Government was much to blame in allowing savings banks to fail, and thus rob the poor.

These banks were : The Guardian, Wm. M. Tweed, President, failed November 18, 1871 ; The Bowling Green, Police Commissioner Henry Smith, President, failed November 18, 1871 ; The National, John McBride Davidson, the Tweed safe-maker, President, failed November 18, 1871 ; The Market, Wm. Van Name, President, failed January 21,

1872 ; The Central, Charles Peck, President, failed January 4, 1872.

The Trust Companies were : Brooklyn Trust Co., Ethelbert S. Mills, President, failed January 19, 1873 ; The Union Trust Co., failed September 20, 1873.

The Stuyvesant people blamed the Chicago fire. The Bull's Head was robbed of $257,000—thief never known. It recovered. The Ocean was first crippled by a big burglary of $100,000 through a tunnel. The Union Square and Eighth National were upset by the Ocean. The Atlantic was robbed of $400,000 by F. L. Taintor, cashier. He went to jail. The Commonwealth was broken by Edward Haight & Co. overdrawing $225,000 before their failure. The three Tweed banks need no explanation. Henry R. Conklin, Secretary of the Market, stole $550,000 and went to Canada ; the President, Van Name, went to Ludlow Street jail. Was there when the article was written. The Central was crippled by the Ocean. The Brooklyn Trust Co. was in bad hands : the President Mills, the Secretary M. T. Rodman, and the Treasurer Sprague, were all apparently defaulters. Mills was drowned (suicide, I believe). Sprague and Rodman—who were Treasurer and Deputy Treasurer of Brooklyn—were in durance vile when the article was written. The Union Trust Co. was broken by the theft of $400,000 by C. T. Carlton, Secretary. It has since been set up in great shape under Edward King, of James G. King's Sons.

This picture is given as a specimen of the liveliness of the frisky days of Tweed, Fisk, Gould & Co.

A WISE ENGLISH OPINION.—In 1873, the *Westminster Review*, in an article on "The Mint and The Banks" uttered these wise and weighty words :—In breaking this monopoly of the banks, we should be taking great strides toward the attainment of that ideal system of currency which Sir Robert Peel must have had in his heart [certainly not in his head! —S. L.] when he passed his currency laws ; a system in which the State shall be the sole fountain of issue ; under which no money shall circulate on credit ; or, if it does, shall circulate on the credit of the State ; all bank notes as well as coins, bearing the image and superscription of the head of the State ; and under which all profits upon the issue of money shall form a part of the imperial revenue, * * * The power of issue now exercised by the Bank of England, and by the

English, Irish and Scotch banks [all private corporations] is
a relic of feudalism. * * * The private manufacture of coin
has been suppressed long ago ; but the manufacture of paper
money still remains.   And the profits of this manufacture are
allowed to remain in private hands : the State taking upon
itself the manufacture of *the only part of the currency upon
which there is, and can be, a loss.*   It is high time this state of
things ceased ; that all right of issue were gathered into the
hands of the State ; that the debt of the Bank of England
were paid off ; that all notes but those of the State were
suppressed ; that the power of issue, now exercised by the
banks, were vested in the royal mint, * * and that the profits
upon paper currency were claimed by the State and appropriated, * * to the reduction of taxation.

1874.

LITTLE CHIT ON BANKS.—A rich Brooklyn conservative—
Congressman Chittenden, said before the Committee of
Banking and Currency of the House, January 16, 1874 :—I
believe that of those 1900 National banks there are not two-
thirds of them sound to-day.   I mean not two-thirds in number.   In the vast proportion of them, the capital is very
small.   I know, for instance, how one National bank was
established, and I presume there were hundreds established
in the same way.   I say I know a National bank of $100,000
capital, whose broker in New York purchased $100,000 of
Government bonds, and paid for them.   The owners of the
bank furnished the margin between the 90 per cent. in currency, which they were allowed on the deposit of the bonds
and the cost of the bonds ; and that margin was all the
capital that was ever put into the bank.   The broker sent
the bonds to Washington, got his 90 per cent. on the dollar
in currency, and got the margin from the gentlemen who
established the bank.   That bank, in the late crisis, was one
of the first to suspend ; but resumed again shortly, and is
going on as before.   It has a banking house which cost over
$30,000.

Gen. John A. Logan was once a zealous Greenbacker—
which is nothing to his discredit, as many of the ablest men
of which the Republican party can boast were Greenbackers.
On January 19, 1874, Logan made one of his roaring speeches

in Congress against the resumption of specie payment, and making gold a monetary standard. He said "The Greenback is the true standard of value, and gold is merely an article of commerce."

MUST TRADE IT OUT OVER THE COUNTER.—Secretary Boutwell testified in the Senate, January 22, 1874, that when $121,000,000 coin accumulated in the Bank of England to the credit of the United States,—from bond sales,—the bank notified our Treasury Department that *its whole power would be used* to prevent our taking it in that shape. "So," says Boutwell, "we were compelled to take other bonds." The same game was played with the $15,000,000 of the Geneva award. J. G. Drew said in 1874, "We now find that we have parted with about one billion dollars of our National bonds to Europe, exhausting ourselves of currency even to do our daily marketing, to make up the pile ; and that it is there in Europe ; for which, as by the foregoing testimony of Prof. Price and Secretary Boutwell, we can get no specie ; but any amount of dry-goods and knick-knacks."

PULLING DOWN THE AMERICAN FLAG.—It was by such *touching* appeals as this from poor old Poppy Dix, that Grant was induced to re-rivet the chains upon this people.

STATE OF NEW YORK, EXECUTIVE CHAMBER,
Albany, March 30, 1874.

My Dear Sir,—I am very much concerned on account of the action of Congress on the currency question ; and I cannot forbear to express to you my earnest hope that you will, by the interposition of your veto, prevent the disastrous consequences which must result from any further increase of the paper circulation.

Money can now be borrowed in the city of New York, on the best security, at four and five per cent. interest. I believe I speak within bounds when I say that one-half of the paper currency of the country is absorbed in stock and real estate speculations. Every addition to it must run into the same channels, and only serve to multiply and aggravate prevailing evils. The action of the Senate, sustaining the action of the House of Representatives, has already degraded legal-tender notes below the standard of specie from one to two per cent. more than before. And if the maximum of four hundred millions proposed by Congress is reached by further issues, I am confident the measure will bring on, within the next two years, a revulsion, which will be fatal to your administration, and ruinous to the interests of the country, if not to the public credit.

JOHN A. DIX.

The old " War Governor " was thusly doing his best to " pull down the American flag." But nobody " shot him on the spot."

VICTORIOUS GRANT CONQUERED.—Congress, warned by the Panic, passed, early in April, a bill authorizing the reissue of the $44,000,000 Greenbacks, which had been retired ; and fixing the amount of the Greenbacks at $400,000,000. This bill was denounced by the money power, as an " inflation " measure (see Dix Letter) ; and accordingly was vetoed by President Grant, April 22, 1874.

. The story of the way in which Grant first snubbed and then yielded to the bankers in 1874, is very instructive. It is told by J. G. Drew, in " Our Money Muss." Frightened into temporary decency by the panic of September, 1873, Grant, in his December message made an elaborate Greenback and convertible bond argument, with the following points : 1st. A clear avowal that specie basis can only be " reached and maintained " by securing the foreign balance of trade in our favor. 2d. That said balance of trade can only accrue by sufficient currency. 3d. That such sufficient currency does not exist, even for the dullest part of the year. 4th. That much more currency is required in the fall and winter months. 5th. That some automatic system is required to prevent the amount which would be proper for the active season from glutting the market in the dull period. 6th. That Government should loan the amount of the face value of bonds to banks at four per cent. per year, payable at the option of the borrower. 7th. That our " currency, based on the credit of the nation, is the best that has ever been devised," and comparing it with gold itself.

Congress, in April, 1874, prepared and passed a pretty good bill in accord with these views. Then the telegraph flashed through the land that Wall Street was up in arms. There was a meeting of the bankers, etc., calling upon Grant for a veto. Peter Cooper presided. This was probably the last time that the bullionists got the old man to play figure-head for them. He presently came out as a Greenbacker. After that

the "best people" called him "a superannuated old fool."
At first Grant snubbed the usurers. He remembered how
they had clamored about him for an issue of $30,000,-
000 Greenbacks, to tide over the panic of the preceding
September; and now, they and their organs—such as
Harpers' Weekly and the *Herald* were ridiculing and lam-
pooning the very ideas promulgated by them the previous
autumn.

Meetings of the oligarchists were promptly called, and
proposed action is thus reported to the *World*: "It is proposed to co-operate with movements already on foot in other
States, in forming leagues throughout the country,—first to
unite the people in demanding that our Government shall
redeem every pledge it has given regarding its financial promises; and second, to make clear to the people that a fixed
standard of value is vital to every department of labor and
trade; that self-interest, equally with common honesty,
demand that the promise to re-establish a specie basis for
currency shall be kept. This work requires time, patience,
labor and money. For the latter we now appeal to all who
are in sympathy with us. The most effective speeches and
arguments for sound finance will be printed and distributed;
and also a weekly publication, to inform the people fully
upon this question. Popular lecturers of high standing and
repute are needed to influence public opinion; and in various
other ways the completion of the organization will require
funds. This question of finance is the supreme question of
the hour; and we should consider ourselves the political
opponents of all public men who are not with us: or who are
even undecided upon the matter of public faith; and resolve
to support no such men for any office whatever."

Political ostracism from President to poundkeeper!

Grant could not stand the pressure, and backed down, and
"took it all back." In his veto message he says that
the bill theoretically increases the volume of the currency,
and adds : "The theory, in my belief, is a departure from the
true principle of finance, national interest, national obligations to creditors, Congressional promises, party pledges—
on the part of both political parties—and of personal views
and promises made by me in every annual message sent to
Congress, and in each inaugural address."

THE PUBLIC ROBBERS LET GO.—Private investigation had

unearthed immense robberies of the Government,—reaching
100 millions,—by fraudulent withholding of taxes on tobacco,
whisky, incomes, railroads, banks, insurance companies,
legacies and successions, for seven years. The regular officials had not time, money, or proof for this work. So, May
8, 1872, a law was passed—by aid of the Secretary of the
Treasury—which authorized those having the proof, to go
ahead, and push the robbers for half what they could collect.
These parties had risked their lives and spent much money
in the search.

In a few months after the passage of the law, they
collected $500,000; and would probably have collected 50
millions, within two years, without suit. But the money
was coming from rich men,—capitalists, corporations, politicians and bondholders,—some of whom had overruling political influence. Congress was besieged to repeal the law,
that the collections might be stopped, and both were done
in June, 1874 (Statutes, pp. 18,192). The pretense was that
the officers of the Government ought to make the collections,
without cost to the Government; when Congress knew that
most of the claims had stood without assessment or collection,
for years, and that the Government could not have realized
them by ordinary methods of collection. None of the frauds
detected and punished by Sec. Bristow would have been committed, but for the repealing of this law.

NATIONAL BANK-NOTE REDEMPTION.—The Act of June 20,
1874, provides that National banks need not retain money
in their vaults to redeem their circulation; though they were
required to keep money for their deposits. They were bound
to keep five per cent. in money in the Treasury, in legal
tenders, to redeem their notes, which sum amounted to about
$17 000,000. This law also provided that when banks did not
wish to go into liquidation, but did wish to sell their bonds
at a large premium, they could by depositing legal-tender
notes in the Treasury to the amount of their circulation, lift
their bonds and sell them. This was the means of locking
up in the Treasury a large amount of legal-tender money,
held by the Treasury to redeem National bank-notes; which
the Treasurer could do or not as the Secretary saw proper.
This arrangement kept the bank notes out and the legal-
tender notes in. This law also enabled the stockholders of
banks to sell their bonds (the most of which cost $40 and $50

on the $100) for $120, and returned them their 10 per cent.
of bonds over circulation. After the bonds were lifted and
sold, the Government and the people had no security for the
National bank-notes but the legal-tender notes to the same
amount. We would infer from this that the legal tenders
were better than the bonds, in the estimation of Congress.
Why not bank upon legal tenders, therefore, instead of
bonds?

THE VALUE OF CONVERTIBLE CURRENCY.—That noted
financier, Wm. H. Winder, said, July, 1874, in the N. Y. *News*,
which he used as his organ (paying for the printing of his
articles) :—The reader will bear in mind that, for the purpose of rendering suspension of specie payments an impossibility, and to make steadiness assured, so that no tempta-
tion to undue expansion could be indulged in, the law known
as the " Peel " Act was passed, in England, in 1844 ; by which
the Bank was prohibited from issuing any more notes, except
upon the actual previous deposit of one dollar in gold for
every dollar of paper which should be thereafter issued.
And, in order to render this provision effectual, the gold thus
deposited was held, not by the Bank, but by an officer who
held it for the sole and only purpose of redeeming notes
issued by the Bank.

All this was in the creditor country of the world. England
had claims on her debtor countries, over and above all
she owed, of more than $3,000,000,000 ; a sum five times
over all the gold in all the banks of the world : besides which,
the Peel Act required the deposit of a dollar of gold for
every dollar of paper thereafter issued. Yet, with supreme
advantages in every respect, necessary to make a convertible
currency permanent, assured, steady, free from fluctuations,
and a safeguard against industrial and commercial disasters,
read what the Parliamentary Committee say of a convertible
currency, after the Panic of 1847 :

"It is true that to those who may have expected that the
7 and 8 Vict., cap. 32 (Peel's Act requiring the Bank to keep
specie to redeem her bills), would effectually prevent recur-
rence of cycles of commercial excitement and depression,
the contrast between the years 1845 and 1847 must produce
grievous disappointment.

"To those who anticipated that the act would put a check
on improvident speculation, the disappointment cannot be

less, if reliance is to be placed (as its committee are confident it may) on the statement of the governor of the Bank and of other witnesses, that speculations were never carried to such enormous extent as in 1846 and the beginning of 1847.

" If the act were relied on as a security against violent fluctuations in the value of money, the fallaciousness of such anticipation is conclusively proved by the fact that while the difference between the highest and lowest rates of discount was, in the calamitous years of 1837 and 1839, but two and a quarter to two and three-quarters per cent., the difference in 1847 rose to six and three-quarters.

" If it was contemplated that the number and extent of commercial failures would have been lessened, the deplorable narrative of the governor of the Bank, recording the failure of 33 houses, comparatively in large business, in London alone, to the amount of £40,000.000. is a conclusive reply.

" If the power of obtaining banking accommodation on moderate terms was considered to be promoted by the acts of 1844, it cannot be said that this important object has been attained ; since it appears in evidence, that in 1847, in addition to an interest of nine or ten per cent., a commission was also frequently paid, raising the charge to ten, twenty or thirty per cent., according to the time which bills had to run."

Thus it will be seen that this committee (like the committee during the suspension, 1797 to 1821, of the Bank) reports that a convertible currency secures no benefit whatever over a properly guarded paper currency. But, on the contrary, the famous " Bullion Committee,"—appointed to prove the great advantages which would accrue to Great Britain by an immediate or early resumption, so as to render the currency "convertible," in their report state explicitly that the history of convertible currency shows it has never prevented any evil, has never secured any advantage over their paper currency ; but that the reverse is true ; the history of the currency during suspension of specie payment would compare favorably with the periods of convertible currency. It is true a boundless or unlimited issue of paper currency may culminate in great disasters ; but a judicious control of paper and of loans by banks, can, beyond all possibility of denial, secure a steadiness of volume and a security against all those evils caused by a fluctuation of volume, which is utterly unattainable by a convertible currency.

BANK CURRENCY FOR SIXTY YEARS.—Under date August 14, 1874. P. Muncy sent a strong letter to N. Y. *Tribune,* advocating Greenbacks. He gave these statistics of expansion and contraction from 1811 to 1873,—as giving an important cause of periodical commercial crashes:

Bank currency in 1811 . . . . $28,000,000
  " " " 1816 68,000,000
Contraction 1816 to 1820 23,000,000
Bank currency in " 45,000,000
  " " " 1837 141,000,000
Contraction 1837 to 1843 83,000,000
Bank currency in " 58,000,000
  " " " 1854 204,000,000
Contraction 1854 to 1858 49,000,000
Bank currency in " 155,000,000
  " " " 1860 207,000,000
Contraction 1860 to 1862 23,000,000
Bank currency in " 184,000,000
  " " " 1863 202,000,000

Total amount of money, currency and circulating medium on Sept. 1, 1865, exclusive of coin :

[Differing only from Moses W. Field (who was probably right) in the amount of National bank-notes, he makes this] :

                  $214,678,680
Circulating Medium, Dec. 1, 1873 765,679,685

Contraction Sept. 1, 1865, to Dec. 1, 1873 . . . . $1,345,998,995

The above amount of circulating medium thus contracted was placed into bonds bearing six per cent. interest per annum in gold, which, in a great measure, took from the people facility of carrying on business, and is manifestly the cause of the crash which commenced in October, 1871, and culminated in September, 1873, causing the ruin of thousands upon thousands of business men.

$2,100,000,000 of circulating medium in 1865, gave a wonderful impetus to business, and enabled the people to pay enormous amounts of taxation. The amount of money accounts for the unexampled "prosperous times," at the close of a very destructive civil war ; which prosperous times would doubtless have continued but for the fearful contraction of nearly $1,400,000,000 of circulating medium.

THE THREE PER CENTS.—Wm. D. Kelley said in 1875 :—

Americans had shown their willingness to loan the Government at three per cent., so long as the Government would promise to return the money whenever they wanted it. The three per cent. certificates were convertible bonds. The Government took $120.000.000, on the terms that, at any time after ten days, the depositor or his transferee, could call for the money deposited with accrued interest. These three per cent. convertible certificates or bonds were never voluntarily presented for redemption ; and finally, under McCulloch's process of contraction and the cry for specie payments, Congress forced the Secretary of the Treasury to call in and redeem that three per cent. currency loan, though he had to sell five per cent. gold bonds to get the money with which to do it [Laughter.] That is so. So, too, gold bonds were issued to get the money with which to redeem the 7–30's, compound interest notes, and other forms of currency indebtedness. The American people were, as I have said, willing to loan the Government for proper interest and at low rates. There are $64.000.000 of bonds now outstanding which always command the highest price, or stand next to the highest in the list of sales. Yet they are payable, principal and interest, in currency. They are long tax bonds. They had 50 years to run when issued ; and every fool knew that specie would enter into our currency before 50 years would pass ; and these currency bonds stand at the head of the market. That they stand there is absolute proof that the American people were, so long as they were permitted to be prosperous, ready to hold the national debt, and to hold it with proper interest. Why were they not permitted to hold it ? There was no room for speculation under that system. No sending syndicate agents to Europe [Applause]. No commissions to be made by dealing with foreign bankers ; or by Indiana men who might go to London to establish banking-houses [Applause].

HORRORS OF RESUMPTION.—After the Resumption misery was fairly started, a candid observer wrote :—Every country merchant would tell you that his old accounts were being paid up in 1865, 6 ; that monthly his cash sales, as compared with credit, were increasing. Every city merchant would tell you that six months' men were buying on four months—that four months' men were buying on two months, and the two months' men were buying for cash ; and that we were fast eliminating credit, with its attendant extravagance and horrors, and getting on a money basis.

Now, the reverse is true. The capitalist no longer seeks the borrower, but the latter must find the former, spider-like in his den, giving audience to crowds of anxious applicants, the last overbidding his predecessors, and promising five times the earnings of money for its use. The country merchant finds his ledger crowded worse than ever ; the wholesale dealer tells you that we have flopped back to much worse than the old times. Even Boston feels the pressure ; as evinced by the following extract from the *Globe* of that city : As facts and truth are the basis of all sound reasoning, I will relate some items of my own experience within the last few weeks. While in the office of a money agent and lender, a gentleman came in and made application for a temporary loan on some houses he was building ; and on which, when finished, he was to have a permanent loan. The security was satisfactory, he could have the money, but not for less than two per cent. per month. They were getting that for short loans. A day or two after, speaking with a gentleman on the contraction of the currency, and of business, he mentioned a near relative of his whom he had just learned had, for four months, been paying $15 a month for the use of $300, with everything in his house, gifts of friendship and all, mortgaged for its security. But business was dull, and his receipts less than his expenses, and his family in need. My own business had led me, a few weeks before, to look at the public records of mortgages of personal property, in reference to a tenant who wished to give security for his rent. I found all the machinery and apparatus of his trade (he was a good mechanic) mortgaged to procure a loan at three per cent. per month. He said he must have some money ; business was dull, and could find no one who would let him have it for less. I took occasion to look over the recent record of mortgages ; and saw records to secure loans as high as five per cent. per month ; and the register remarked that some had been as high as ten per. cent. He thought they would average three per. cent a month. His humanity found expression in the words, " It is awful !" * * *

WHO USE SAVINGS BANKS.—One great argument against the demands of workingmen is found in the vast sums deposited in these banks, and supposed to belong to the workers. Geo. E. McNeill brought down the wrath of the monopolists upon him by showing, while at the head of the Massachusetts Labor Bureau, that the money belongs mainly to well-off people. In 1875 even the N. Y. *Tribune* confessed this as follows :—The aggregate amount due to the depositors in 158 savings-banks of this State now reaches the enormous total of $304,000,000—having increased $18,400,000 from January 1, 1874, to January 1, 1875. This seems an astonishing sum, and doubtless many persons find it difficult to account for so large an increase in twelve months of such depression as now prevails in almost every branch of trade and industry. The fact is that the depositors in savings-banks are far from being confined to the humbler walks of life. The mass of deposits is owned by persons of the middle-class —by those who are generally recognized by their friends as "well-off."

An editor said in 1875 :—There is no comfort in the reflection that we have had hard times in this country before, and survived them. The debts are the great obstacles at present. There were hard times in 1840 and 1857, and at other times ; but then there was little or no debt or taxes. There were no railroad debts then. There was but little Government debt then. There were no municipal debts then, and taxes were hardly felt. It is not so now.

H. Bronson said in 1875 :—I do not understand why an inanimate dollar is not as fit a subject for conscription as a human soul. We laid our Governmental strong hands upon the fathers and sons, perhaps the main-stay of the household, and left their bones to bleach upon the battlefield : then we got on our knees to borrow from the bondholder ragged dollars for our gold bonds, upon his own terms ; when he should have been sent to the front, money-bags and all. We issued Greenbacks—"dishonest money" to buy human life with and gold-bearing bonds to buy shoddy. We took the income tax from shoddy, and put a heavy tax upon the returned soldiers' shirts, boots, coffee and tobacco, to raise gold for the bondholder ; and thus, whether the soldier fell in battle or returned to his humble home, he dies or lives for the bondholder !

WHAT THE HUNGRY DEMOCRATS DID.—The Panic of 1873 resulted in the Democrats getting a majority in the House of

Representatives in Congress, in the Fall of 1874. But, after all their blowing against the Republicans—the hungry creatures at once, with cheerful alacrity, sold out to the money-kings : and began by electing Kerr, a gold-bug speaker. They did even worse than the Republicans. They showed their caliber again on the silver question, under Cleveland.

A NATIONAL DEBT A NATIONAL BLESSING.—In 1874, Henry Carey Baird printed the following very striking and original argument in favor of the idea that "a national debt is a national blessing : "—

One might naturally infer that a measure which had proved itself so powerful and so beneficent in the hour of national trial, amid war and destruction, might be equally so in peace, in building up that which war had pulled down. Not so, however, have thought our great finance ministers and other statesmen—our McCullochs, Boutwells, Richardsons, Shermans, Joneses and Grants! As soon as, by the combined operations of a cessation of war and of the wringing of taxes from the people, the National Treasury had become strong enough to have no fear for its own future,—and giving no heed whatsoever to the people,—the Greenback was denounced as a "forced loan," inflated, irredeemable paper, etc., etc ; and efforts, to some extent successful, were made to retire it. The consequences have been nine years of societary paralysis, which has cost the country ten times the pecuniary cost of the war ; and left the people so much prostrated, and in such a state of financial exhaustion, that they are unable any longer to carry the indebtedness of their Government ; which latter is now obliged, in peace, to call upon foreign credit-mongers to do for it that which, in the midst of war and ruin, its own people were able to do, and did with so much alacrity. Seeing, then, how much more ruinous than war itself are incompetent rulers, when their hands are not tied by the force of public necessities and considerations, is it in the least to be wondered at, that the idea should have gone abroad that a "national debt ",—when so great and so pressing as to overrule and control the ignorance and incompetence of public officials,—is "a national blessing."

THE PRESIDENT OF METROPOLITAN BANK SPEAKS OUT.—John G. Drew said in 1874 :—And that a. currency famine does exist, we demonstrate by another quotation from John

Earl Williams, whose position as President of the Metropolitan Bank, the redeeming center for the country banks, gives him a better chance to judge than, perhaps, any other man in America. He said : " And most prominent of all the vain efforts to resume specie payments by banks, as heretofore, including alike bills and deposits ; which always has been, and, in the nature of things, always must be, sooner or later, a failure."

DREW VS. WELLS.—John G. Drew said in 1874, of the enormous cost of Resumption, and in reply to David A. Wells :—Mr. Wells is an excellent mathematician. He can undo much of the mischief which he and his school have done, if he will figure what the cost of our war would have been with full legal-tender as taught and practiced by French statesmen ; and then compare the same with our disbursement footing. After obtaining that result, multiply each day, for the past three years, by five millions, which is the minimum cost per day, in dollars, for the enforced idleness of our productive industries. Add those two results together, and he will have an approximation to the cost to date for this war of the specie advocates upon the nation. It has already cost the nation five times what slavery cost us to subdue it ; and the end is not yet.

What is the plainer English of this very plain English? It is this : That while our producers have begged, almost on their bended knees, for the privilege of the right to labor, and to be paid for the same in national certificates of indebtedness, called Greenbacks, without interest : our infatuated Government has insisted on having its work done by subjects of European monarchies, and to pay for the same in interest-bearing bonds : and that our mechanics are leaving our shores to find that employment which we have banished across the ocean. If that has not been practically levying a tariff upon our home productions, or offering a bonus for foreign importations, we have forgotten what little cyphering we ever knew. * * * The British Lion, having thus seduced us by gentle roaring, moral precepts and big scientific demonstrations, to thus drop our national resources into his open jaws, he shuts them together with a snap ; and when we demand our specie, we are laughed at for gulls, and told to " go to the store and trade it out " !

GOLD, FLOUR AND BEEF.—The following statistics compiled

by W. Kimball of New Haven, Conn., show the price of gold, flour and beef, from 1860 to 1874; during which period the volume of currency swelled from about $400,000,000 to near $2,000,000,000; and was contracted again to $779,000,000; and the gold dollar fluctuated all the way from $1.00 to $2.85.

	Gold	Flour	Beef
1860	$ 1.00	$5.25	$10.75
1861	1.00	5.50	9.00
1862	1.00 to 1.37	5.47	12.00
1863	1.37 to 1.72½	5.87	12.50
1864	1.72 to 2.85½	6.30	13.25
1865	1.46¼	9.72	20.00
1866	1.41	7.60	19.00
1867	1.37	9.42	13.50
1868	1.36	8.70	15.00
1869	1.24	5.70	14.00
1870	1.10	4.92	14.00
1871	1.08	5.50	12.50
1872	1.11	6.00	10.00
1873	1.12	5.55	11.00
1874	1.13	5.95	10.37

FIVE MILLION DOLLARS A DAY LOST.—J. G. Drew said in 1874:—The productive capacity of the nation, with anything like a fair chance, is indicated by the census $7,000,000,000 per year: or, in round numbers, $20,000,000 per day. The loss by the present enforced stagnation, is variously estimated at from one-fourth to one-half that sum. Take the smaller figure, one-quarter, and we find that we are paying $5,000,000 per day for the luxury of our present idleness, bankruptcy and starvation; equal, as above stated, to the cost of the late war *on both sides*, at the time of its greatest intensity.

At great cost, we convulsed all civilization for years, to obtain an indemnity from England of $15,000,000; and glorified our Government for the achievement; while the same Government was wickedly exhausting the nation to the same extent *every three days!*

1875.

THE RESUMPTION ACT SCORCHED.—Judge W. Martin gave a scathing review of the Resumption Act of January 14, 1875, in his "Money of Nations." He bewails the first

provision of the act, which calls in the 45 million fractional currency and substitutes silver at a cost of $2,500,000
per annum. He says:—Thus we see that a bullion and
bond-worshiping Congress fought and still fight to the death
the payment of bonds in silver of full weight: and insist that
the people shall use a subsidiary money,—seven per cent.
light,—and pay five per cent. per annum for the privilege of
using it. It is true, with Congress, as Senator Sherman
said, "The gold is for the rich and the silver for the poor."
* * So is it in England, where gold is the money of the rich;
and worn, sweated and clipped and light subsidiary silver and
heavy copper coins is the money of the poor.

The second provides that gold bullion shall be coined
free: but makes no provision for the recoinage of the worn
silver.

Section 3 repeals the law limiting the National bank circulation. All disguise is thrown off. As fast as National
bank-notes are issued, legal tenders, to the amount of 80 per
cent. thereof are to be redeemed. 400 millions of five per cent.
bonds were to be sold for this purpose.

On and after January 1879, the 300 million legal tenders
must be redeemed in coin. The 5, 4½ and 4 per cent. bonds
would cover this redemption. There was to be an annual
tax of $38,200,000 (bond interest) to rob the people of the best
money they ever had.

There is no provision for redeeming the National bank-
notes. They knew well that resumption did not apply to
them. They had $8,000,000 gold, to a billion liabilities.
They now sold their gold—having no farther use for it.

DEAD WENDELL PHILLIPS SPEAKETH.—Here speaks Wendell Phillips on Resumption:—The money kings and coin
mongers of London and New York are the thieves. Watchful and keen, they saw at the end of the war that our bonds
were the best investment in the world; and that our finances
could be most easily wrenched to make the rich richer, and
to crush the poor into slavery. Joining in conspiracy, and
shutting Boston and Philadelphia out of the scheme, they
proceeded to derange our currency—demonetize silver—and
to change the basis and conditions of our bonds: so as to
double their own wealth, and double the weight of our
national debt, leading our obsolete financiers, wise in their
own conceit, a fools' chase. * * * But is God dead? Have

seed-time and harvest failed ? Has the hand of man lost its cunning? Does this blight cover the whole world? No! there is a nation which a merciless foe has just trampled in the dust, eating up and carrying off its garnered wealth. Exhausted with this foreign drain, civil war is eating out her strength. Angry parties stand ready to fly at each other's throats. By all the rules that obsolete political economy prates and babbles about, the people of such a nation ought to be starving. Her ships idle, her granaries empty, her trade annihilated. Not so! That nation is France. France has just paid suffering Germany $1,000,000,000. Her chief cities have been sacked and plundered—humiliated by defeat, torn by civil dissensions, she laughs, while all the rest of Christendom wade through the mire of bankruptcy. Her ships are full busy : and what little other nations do, is in carrying to and fro her manufactures. Her homes are happy, her streets crowded with passing trains laden with goods ; all her mills hurrying night and day, to get even with the demand upon them. Labor walks rejoicing, and capital sleeps easy, fat with its gains. What magician has done this? Paper Money. Like the rest of the nations she ran to its protection during the stress and storm of her German war. Unlike and wiser than the rest of us, she has not hurried back to coin. Wiser than we, she received the paper that she offered to others. That honesty had its reward. Her paper is to-day more valuable than gold, and she strides valiantly forward in her path to wealth and peace, spite of all drawbacks. Now, if fanaticism is feeling without facts, and wisdom means facts governing theories, which party are the fanatics, and which are the wise men ?

Judge Kelley said, in a speech in 1875 :—What has produced this unhappy condition of affairs ? My friends, it is self-imposed. It is the result of our devotion to an idea— to an abstraction. There are millions of us who think that Andrew Jackson is still President, and still fighting the United States Bank ; and that we ought, therefore, to go for hard money. This is neither jest nor exaggeration. We meet men daily who say " I am a Jackson man, and I go for hard money." I have met 50 such. Then there are theorists, doctrinaires as they are pleased to be called : who pooh-pooh at me as a sort of responsible lunatic, who has never read the " Bullion Report," or the writings of such flatulent egotists as Bonamy Price of Oxford. They cry, " consider what Ricardo says." Well, consider what Ricardo says and who he was. He was a bond and bullion monger and argued his own cause. I have studied his theories, and denounce them as selfish fallacies. I go for what old Ben Franklin says—Ben Franklin, who has more wisdom in his great toe than Ricardo had in his brain ; and less selfishness in his whole body than Ricardo had in his great toe.

I am a follower of Benjamin Franklin and Horace Greeley on this currency question. Mr. Greeley, notwithstanding the fact that the *Tribune*, founded by him, by turns satirizes or denounces my opinions on this question, was the first man to convince me of the propriety and necessity of resorting to the interconvertible bond system. * * * Who was Ricardo ? He was a banker who, being rich, secured an election to Parliament, and did for himself and Robert Peel, the son of the first Sir Robert Peel, and other British bond-holders, what Congress is doing for the banks and other holders of our bonds of to-day—transferring the property of the men of toil and of enterprise to men of bonds and gold. The Peel family has had its story ; and it should be studied by every American farmer, manufacturer and laborer.

The first Sir Robert Peel was a manufacturer of fabrics, and contracted for clothing the army. He was a patriot ; and proved his loyalty by putting all his profits into the depreciated bonds of the Government. He said, " I stand with the Government, and, make or lose, I give it the use of my capital." And when the war was over, he was one of the heaviest holders of the national debt. He and his son, Mr. Robert Peel, were both in Parliament. The son united with Ricardo, in forcing through the act providing for the resumption of specie payment at the end of four years ; of which the act passed by Congress is, in good measure, a copy. They carried it, and Sir Robert, who had stoutly opposed it, said to his son, " Robert, you have made the fortunes of your family, but you have ruined your country." And it was so. The bonds went up, and factory and every other species of productive property went down. The Peels and Ricardo sold at par the bonds they had bought at 40 per cent.; and put the proceeds into real estate at one-quarter or one−fifth of its intrinsic value. In these facts you have the secret

13

of the great landed estate of the Peel family ; and an illustration of the method by which the landed property of this country is to be concentrated in a few families. Men who bought our bonds at 40 per cent. are howling for resumption ; in order that they may get 100 for them ; and that factories, farms and mines may be without marketable value, until they shall come to own them, and again set industry in motion by expanding bank credits.

DEBTOR AND CREDITOR NATIONS.—Wm. H. Winder, now dead, has been our greatest authority upon the relations of debtor and creditor nations. In 1875 he spoke in his hot, just wrath thus :—After describing how we fought through the war without foreign aid, and our wisdom in so doing, he said ; Is not this position impregnable ? Just here comes in that ever damnable foreign influence, which has always been the bane of fiscal policy. As usual, that greediest of creditors, London, struck up the cuckoo note of specie payment and depreciated currency; and the wonderful, the vital importance of a good credit in that great banking center ; which credit, it was alleged, must be sought only by a return to specie payments, through the channel of contraction ; although the whole distance should be lined with an endless series of wrecks. The asses in this country brayed forth from a thousand throats the same mad doctrine. The parties under foreign tutelage,—some willfully dishonest, many honest,— would not listen to the suggestion that all values had accommodated themselves to the increased volume of currency ; and that to change it by a series of contractions would be a general slaughter of all values, for the sole benefit of monied men and the foreigner ; that a steady contraction was synonymous with the gradual but inevitable smothering of the industries at work ; and a perfectly assured guarantee of failure and disaster to all new enterprises which might be inaugurated in a shrinking market ; that, as we had prospered, as employment was abundant and profitable to all under the currency, as it then stood ; if left alone, there was assurance of a continued activity.

But these knaves and madmen were deaf to every appeal of reason and experience ; and would listen to no other suggestions than those from London, which said, if you want any high credit here, you must forthwith return to specie payment. To court favor with London, not being able

forthwith to resume specie payment, these wise men, being
in Congress, and urged on by the false teaching of the
foreigner; and under the delusion of being able to secure,
in the future, loans in London,-- made the greatest sacrifice
of the rights and interests of the people of the United States,
which the world has ever known one country voluntarily to
make to another; and without the shadow of consideration
therefor. In the preposterous expectation of propitiating
the foreigner to make future loans, should this Government
ever need foreign loans, Congress voluntarily, wantonly,
wickedly, committed a most gigantic fraud on the rights and
interests of the people, by changing the redemption of the
bonds from Greenbacks into gold, and inaugurating a silly
and most pernicious contraction.

Thus, this was the source of all our woes. The result
was, the foreigner purchased our gold bonds at about 40 to
50 per cent.; and paid for every dollar of them in commodities—not a cent of money was ever received here. Then
contraction began to choke our industries; and the foreigner
getting our bonds at 40 to 60, could pay us in commodities,
at rates which would undersell our producers. By means of
the accursed legislation of Congress,—in contraction and
changing payment of bonds from Greenbacks into gold,—
we were seduced to purchase three billion of dollars of
commodities from the foreigner *more* than he purchased
from us. We paid by a thousand millions in gold, and
two thousand millions in, gold-paying securities. The
addition of this thousand million of gold to the foreign
market gave rise to vast money enterprises; and the
purchase of three thousand millions of commodities by us,
gave extraordinary activity and prosperity to the foreign industries. The thousand million of gold enabled the creditor
countries of Europe to lend money to other countries; which
countries, like the United States, also negotiated their bonds,
to great extent, and received in return commodities, as did
the United States. If these countries of Europe had continued to take our securities and the securities of other debtor
States, the seeming prosperity would have continued. But
a stop having been put to any further purchases of bonds;
and a demand being made for the payment of many of
those already had by the foreigner; a sudden stop has been
put to this state of things; and we and all debtor countries,

find ourselves plunged, necessarily, into all the troubles which envelope us. The immense demand for commodities from the foreign creditors has ceased; and consequently his industries feel the loss of custom, and have suffered. These are the so natural consequences of that frightful legislation of Congress, that no one can close his eyes to the truth of it. [He then showed that to get out of debt we must make our exports greater than our imports. He saw with wonderful clearness the relations of debtor and creditor nations; but had not the widest vision in other respects.]

In another article he says:—Under a decision of the Supreme Court that coined metal or bullion alone is money, this fact would stand transparent, that every dollar of money in the country would virtually belong to the foreigner; and we should be indebted to his policy or indulgence for whatever portion of it might remain; it would in truth and in fact be a loan on call by the foreigner. This statement is unqualifiedly true as it is pregnant.

The corollary is that a decision by the Supreme Court that the Constitution restricts both Federal and State Governments from acknowledging or constituting anything as money, save and except coined bullion, is *to convict the framers of the Federal Constitution* of the stultification of rendering the people of the United States wholly and helplessly dependent upon the foreigner's policy or caprice for every dollar of money. They are inexorably excluded from any money except what the foreigner may vouchsafe to lend and recall at will. [The British thus seized all our money before the Revolution.—S. L.]

It may be said that since the peace of 1814–15 the foreigner has owned our bullion; and our experience from that time to 1863 has been that about every five or seven years he has exercised his right of ownership by draining our bullion; and causing perturbations and convulsions in our money market to such an extent, that the result may be safely stated to be the failure of 95 per cent. of all parties engaged in business, including the periodical crushing of our manufactures. Amos Lawrence, of Boston, in his diary, states as the result of his observations, among his own acquaintances, that 97 per cent. of them succumbed. This fearful record of the foreigner's fatal power over all our interests, given him by limiting ourselves to metal money, was during a period when our indebtedness to the foreigner rarely, if ever, exceeded 200 millions of dollars. What, we significantly ask, may not be apprehended from that same foreigner, with a claim against us of ten times that amount?

Again the right to issue bills of credit is as inalienable as it is an indispensable attribute of sovereignty; and as it is expressly denied to the States, must, as a matter of course, reside in the Federal Constitution.

SOLON CHASE AND THEM STEERS.—This earnest worker, who started the Greenback movement in Maine, and long fought manfully against fusion there, was popular enough to be a prominent candidate for nomination to the Presidency by the Greenback Labor Convention of 1880. The following description of his ideas is by Judge Kelley:—In illustration of this point, and as a further demonstration of the effect of contraction upon the condition of the farmers of the country, let me recall an interview I had with Mr. Solon Chase, of Maine, during a day that he did me the honor to pass under my roof, when returning to his home from a Western stumping tour. I had seen in New England papers many allusions to " Solon's heifer "; and in his own paper the assertion that the same stroke that had struck " Solon's heifer ", had struck a savings-bank or other corporation that had failed; and at a later day I had found occasional allusions to " Solon's Steers "; and I took the liberty of inquiring of Mr. Chase whether they were his heifer and his steers that had become so famous; and, if so, what made them remarkable? He said that there was nothing remarkable about the heifer, except that he had given it some prominence by making it an example to his brother-farmers of the double wickedness of the contraction policy.

He also said, in substance, that having been a hard-money man, and spent some months in endeavoring to answer a Congressional speech against contraction, he had seen that the arguments of that speech were unanswerable, and had set about starting a Greenback movement in Maine. His efforts, for the first year, were confined chiefly to his own county, and, indeed, largely to the towns of Turner and Buckfield, the people of which were farmers. Their land was poor, their season short, their products few and simple; but, as a means of increasing their gain, it was customary among them to keep breeding-stock for the dairy and farm

use; and instead of selling their hay to advance it into
meat. They never sold a calf for young veal, if they could
advance it to a yearling; or the yearling, if the demand
for money or taxes or other imperative purposes would permit them to feed it until it should, as a two-year old, be
worth more than twice the price of a yearling. When, however, he attempted to sell his then last two-year old, he had
found that he could get no more for her than he could have
got a year before. He also found that this was true of all
the other two-year olds in the neighborhood. So, going before his neighbors, he told the story of his heifer, and asked
them whether it was not the story of their two-year olds;
and when answered in the affirmative, he asked them, "*Who
gets the hay?* For whom have we worked? We have fed
these heifers and tended them for a year, and have done it
for the benefit of somebody. We have not enriched the
town, or county, or State. I have not worked for my poor
blind boy whose eyes, as you know, were shot out while
fighting for the maintenance of the nation; or for other
members of my family; yet you and I have worked, and
worked faithfully. Our land has yielded, and yielded well;
but who takes the yield of our labor and our land? Let us
see if we can find out. As we must sell our two-year olds
for what was freely offered a year ago for yearlings, somebody is benefited. As we can get but one-half the value of
our products, the man who buys them takes two dollars
worth for one; and it is for him, whether his capital be invested in National banks or in the untaxed bonds of the
Government, for whom we work. Our toil and enterprise
do but impoverish us, while the idle rich man, who buries
his money, or puts it in a vault, grows rich at the rate of 100
per cent. per annum. Labor, enterprise and production
have thus become the road to poverty; and all capitalists
are warned that the true way, the rapid road to wealth, is to
withdraw capital from productive business and put it into
bank-stock or untaxed bonds."

The story of Solon's steers was an equally apt illustration
of his whole argument. It was this: In 1875, he was attracted by the beauty and symmetry of a yoke of three-year-
old steers, and bought them, as he and his neighbors thought,
at a great bargain, for $100. I was delighted with the en-
thusiasm this simple farmer exhibited when he spoke of the

beauty, docility and strength of those steers. They had for
two years been objects of his care and solicitude. They
were to win him the approval of his fellow-citizens, if not a
premium at a State fair; and, when five years old, were accordingly exhibited at such fair and commanded universal
admiration. The time had now come to sell them, and he
attempted to do so, and found that $90 was the highest sum
offered for them. He had fed and cared for and disciplined
them through two of the long winters of Maine, and two of
her short and fruitless summers; and the net result of all
his labors, tested by the market values of 1875 and 1877,
was the loss of $10, of the little stock of ready money he
had been able to command in the former year. Another
political campaign had opened; and he went again to his
fellow-citizens asking them, who had got the hay or was to
get it? For whom were they at work? Who gathered in
the fruits of their land and labor, as effectually as though
they owned the land, and employed the farmers to work it,
or rented it to them as tenant farmers under the British system of agriculture? And, again, as he said, he pointed out
to them, how contraction impoverished labor, and swelled
the profits of capital, and was building up a plutocracy in
the United States, which must not only be dangerous to
popular liberty, but promised to rival in splendor the plutocracy of England. With the inevitable results of Mr. McCulloch's financial policy,—in obedience to which the resumption act was passed and maintained,—so pertinently illustrated by this farmer, is it wonderful that more than 43,000
citizens of Maine sundered old party ties, and sought to
emancipate themselves, and the country, from a system
which is ruining them, and threatening their liberties and
those of their posterity?

GOLD BUG TRICKS.—During the long agony that preceded
gold resumption, all sorts of subterfuges were used by the
wretches who caused the agony, to hoodwink the people.
Judge Kelley showed in 1875, that the statement that the
Secretary of the Treasury was selling surplus gold, at the
rate of $5,000,000 per month, was humbug. He would make
such an announcement, because he would not get enough
currency from the revenues to meet expenses, and so sold
some of his little hoard of gold, which he was trying to save
for resumption in 1879.

BEN BUTLER AND BUTLER DUNCAN.—Gen. B. F. Butler, in August 1875, said, in his response to an invitation to address the N. Y. Legal Tender Club :—" Regretting that I cannot be with you and elaborate these views, as I should be glad to do in New York City ;—whose docks are deserted by shipping, whose stores are unrented, and whose dwelling-houses have been so depreciated as hardly to meet the mort-gages upon them ; and where, I think, sound financial doc-trines are as much needed as anywhere ;– my necessities com-pel me to forego this, which would be a pleasure to me, and, I trust a profit to others. I am informed that Mr. Duncan, of Duncan, Sherman & Co., went to Washington when the currency bill was before the President, to advise him to veto it ; because it was necessary to depreciate values. The President did veto the bill. Values have been depreciated, I trust, to an amount entirely satisfactory to Messrs. Duncan, Sherman & Co., *however little their creditors may relish the process !*

" I have the honor to be, very truly yours,

"BENJ. F. BUTLER."

I was walking in Nassau Street, New York, at the moment when the news of the failure of Duncan, Sherman & Co., struck the " Street." The instant rushing to and fro of men and boys, which continued for hours, reminded me of the frantic motions of a colony of ants, when the flat stone under which they lived has been turned over. All push, loaded and unloaded, for a new hiding-place.

MONOPOLY'S PANDEMONIUM IN CALIFORNIA. — One of the most disastrous exhibitions of human greed ever seen in this country, took place on the Pacific coast in 1875. It resulted in transferring the greater part of the wealth of California into the hands of a few individuals, who have ever since borne down on the people of that State with such relentless oppression, that revolution has been imminent, and was only prevented by the partial success of the people at the ballot-box, in thwarting the designs of their oppressors, and staying them in their unbridled career of robbery.

· These speculations, be it remembered, were not based on paper money of any kind, nor on silver. Neither were they based on a redundancy of money of any kind ; for the total amount of currency of all kinds in circulation, and held as reserves (as shown by the report of the Secretary of the Treasury) only amounted to $773,646,728.69.

These speculations and grabbings, wild as they were, were based upon gold banks and gold bank credits, and a currency contracted to a specie basis. The remedy for the prevention of wild speculation and extravagant indebtedness must be sought in some other direction than contraction to the specie basis or gold standard.

I have given a full account of this epoch in California in " The Cyclopedia of Money and Finance."

GREENBACKERS ORGANIZED.—On December 1, 1875, the Greenback party was first formally organized in Farwell Hall, Chicago. Strong Greenback and Anti-Monopoly resolutions were passed. Chairmen of State committees were appointed. Samuel Leavitt is proud of the fact that he was ·appointed for New York State.

1876

FRANTIC DIABOLISM.—Here is a specimen of the frantic diabolism with which such papers as the N. Y. *Tribune* were driving the nation through the dark valley in the " hard times." This editorial is from the *Tribune* of January, 1876. It is written with the fanatical zeal of a heretic-burning Torquemada. I know of no man more likely to write such rot than W. M. Grosvenor, once of St. Louis. He really seems to *think* in that way. " *Non tali auxilio, nec defensoribus istis, tempus egit.*"

[N. B. Fourteen years later, in 1890, I find that Grosvenor is an editor of the *Tribune*.]

" How long, O Cataline, wilt thou abuse our patience ? "

Congress and Contraction.—" Go, my son, and learn with how little wisdom the world is governed ! " The counsel of the French father has lost none of its force. The American who wishes to learn how stupidly it is possible to act, in dealing with the affairs of a great nation, must visit Washington, and talk with members of Congress about the money question. Contraction is the great bugbear. Everybody is afraid of it, and the average member would about as soon think of jumping from the railing that surmounts the dome of the capitol, as of defending contraction in any form or degree. Rascally demagogues have joined with timid and unreasoning business-men, to make the people believe that any reduc-

tion in the volume of the currency would bring indescribable
horrors. A vast number of persons, whose sincerity of purpose is as obvious as their want of information, and whose
ignorance is past hope of cure, because they fancy that they
perfectly understand the whole subject,—join in a clamor
against any form of contraction. Congress was elected at a
time when this panic was at its worst; and fully represents
all its most stupid phases. And this is the body of men by
whom the welfare and honor of the country are to be guarded,
so far as they depend upon legislation.

Accordingly, whether a member calls himself an inflationist or a resumptionist, he usually begins and ends his statement by declaring his unalterable hostility to contraction. It
is a most disheartening fact, that the few sane men in Congress—who know what the country needs—are often too
timid to confront what they suppose to be a settled public
conviction ; and so they go about seeking for some mode of
"resuming specie payments without contraction." Cursed
for eight years by the theory of Mr. Boutwell—that it is possible to "grow up to specie payments,"—the country counts
the 7,000 commercial wrecks which that bit of financial
idiocy has caused within a single year, and yet fails to see
that mere standing still involves ruin, because it involves
prolonged and fatal uncertainty. It is perfectly marvelous
that members of Congress—many of whom must know, as
practical business men, that this uncertainty does more harm
to trade than could be done by any settled policy whatever
—cannot be made to see that doing nothing is the very
worst thing. Bankruptcy and repudiation are the worst results, and prolonged uncertainty is bringing these with terrible certainty.

This land cries out in agony for a ruler [hear! hear!—S.L.]
One man of wisdom and power—who would give the country
a settled financial policy—would be worth more than can be
computed in millions. But the country looks to Congress,
thus far in vain. The hard-money Democrats in the House
are so overawed and overpowered by their associates that
they *even talk of repealing and repudiating the pledge of resumption* [ah!] ; and propose, of all conceivable methods, exactly
that which everybody knows must be the most harmful in
operation and the most uncertain of success—the slow accumulation of a monstrous hoard of idle coin. Meanwhile, all

the small demagogues are preparing their speeches against contraction; and all the half-statesmen are getting ready to say, with fear and trembling, " Let us try to resume without contraction." Where is the man who will have the sense and the courage to defend stoutly the manly policy which the Secretary of the Treasury suggests? Who will show what it means, and why it meets the necessities of our condition, as no other yet advocated does? If such a man should come forward, with the pluck to tell the people what they ought to know and to do—and with the ability to make even a dull Congress listen and understand—who can measure the good that he can do? But the country waits; uncertainty continues; doubt slaughters merchants and manufacturers every week; hope dies away, and the last opportunity of saving the honor and restoring the prosperity of the nation, by legislation, before the next Presidential upturning, are vanishing fast. There is a strong and clear-headed man at the Treasury. But what he will have power to do no man can say until Congress has adjourned. [The Chicago *Tribune* never now utters a more infernal tirade than that.]

GLADSTONE VS. GOLD BASIS.—James Harvey, of England, wrote thus in 1878 :—Even Mr. Gladstone, the chosen disciple of Sir Robert Peel, could plainly see that this gold system would not work, and that periodical panic showed it to be wrong in principle, and therefore impracticable in the working. These were his words in February, 1876, two months before the Gurney Panic, which took place in May: "The bill (of 1844) cannot stand as it is. I cannot consent that trade should be devastated by these continually recurring convulsions. The bill of 1844, damaged in 1847, was utterly shattered in 1857."

Harvey adds :—May I ask Mr. Gladstone what was its state after the panic of 1866? The Bank of England was saved by the interposition of the Minister, who allowed it to issue interconvertible paper (this for the third time); and yet by Peel's bill to be unable to pay your debt in gold is—bankruptcy.

TRADE DOLLAR REPUDIATED.—A joint resolution of Congress approved July 22, 1876, provides that "The trade dollar shall not hereafter be a legal tender." .

POSTAL CURRENCY GONE.—The Acts of April 17, and of July 22, 1876, provided for $50,,,000000 subsidiary silver coin to redeem fractional paper currency. These small notes were redeemable in legal-tender notes, in sums of $5 and more. It was an outrage upon the people to impose this silver money upon them at a cost of $2,500,000 a year, for such a purpose. The silver money, under the law creating it, was not redeemable in anything.

John G. Drew received this short, sharp and decisive note from Mr. Spinner, late U. S. Treasurer :—

MOHAWK, Aug. 17, 1876.

DEAR SIR.—Your letter of the 15th inst. has been received. In answer, I have to say that the 7-30 Treasury notes were intended, prepared, issued and used as currency.

Very Resp'y yours,

F. E. SPINNER.

SECRETARY FOSTER AND 7-30's.—The following, added in 1893, after the failure of "Calico Charley," is very interesting reading. We know now why Foster was so anxious to please Wall Street.

To the Editor of The Advocate.

As there has been considerable of time spent and writing done, contradictions, affirmations, etc., in regard to the 7-30 Treasury notes being used as money and circulated as a part of the currency of the country, I now claim to have positive proof, Secretary Foster to the contrary notwithstanding, that they were used, and that Secretary Foster used them himself. The following letters will explain :—

JEWELL CITY, KAS., Oct. 3, 1892.

Mr. G. L. Daniels, Gibsonburg, Ohio.

DEAR SIR.—I understand that you purchased a farm from Mr. Foster (who is now Secretary of the United States Treasury) in 1866, paying him 7-30 notes for the same. Enclosed find stamp for reply, and you will do me a favor by answering if the above is correct. Give a detailed answer of purchase and payment, and oblige.

FRANK R. FORREST, Jewell City, Kas.

In reply to the above, is the following :—

GIBSONBURG, OHIO, Oct. 17, 1892.

Mr. Frank R. Forrest, Jewell City, Kas.

DEAR SIR.—In regard to enquiries enclosed to me, will say

that in 1866 I purchased 80 acres of unimproved land of Hon. Chas. Foster, now Secretary of the United States Treasury, for the sum of $800, and a part of first payment was made in 7-30 notes ; the exact amount I have forgotten, but it was not less than $150, and not more than $200. After Mr. Foster received said notes, he gave me a $10 bill as a part of the accumulated interest. I do not know how the deal between Mr. Foster and myself ever became public, as I have no recollection of ever mentioning it to any one, and if I did it must have been years ago, and then only in a casual way, viz : that they were the only bonds I ever saw.

Respectfully,

G. L. DANIELS.

The above is an exact copy, *verbatim et literatim,* and I have the genuine letter in my possession. Any one doubting the same can write the Register of Deeds of Jewell County, Mankato, Kas.

FRANK R. FORREST.

It was the late Gen. Kilpatrick who immortalized himself in 1876, by declaring that the Greenbackers of Indiana were "poor, needy and in debt ; " and that " a bloody shirt campaign, with money, and Indiana is safe."

GRANT DOES UNINTENDED GOOD.—This is the way in which the New York *Sun* talked in 1876 about the Legal Tender Decision by the Supreme Court of the United States. If Grant thought that he was playing sharp in this case (and he was none too good for such trickery), he simply stumbled upon the perpetration of a very proper deed : in appointing judges who decided rightly. This decision, legalizing the Greenback as money, was one of the best things that ever happened to this country. The *Sun* said : " In the legal tender cases did not General Grant pack the Supreme Court with Bradley and Strong, expressly to change the former decree, while the record was still fresh ; thus postponing specie payments for years ? That infamy was perpetrated to benefit certain corporations, whose obligations for gold payments were maturing. They paid in paper, and pocketed a large difference by this scandalous prostitution of the judiciary to a selfish end."

Such corporations may have been benefited ; but the clamor of the plain people for justice was the basic cause of this decision. Hatred of Grant blinded Dana's eyes to facts which he now dimly perceives.

FOOLISH CALIFORNIANS.—A California correspondent said in 1876:—The independent papers that were the supporters of Newton Booth have not dared to follow in his wake on the Greenback question; and, indeed, it would hardly be safe to do so, so strong are the prejudices here in favor of a gold currency, among all classes except the farmers. Even in the country towns, the traders—who control all the advertising—will not allow the local press to speak out upon this question. The working-classes, and all others working for wages, see in the adoption of a Greenback currency for California, only this—that whereas we now receive silver for our wages, at only three to four per cent. discount, we should receive the same sum in Greenbacks at twelve per cent. discount; and beyond this they cannot reason. They do not see that a high rate of interest and scarcity of money paralyzes our industries. The loss of population during the Rebellion, caused by rejecting the legal-tender currency, was too apparent to escape notice; but the money monopolists comfort us by saying, that, though it might have been a good thing then, it is too late to remedy the evil by adopting it now. They whisper, however, that to put a strict construction upon our refusal to receive the notices and obligations in the hour of her peril, was giving aid and comfort to the enemy; and was therefore treason to our country.

DEMOCRATS REPUDIATE RESUMPTION.—The Democratic House of Representatives passed an act at the session of 1876, repealing the Resumption Act, as the convention in St. Louis required should be done, notwithstanding the opposition of a few Democratic bondholders and advocates of National banks; but the friends of the British bondholders prevented its passage in the Senate.

THE BOND AGE—$150,000,000,000.—The interest-bearing burden of Europe and America, in this " Bond Age ", is calculated at at least one hundred and fifty thousand million dollars. A. J. Warner, of Ohio, has published a carefully prepared statement showing the increase of the municipal indebtedness alone, of the United States, from 1866 to 1876. His figures giving the conditions of 130 cities, show that, during those ten years, their average debt was increased

200 per cent. ; taxation 83 per cent. ; valuation 75 per cent. ;
population only 33 per cent.

COIN AND BULLION IN EUROPE.—The following was given
as the gold, silver and base metal coins ; and gold and silver
bullion in circulation and in banks in all Europe about 1876 :

	GOLD.	SILVER AND BASE METAL.
Great Britain	442.500,000	80,000,000
France..................	650,000,000	350,000,000
Germany................	380,000,000	370,000,000
Austria................		200,000,000
Russia...		250,000,000
Italy..................		145,000,000
Spain	300,000,000	200,000,000
Sweden...............		70,000,000
Belgium		38,000,000
Switzerland		5.000,000
All other States of Europe.		360,000,000
	$1,772,500,000	$2,068,000,000

1877.

MONEY MARKET EASY IN THE HARDEST TIMES.—In or
about 1877, in the House of Representatives, Judge W. D.
Kelley asked the house to wipe out the ruinous statute
calling for Resumption in 1879. He said : " It stood a
menace to confidence—the steady destroyer of credit. It
was notice to every capitalist that the body of money was to
be contracted ; that the banks must hoard specie for resumption ; that prices must fall ; and that, therefore, the best use
for money was to bury it, either in their own cellars or in the
vaults of the banks. It was no wonder, therefore, that the
gentleman from New York (Mr. Chittenden) could say yesterday that *there never had been so much money to lend.* There
was no use for money, when men saw that that which they
produced must be sold at less than cost. On what could
men borrow money ? Could they borrow money in Philadelphia on Reading Railroad stock, on Delaware and Lack-
awanna, on Jersey Central, or on any other railroad stock ?
Could money be borrowed on farms, factories, forges or fur-

naces? No! And why? Because under the Resumption
Act their value must shrink. He had heard of moneyed
institutions in New York that were not only foregoing interest on mortgages, but were paying the taxes on the mortgaged
property, rather than take it in at its present depreciated
value, and thus tie up their working capital. He knew of
similar instances in Philadelphia. He knew of mortgagors
who were begging the mortgagees to take the property, and
free them from the resulting judgment, which would blight
the hopes of their future life. In conclusion he said: Repeal that act; restore confidence; allow the tramps and the
millions of working men and women, who are now living in
despair, to go to work on your raw material, and supply each
other's work. No nation, no individual, was ever freed from
debt by idleness and want of industry. Set the miners
of Pennsylvania and the other coal States at work in producing power. Let the coal which they mine quicken your
machinery. Let wages be earned by the working-people,
to enable them to pay their debts, and to consume dutiable
and taxable commodities. We have gone at this thing bull-
headed; and have thus effectually disabled ourselves; deprived ourselves of confidence; impoverished our people;
diminished the revenues of the Government, and put ourselves in a position that, in the midst of abounding crops,
our people are hungry. With our cotton (the largest crop
that we ever produced) they are naked or in rags. *The
examples of France are worthy the study of American statesmen.*
Let them study those examples—not books written by *petits
maitres*,—men who hold seats in colleges,—who have read
Ricardo or Adam Smith; and who begin, at once, like an
apothecary, to compound prescriptions for sick nations, by
putting in a little from each bottle, and giving it a common
title. Take the management of a nation; study the details
of history for a series of years; grasp the subject; remember that Hugh McCulloch does not know what a boy of ten
years does know—that a promise to pay is not money. I
trust that no other citizen of Indiana is so ignorant. Remember that you are to deal with five thousand millions of
indebtedness."

THE SILVER COMMISSION AND THE CAUSE OF HARD
TIMES. On the 15th of August, 1876, a law was enacted
creating what was known as the Monetary Commission. The

law specified various duties for the commission, and among others, one was to solve the question of the disaster of '73 and the fearfully hard times and sufferings which followed. The commission was made up from the United States senate, John P. Jones, Lewis V. Boggy and George S. Boutwell. From the house of representatives, Randall L. Gibson, Geo. Willard and the following gentlemen were appointed secretaries : Wm. G. Grosbeck of Ohio, Prof. Francis Brown of Massachusetts and George M. Weston of Maine. This committee held meetings in all the principal cities of the union, exhausted every resource that was possible to discover the cause of the hard times, and in their report of March 2, 1877, they make use of the following extraordinary language : " The true and only cause of the stagnation in industries and commerce now everywhere felt, is the fact everywhere existing of falling prices, caused by shrinkage in the volume of money." They also declare that " an increasing value of money and falling prices have been, and are more fruitful of misery than war, pestilence and famine."

Silver demonetization was thus treated by the Silver commission :—" The effects of the demonetization so far accomplished, and of the resulting disturbance of the relative value of gold and silver upon trade, commerce, finance and productive interests,—in this country and throughout the commercial world,—have been signally disastrous : and especially to the countries that have recently demonetized silver ; or in which the gold standard was already established. In all commercial countries, the same phenomena are simultaneously presented—of falling prices of commodities and real estate ; diminishing public revenues ; starving, poorly paid and unemployed laborers, and rapidly-multiplying bankruptcies. These facts, existing everywhere, must arise from some cause operating everywhere. And no such cause is or can be pointed out, except the decrease of the metallic supplies from the mines ; and consequently the decrease of metallic money relatively to population and commerce since about 1865 ; and the larger and more sudden decrease of metallic money, caused by partial destruction of the money functions of one of the precious metals. This distress dates with the law of the United States of February 12, 1873, and the law of Germany of July, 1873,—giving practical effect to a previous decree of that empire of December 4, 1871, for the establishment of a single gold standard."

Senator Jones has, since then, broadened into the knowledge that not lack of silver only, but of *money*, was a leading cause of the woes described. The report concludes thus : Finally, the commission believe that the facts that Germany and the Scandinavian States have adopted the single gold standard, and that some other European nations may possibly adopt it, instead of being reasons for perseverance in the attempt to establish it in the United States, are precisely the facts which make such an attempt entirely impracticable and ruinous. If the nations on the continent of Europe had the double standard, a gold standard would be possible here : because, in that condition they would freely exchange gold for silver. It was that condition which enabled England to resume specie payments in gold in 1821. The attainment of such a standard becomes difficult precisely in proportion to the number and importance of the countries engaged in striving after it ; and it is precisely in the same proportion that the ruinous effects of striving after it are aggravated. To propose to this country a contest for a gold standard with the European nations is to propose to it a disastrous race.

" A MAD, MAD WORLD, MY MASTERS ! "—In the time of our greatest financial misery, the then bold, brave Gen. Thomas Ewing, uttered the following thrilling words in Congress. Beaten, humiliated in running for office, and impoverished, he afterward came to hide himself in New York,—trying by law practice, like Conkling, and other disappointed ex-leaders, to " make money". He spoke thus :— Mr. Ewing pointed out the depreciation of values, which he estimated at one-third of the whole. The Resumption law was a practical confiscation of $3,500,000,000 of property. Three-fourths of all classes of the people of this country were debtors ; and it was their hard-earned accumulations that were being wrested from them, by this robber-law. The loss of the laboring classes was $3,000,000 a day, or $900,000,000 a year. The President of the Dayton and Southeastern R. R. told him that *hundreds of men had been offering to work on the road for bread and meat.* Nothing for clothes : nothing for wives and children ; nothing to lay up for winter ; merely enough to keep the poor human body, that was doing the labor, able to exercise the necessary force.

"O God, that bread should be so dear, and flesh and blood so cheap." [Sensation and applause.] The law was not going to stop with that fall in values. The bottom had not been touched. A further fall of values had to be witnessed. An increase of poverty and suffering, the practical confiscation of property, and the repudiation of a large part of the public debt. He appealed to the moneyed men. Had they not heard enough to warn them that they had better stop? What was the meaning of the labor riots—that almost civil war six months ago? The meaning was that labor had been trampled on as much as it could stand.

Go to any of our cities and see the hundreds and thousands and tens of thousands of pale, wan, ragged and hungry people. I have seen them clubbed out of the parks of New York city at night; men who went there hoping to lie down on the grass and get a little fresh air, and a cool and smooth resting-place. The thing has been pushed just as far as it will bear. What are we to gain by inflicting such losses on our industry and labor? What is the great advantage to be accomplished? It cost this country in the loss of productive industries, in the unjust transfer of wealth from the debtor to the creditor, in the unjust increase of taxation, in the loss of labor, more than all the wastes of the rebellion combined. We are to get back the banking system that existed before the war, modified a little, a little better in one respect than the old State bank system; but a system the very genius of which will be panic; a system which in the very nature of things cannot be stable.

No greater question than this was ever presented to an American Congress for its action. It touches the happiness, the prosperity, the future, of three-fourths of the men, women and children of this land. Thousands of men have been driven by the Resumption law to insanity or suicide. Hundreds of thousands have been cast down from competency to poverty. Millions have been deprived of employment for their labor, on which rests the dependence of their families. It is now too late to right the wrong; but we may avert any greater wrong from them and other millions by prompt action on the part of Congress and the President. I do not appeal to that money-power which seeks its fortune over the wrecked happiness and accumulations of its fellow-men—a power to which our unhappy civil war gave birth; which has grown so enormous, through unjust financial legislation; which

now bestrides us like a colossus ; which subsidizes the press ;
which captures statesmen and parties, and makes them its
subservient tools ; which hounds down and vilifies every public man who dares to raise his voice against it. That power,
in the flush and arrogance of its enormous and ill-gotten gains,
has a heart of stone—not to be touched by any human sympathy and compassion. I appeal to the masses, to their faithful representatives (I thank God !) of both political parties on
this floor. The true aim of government is the greatest good
to the greatest number ; and whoever, by legislation or otherwise, changes the value of a contract, is as accursed as he
who removes his neighbor's landmarks. For twelve years
past, the financial legislation of this country has been dictated,
one would think, in Lombard Street or Wall Street; and the
people have been plundered by every fresh enactment. They
have suffered the fate of Gulliver when tied down by the
Lilliputians. Thank God they are now about to rise ; to burst
the bonds which their petty foes have fastened upon them
when sleeping ; and to walk abroad again in their own maj-
esty. [Applause.]

Hon. Francis Gillette of Connecticut, said :—Most of my
enterprising neighbors have gone down, or are still afloat at
the cruel mercy of capitalists ; who hesitate to foreclose upon
them, lest they should fail to realize enough to pay first mortgages. Despondency and gloom cloud the faces of our leading men of business enterprise. The road of our hard-money
financiers toward " a gold basis and specie currency " is a
hard road to travel. Like that from Jerusalem down to Jericho, they find it rough and rocky, and infested by thieves and
usurers.

THE BUELL CIRCULAR.—An apparently authentic circular
got into the papers which was dated in New York, September
19, 1877, and was signed by Jos. Buell, Secretary of the Bankers Association. It calls upon bankers to make every effort
to sustain all papers that oppose Greenbacks; and to with-
hold all patronage from Greenbackers ; as " they wish to provide the people with money other than our own supplying;
and [if successful] would seriously affect your individual
profits as banker or lender." ! ! !

STUPID ASTONISHMENT OF THE GOLD BUGS.—An editor
said in 1875 : " There is no comfort in the reflection that we
have had hard times in this country before and survived them.

The debts are the great obstacle at present. There were hard times in 1840 and 1857, and at other times; but then there was little or no debt or taxes. There were no railroad debts. There was but little Government debt then. There were no municipal debts then, and taxes were hardly felt. It is not so now."

The following from the Chicago *Tribune*, 1877, is a fair specimen of the stupid astonishment displayed, every Spring and Autumn, by the bullion papers, all through the hard times; because of the continuance of depression. "And still Pharaoh hardened his heart, and would not let the people go:"—

The continued dullness, is, for the season, unprecedented. Never in the history of the city, probably, have the most carefully-matured opinions, even of our most conservative men [ah !] in regard to the Spring business, been so greatly at fault. Everybody expected a fairly active trade in our leading staples, instead of the dullness so long continued that it has become decidedly oppressive. Last year's crop, in most sections, was a fair average in amount, and of good quality. Money in all business centers, was never so plenty and so cheap. And right here we are likely to find the cause of the stagnation which seems to have fallen upon the channels of trade. Not only in the cities, but among the people in all the surrounding States, money has been and still is plenty. Hence they have sent it here to be used as margins; and the vast amount of farm products in store here is due more to the nerve and the money of country dealers than to those in our own city. Within the last few days, their margins have been wiped out at a lively rate ; and how long they will " put up" nobody can predict.

New enterprises are generally avoided ; and capitalists are at their wit's ends to find some profitable employment for their funds. Several have been here during the week. Satisfactory loans could not be had. Some have left, while others are looking for real estate, generally near the business center of the city.

Our commercial columns show that transactions on the Board of Trade are mainly in options. Those in grain for shipment are merely nominal. The cattle-yards furnish nearly all the Eastern exchange upon the market.

WHAT GENTLEMAN GEORGE SAID,—George H. Pendleton

of Ohio tersely assailed the Republican party in 1877. After denouncing the National banks, because they are liable to become "a great political machine, the ally and support and money-lender and master of the party which sustains it "—he arraigns the Republican party for the financial measures, adopted during and after the war. He says they "unnecessarily [?] abandoned specie payments [?] and most unwisely degraded the Greenback currency. THEY ENHANCED THE BURDEN OF THE PUBLIC INDEBTEDNESS BY MAKING A HOME DEBT A FOREIGN DEBT; BY MAKING A PAPER DEBT A COIN DEBT; BY EXTENDING THE TIME OF ITS PAYMENT; BY MAKING A COIN DEBT A GOLD DEBT: by contracting and hoarding, and selling bonds. And all this they did without other apparent reason than the demands and the profit of the holders of bonds."

THE "LEADING PAPERS."—The following item, current during the hard times, is, as Horace Greeley would say, "very interesting reading." It will be interesting to the Western people, generally, who,—as far as I can judge from considerable experience during the last four seasons, in Ohio, Indiana, and a part of Illinois.—believe in the nation having the profits of the paper circulation, to be informed that the six or seven daily journals of most influence in New York, about two years ago, entered into an *explicit understanding* to advocate an extinction of the legal tender circulation. These journals were all in FAVOR OF IT, until the decease of the founders of the three chief morning papers—the *Herald, Times* and *Tribune.* These, and all the others, are now controlled by new men, and capitalists who have large interests in National banks, and derive a vast annual income from advertisements from this source.

The N. Y. *Tribune* held high carnival in 1877. The N. Y. *Sun,* before it became a Greenback paper (for a time) said : " No wonder the inflationists make capital of the fact that the *Tribune,* the pretended champion of hard money for the good of all, is only the tool of Jay Gould ; and works in his stock-jobbing interest. Jay Gould and his stool-pigeon are a load the advocates of a sound currency cannot afford to carry. The former work for their personal greed, the latter for *a great principle.* We repudiate the stool-pigeon and his master ! "

Mark how the cold-blooded wretches who run the *Tribune* jeered at " the hungry and homeless wanderers," who, as they well knew, filled the highways of this land in 1877 :— " Mr. Ewing's speech in favor of repealing the Resumption Act was a fine example of emotional treatment applied to financial questions. And if such questions were best settled by a show of hands, at an Ohio town-meeting, nothing could be more effective, before such a tribunal, than Mr. Ewing's effort. Mr. Ewing's vivid pictures of despoiled labor and hungry and homeless wanderers,—and the general intensity of his rhetoric.—would be well calculated to rufile up the spirits of the unthinking ; and incite a mutiny against some *imaginary oppressor;* even if he should not condescend to any appearance of an argument, or if, as was really the case in this instance, his entire argument, so called, was bottomed on the hollow fallacy that a promise to pay is money."

No wonder that Ewing, like so many others, grew selfish ; and concluded to come to New York and " make money."

Here was a characteristic piece of impudence in a *Tribune* editorial. The editor began thus : " Even in the worst cause, unflinching courage commands admiration. The soft-money lunatics merit contempt by the amazing folly of their belief. But they are so thoroughly in earnest ; they have so fully the courage of their opinions ; they are so persistent, resolute, and ready to face all possible consequences, partisan or personal, in fighting for their notions,—that it would be a great mistake to despise them. Men of that stamp generally make themselves felt. * * * Of men who thoroughly believe in the soft money heresy, avow that belief on all occasions without hesitation ; and in any sharp contest on that issue are impelled by that belief, there are many hundred thousand.

" They band together as naturally as the devotees of Slavery did in years before the war."

That last touch is good ! If he had put in the " Anti " it would have been right.

In that same terrible 1877, the *Tribune* amused itself thus : " No cautious gentleman can retire to rest with any comfort now-a-days, without going through a rigid course of self-examination, to convince himself that he has not been stealing something, or committing a forgery or so, during the day.

As a prophylactic measure,—during this epidemic of financial inpropriety,—it would be well for any operator who is compelled to expose himself, to hire a private detective to watch him—at least during business hours."

I wrote at the time: " As true as it is funny and sad ! Try it yourself, Jay ! "

Again that paper said :—Time was when exposure of such frauds as those of Morton in Philadelphia, and Gilman in New York, would have shaken the commercial fabric to its very foundations.

It is not altogether a favorable symptom, that these disclosures create so little alarm. For it proves that commercial confidence has sunk so far, that scarcely any dishonesty in men of the highest standing, and scarcely any carelessness on the part of those who manage the funds of others, can depress it much further.

The Norristown, Pa., *Herald* said : " To save composition, every well-regulated newspaper office should keep the fol lowing form in type : The————savings bank of————suspended yesterday morning. The president Mr.————, who is a defaulter to a large amount, has disappeared, and it is believed that he has sailed for Europe."

These " conservative " papers were largely responsible for all this villainy.

No More Trade Dollars.—October. 15, 1877, John Sherman ordered the Philadelphia Mint to stop coining trade dollars. Silver had so depreciated that speculators were making money, shoving them on the people.

Our Per-Capita Currency.—The following table, compiled from official sources, by B. S. Heath, shows, the amount of our circulation per capita; and its contraction from 1865 to 1877 :

Year.	Currency.	Population.	Per Cap.
1865	$1,651,282,373	34,819,531	47.42
1866	1,803,702,726	35,537,148	50.76
1867	1,330,414,677	36,269,502	36.68
1868	817,199,773	37,016,949	22.08
1869	750,025,989	37,779,800	19.85
1870	740,039,179	38,558,371	17.19
1871	734,244,774	39,750,073	18.47
1872	736,349,912	40,978,607	17.97

Year.	Currency.	Population.	Per Cap.
1873	738,291,749	42,245,110	17.48
1874	779,031,589	43,550,756	17.84
1875	778,176,250	44,890,705	17.33
1876	735,358,832	46,284,344	15.89
1877	696,443,394	47,714,829	14.60

N. A. Dunning, in "The Philosophy of Price," gives a similar table, with the amount of currency decreased by from 30 million in 1868 to 90 million in 1877, through some discrepancy in their calculations. Dunning continues thus:

Year.	Currency.	Population.	Per Cap.
1878	$549,540,187	48,935,306	11.23
1879	534,424,248	50,155,783	10.65
1880	528,524,267	51,660,456	10.23
1881	610,632,433	53,210,269	11.48
1882	657,404,084	54,806,577	11.97
1883	648,205,895	56,450,714	11.48
1884	591,476,978	58,144,235	10.17
1885	533,405,001	59,888,562	8.90

DEBTS IN THE UNITED STATES.—The Act of Feb 12, 1873, took from silver its "lawful money" quality in sums above $5, and the law of May, 1876, totally demonetized the trade dollar,—leaving nothing but gold with which to pay debts, taxes, interest, and for the redemption of bank bills. The following figures do not overreach the actual amount of the individual, municipal, corporate and national indebtedness of the country in 1877:

Greenbacks to the amount of.....	$350,000,000
National bank currency.	300,000,000
Notes payable in bank.	900,000,000
National bank deposits.......... ...	1,000,000,000
Savings bank deposits........... ...	1,500,000,000
Mortgages, not less than......... ...	3,000,000,000
Railroad bonds................. ...	5,000,000,000
Public debt................... ...	1,700,000,000
Private indebtedness............. ...	200,000,000
Municipal bonds................. ...	375,000,000
	$14,325,000,000

It is no wonder that, with statements like this before them, our people hustled to get silver remonetized.

THE ENGLISH VIEW OUR AMAZING FOLLY.—After review-
ing the state of trade in Great Britain and Germany, the
London *Telegraph* says, with reference to the United States :
—In 1876 thirty American railways, covering 3,846 miles in
length, and representing $217,848,000 of invested capital,
were sold under foreclosure of mortgages. Receivers in bank-
rupty were appointed or foreclosures determined upon in the
case of 46 other lines, extending over 7,576 miles and involving total expenditure in construction and maintenance of
$536,000,000. Ten railway companies figure in the list of
defaulters for the same year, whose aggregate lines measure
2,757 miles, and show $156,661,000 to have been invested
in them. This making a total of 86 railways, consisting of
14,179 mileage, and exhibiting a loss to the shareholders of
$912,509,000. The list, therefore, as far as it has been made
up, discloses the painful fact that, during the past year, one-
fifth of the entire railway mileage of the United States,—
representing a similar proportion of the total railway capital
of the country,—was brought, from various causes, into a
state of insolvency. But this melancholy revelation naturally
awakens our curiosity to learn how far the business classes
proper shared in the general financial visitation.

Out of 630,099 firms in the Union reported to be engaged
in business in 1876, no fewer than 9,002 became bankrupt :
and the gross amount of their liabilities reached the sum of
$191,117,786. The increase in the number of failures com-
pared with 1875 was 1,350 ; while the latter year showed
the number to be 2,000 more than in 1874. The total indebtedness of insolvents in 1876, however, notwithstanding the
augmented number of failures, was less than in 1875, by
nearly $10,000,000. But the description of firms which col-
lapsed last year, combined with the reduced average liabilities chargeable upon the previous year, plainly indicates that
the wave of financial embarrassment is not yet spent ; and
that, after engulfing the mammoth houses, it has been gradually swallowing up the smaller traders. It is, moreover,
significant of the manner in which business has been conducted in the several divisions of the Union, that the failures
in the Middle States are one in every 57 trading firms, and in
the Western States one in every 72. In the Eastern States,
notwithstanding their reputation for wealth and stability,
one in every 59 firms has succumbed ; while in the Southern

States which have been depopulated and exhausted by the civil war, and are still laboring under heavy political disabilities, the percentage of failure is one in every 64.

1878.

A YEAR OF NATIONAL SHAME.—Under this head the N. Y. *Herald* descanted as follows early in 1878 :—The year that has just closed is altogether the most disgraceful in American annals ; if disgrace is to be measured by the exposure rather than by the perpetration of stupendous breaches of trust. If the year 1877 has any competitor for this bad pre-eminence it is the year 1871, when the monstrous robberies of the Tweed Ring were dragged forth into publicity ; and the rascalities of the infamous Credit Mobilier were fastened by proofs upon their authors and accomplices.—But in those instances the villainy was not so widely diffused. There was one great focus of corruption at Washington ; but the taint and rottenness had not spread into every walk of business, and every kind of private and semi-public transaction. But at present, the whole atmosphere seems reeking with foulness. Every description of fraud and embezzlement is repeated, in every part of the country; until their accumulated magnitude seems like Pelion piled upon Ossa, in the ancient fiction. It is difficult to say whether frauds have attained a ranker growth here in New York, or in Philadelphia, or in Boston, or in Chicago, or in San Francisco, or in some of the smaller towns. In proportion to population and opportunities there would seem to be but little difference.—There is no conceivable variety of swindling which has not been practiced ; but the most execrable of all is the widespread violation of sacred trusts, by institutions and men charged with the care of property belonging to the unprotected and the helpless. There are degrees in the turpitude of theft ; and none is so base as that which takes the bread from the mouth of the widow and the orphan, as so many false guardians and rotten savings-banks and life insurance companies have done.

THE PARTIAL " UPRISING OF A GREAT PEOPLE."—1877 was the hopelessly horrible year. Light began to dawn in the Spring of 1878. The trodden worm began to turn, to some purpose. Then began " the uprising of a great people." The agony was as great as ever, and the misery more appalling. 800,000 of our Eastern middle-class, in despair of any improvement, realized what they could on their small stores, factories, shops and farms; and fled west of the Mississippi,—knowing that if they delayed longer they would soon be going a-foot. The "pound-of-flesh" men were frightened; and yielded a few points, such as the Congress resolution of January 20, 1878, asserting the right to pay bonds in silver, the Bland Act of February 28, 1878, remonetizing silver, the Act of March 31, 1878, reissuing 44 million of Greenbacks; and the decree of John Sherman in October, 1878, remonetizing the Greenback by making it receivable for custom duties. These made some prosperity possible. Of the people who fled West, say a quarter made a new start by living in dug-outs on the prairies; a quarter perished from disease and privation and heart-break; a quarter took wage service; and a quarter wandered back East to finish their lives in various servitudes.

BONDS NOT PAYABLE IN GOLD.—The following resolution was adopted by the Senate January 25, 1878, and by the House January 28, 1878 : the vote being in the Senate 42 to 20, and in the House 189 to 79 :—"That all bonds of the United States issued or authorized to be issued under the said acts of Congress hereinbefore recited are payable, principal and interest, at the option of the Government of the United States, in silver dollars of the coinage of the United States, containing 412½ grains each of standard silver; and that to restore to its coinage such silver coins as a legal tender in payment of said bonds, principal and interest, is not in violation of the public faith, nor in derogation of the rights of the public creditor."

The acts referred to are the Funding Act of 1870, authorizing the issue of 4's and 4½'s for refunding purposes; and the Resumption Act of 1875, authorizing the further issue of the same bonds for resumption purposes. The resolution was a public notice to the whole world, that the nation would pay its debt in silver, if it should so elect. With the exception of $200,000,000 of 4½'s and $75,000,000 of 4's every United States bond outstanding in 1886, was issued subsequent to the passage of this resolution, and was subject to its declaration. Of the excepted bonds, the $200,000,000 of 4½'s became due in 1891.

In spite of the above facts Chas E. Coon, late Asst Sec.

of the Treasury, was urging in the *Herald* in 1886, that " we have agreed to redeem these bonds in gold coin." Coon is one of those coons who start a still hunt for a fat Wall Street berth, as soon as they get into office in Washington. His Wall St. concern—Bateman, and Co., came to grief in 1890 : also a concern in Buffalo in which he was silent partner.

THE BLAND BILL PASSED OVER HAYES'S VETO.—The Act of February 28, 1878, monetized the silver dollar over the veto of the President. Silver dollars of 412½ grains 9-10 fine, are made full legal-tender for everything, unless specially provided to be paid in something else. These dollars are to be coined by and for the Government; not more than $4,000,000 per month, nor less than $2,000,000. The holders of these dollars can deposit them in the Treasury, and receive certificates therefor, which certificates are to be full legal-tender for everything. This is the celebrated " Bland Bill ", that has caused the silver dollar to be called the Bland dollar, the Bland cart-wheel, etc.

––––––

Senator Teller said in his speech of May 14, 1890 :—During the ten years preceding December 31, 1877, we produced in the United States not less than $425,000,000 of gold ; and of silver not less than $270,000,000 ; or a total of gold and silver of $695,000,000. Yet, in the month of February, 1878, when the Bland bill became a law, our total amount of gold and silver, exclusive of subsidiary coin, was less than $180,000,000, of which $167,500,000, was gold. During the ten years named, we had exported $335,000,000 more gold than we had imported ; and $185,000,000 more silver than we had imported ; making $520,000,000 of gold and silver in excess of imports. During the ten years succeeding the passage of the Bland bill, we imported $198,634,763 of gold in excess of our exports ; and we kept at home our own production, amounting to more than $420,000,000. So that, in ten years, we added to our stock of gold more than $600,000,000, less what might have been used in the arts ; and our stock of gold is now estimated by the Treasury Department to be $684,-000,000. We have now of gold and silver $1,038,000,000. Surely the coinage of silver did not drive gold out of the country ; nor did it keep it out.

––––––

February 22, 1878, the Greenback Labor Party, meeting in convention at Toledo, Ohio, formulated an elaborate platform ; the money planks of which have been much used by money reformers since then.

March 31, 1878, Congress authorized the reissue of the 44 millions of Greenbacks that had been destroyed.

Discussion was hot and heavy in 1878 as to whether the U. S. currency was near two billions in 1865. The *Inter-Ocean*, that now stoutly denies it, in 1878 printed the following editorial reference to this subject :—

The anti-Greenback papers of this city are in the habit of stating, every now and then, that the volume of currency has been but slightly decreased, and that the amount per capita in 1865 and 1878 varied very little, being from $14 to $15. We produce below a table compiled from official sources :

Year.	Paper Money	Population	Per Capita
1865	$1,651,282,373	34,819,581	$47 42
1866	1,803,702,726	35,537,148	50 76
1872	735,358,832	46,284,344	15 89
1877	696,443,394	47,714,829	14 60

The currency included in the above amounts comprises demand and one and two year Treasury notes authorized by the Acts of December 27, 1857, December 17, 1860, and March 2, 1861 ; temporary ten-day loans and one year certificates of indebtedness ; Treasury notes payable in two years and in sixty days ; 7-30 three-year notes ; compound interest notes ; three per cent. certificates ; non-interest bearing demand and legal-tender notes ; fractional currency ; State bank notes and National bank notes.

The bulk of these issues were made legal tender by the Government.

We are prepared to prove that all the above issues were employed as currency, and went to make up the volume of circulating medium.

It is in our opinion the highest of folly for the opponents of the so-called National party to deny facts so well established as is that of the contraction of the currency. If that party cannot be defeated by a fair and honest statement of the truth, then it had better be allowed to win.

ERNEST SEYD ON SILVER DEMONETIZATION.—On May 18, 1878, Judge W. D. Kelley referred in the House to a previous speech of his which was: " I avail myself of the two minutes allowed me to reply to the gentleman from Maine, Mr. Frye, and the gentleman from New York, Mr. Hewitt, and to tell them why prices have fallen in every country, why machinery is idle and the laboring people of all countries in poverty, and unable to consume each other's productions, or to contribute to the revenues of their Government. Prices, sir, the world over, had adjusted themselves to the volume of gold, silver and paper money in circulation ; and when Germany and the United States thrust silver, which was about one-half of the metallic money of the world, out of the category of the money metals ; *when Germany prohibited the circulation of any bank-note under $25.00 ;* when the United States contracted its paper money from two thousand millions to practically less than five hundred millions,—they decreed the terrible shrinking of prices, and consequent ruin, which have taken place throughout America and Europe, and thus deprived the laboring people of the world of employment, and of the ability to earn the means to contribute to the public revenue."

He then said that the contractionists and monometalists sitting near had told him that this two-minute speech was " the best joke of his life." To intensify this joke, he would now present to them a paper read April 5, 1878, before the British Society of Arts by Ernest Seyd, F.R.S., one of the most distinguished statisticians in the world. It related to the stagnation of business in England. Mr. Kelley said that though Mr. Seyd did not consider the effect of the contraction of paper money in America and Germany, it was evident that "all the evils accruing from silver demonetization were immensely enhanced by our withdrawal of more than a thousand million dollars of paper money."

Mr. Seyd, after a full exposition of the wealth and financial affairs of England, showed that in 1873, our panic year, which followed three years of wonderful success in England, the balance of trade turned against her. In 1875, 6 and 7, it rose successively to £4,000,000, £34,000,000 and £57,-000,000 against her. He says, truly enough, that in 1873,

Central and South American States began to default on their bonds. This reached, in 1875, $50,000,000. In 1876, Peru and Uruguay bankrupted, with a loss of $150,000,000 to England; and Turkey with a loss of $400,000,000!! The strangest omission in Mr. Seyd's estimates is that of the default on the interest on $500,000,000 of American railway and other securities in our panic years. This certainly had much to do with England's depression. Perhaps, he did not enumerate this because he considered that only the interest was permanently in default. He was about right; as most of them had recovered by 1882; though the stockholders of most of the companies held in the grip of these bonds, had been ruined. The latter-day bond has a tighter hold than the ancient ones; especially when the strongest nations are ready to re-rivet them by aid of army and navy; as the Egyptians have discovered of late. Ah, where are the angels to enter the prison-house and cast off these bonds, as they did for Apostle Peter?

FOURTEEN DOLLARS PER CAPITA.—The circulation outstanding June 18, 1878, is shown as follows, by Secretary McCulloch's report:

State Bank circulation	426,504
National " "	324,514,284
Demand Notes	62,297
Legal-Tender "	346,681,016
One and Two Years Notes of 1863	90,485
Compound Interest "	274,920
Fractional Currency	16,547,768
	$688,597,274

The same statement estimates the population of the United States at 47,483,000 or 48 million in round numbers.

This gives a per capita circulation of $14, or $30 less than in 1864, 1865.

A MILLION AND A HALF GREENBACK VOTE.—The most remarkable occurrence in 1878 was the extraordinary growth of the Greenback-Labor party; which in November polled a million four hundred thousand votes; and elected 20 Congressmen; about 15 of whom remained faithful to the party.

One of the prominent features of this movement was what was called "Peter Cooper's *Advocate*"; though the paper was only under the auspices of Cooper. It attained a cir-

culation of 700,000 real subscribers ; and sent out 30 tons of
paper weekly. The writer of this, Samuel Leavitt, was
managing editor during the six months, March to September, when it was "booming". It afterward went down,
through mismanagement of the proprietor, Walter Shupe, as
rapidly as it rose. I gave a column and a half to the N. Y.
Sun about the paper when I left it in September. Here is
what the N. Y. *Times* said of it :—

In short, the Greenback organization in the South, as in
other parts of the country, is, in different localities, made up
of different material. In North Carolina, the men engaged
in the new movement are for the most part, white mechanics,
and small white farmers who are in debt—men who have
nothing to lose by inflation, repudiation and communism ;
and who believe that they can gain nothing by the success of
either of the old parties. There can be no doubt that the
people of the mountains and the small farmers referred to
have to a great extent been won over to the new party by the
teachings of the *Advocate :* which, at Peter Cooper's expense
it is claimed, has been sent into the remote inland counties
by the car-load. At all events they are in it ; and the Democrats are evidently very much afraid that they will remain
firm in their determination to vote for its candidates.

THE GREENBACK REMONETIZED.—Much has been said of
the quiet, secretive way in which Sherman & Co. demonetized
silver in 1873. On October 1, 1878, in consequence of the
Greenback uproar, voiced specially by Peter Cooper's *Advocate*, he, as boss of the Republican and ruling party, caused
a change of even greater importance, in that sly, sleek, quiet,
unobtrusive way of his. He, on that day, as autocrat of his
party, ORDERED THE GREENBACKS TO BE TAKEN FOR DUTIES
AT THE CUSTOM HOUSE. In this act, sneakingly done, the
Republican party completely changed front, financially ; and
made the specie resumption of January 1, 1879, A GREENBACK
REMONETIZATION. The Democratic leaders were too ignorant
of finance to see the change of the Republican Party's policy,
from a specie resumption to a Greenback remonetization.
The National banks had accomplished this result, to save
them from bankruptcy, and to extend their charters for 20
years longer. The Republican leaders claimed that it was a
resumption of specie payments. *It was simply a change of
the common Greenback into a* LEGAL TENDER DEMAND NOTE,

15

which was always receivable for duties. The Republican leaders soon discovered that the Greenbacks became better than coin ; after they were received for duties. They secretly resolved to support the Greenback system, in order to preserve the National banks, to restore trade and save the party. These results were obtained. The slow-brained Democrats were cajoled by Belmont, Hewitt, Tilden & Co. into rank gold-buggery.

CHICAGO TRIBUNE ON THE FRAUD OF 1873.—There has been much discussion about the fraud by which silver was secretly demonetized here in 1873. The Chicago *Tribune* threw some light on it in 1878. It said that the bill was concocted by " an English gentleman," Mr. Boutwell the Comptroller of the Currency, and two or three other American capitalists. The work of stealing it through Congress was intrusted to Mr. Hooper of Massachusetts, in the House, " who is a capitalist and money-lender ; " and to John Sherman in the Senate. It was not permitted to be read in the House ; and Mr. Hooper deliberately lied, in debate upon it, in response to the inquiry of members regarding its features ; and Speaker Blaine, by extraordinary ruling, helped to force it through the House—only 123 members being present. Mr. Blaine undoubtedly was in the secret of the whole scheme himself. His unheard-of ruling warrants this belief.

———

There was much hot fighting all over the country at this time, as to whether the currency had been reduced, the goldbugs insisting that it had not been. Such leading papers as Chicago *Inter-O.ean*, Cincinnati *Enquirer* and St. Louis *Republican* talked as the *Inter-Ocean* does in the following sentence. After claiming that we had about 1,804 millions of currency in 1866 [see that year] it adds : " We are prepared to prove that all the above issues were employed as currency."

THE LEADING PAPER CAUGHT NAPPING. The N. Y. *Tribune* probably put the following in cold type in 1878, because English of Indianapolis was a Democrat. It is too keen in these days, to print so much truth about usury :—

Any one who has lived in the West during the past five or six years can readily judge what effect English's hard cash and mortgage record will have upon the voters of his section. No class of men have made themselves so obnoxious as the Western money-sharks [except the Eastern.—S. L.]. In the

years succeeding the war, thousands of men who, by industry
and economy, had succeeded in laying up a few hundred dollars, emigrated to the West and purchased a farm, or em-
barked in business. Most of them, trusting to their past
success, gave mortgages on their property, paying from 15 to
30 per cent. interest. Had times continued prosperous they
would have been able, undoubtedly, to meet obligations.
But as soon as the business depression began, they found
themselves at the mercy of their creditors ; who exacted the
last dollar from the poor debtor. The creditor had foreseen
just the financial crisis which occurred. Money at once became scarce and real estate a drug in the market. With their
long purses, they knew they were able to carry the property
until the advent of better times. So, the moment there was
any default in paying an installment, or even the interest,
the sheriff was at the door. The practice became known in
the West as " squeezing ". The wrong lay not in the creditor
asking his just due, but in his taking advantage of the debtor's
embarrassment, to gain a legal title to property worth many
times the mortgage, and it is adding insult to injury when
one of this class asks for the suffrages of farmers and small
traders, from whom he has " squeezed " every dollar possible.

The *Tribune*, which was one of the chief causes of our
" seven years of famine in a land of plenty," printed this in
1878, just before " resumption " :—While the laborer, whose
wages were reduced,—or the capitalist, large or small, whose
money was invested in manufactures or stocks which depreciated in value,—has suffered severely, there is a very
numerous class who have become much richer by the
changes in values. Men whose capital was invested in
mortgages, for example, receive the same secure, and in
most cases, undiminished income ; while the actual cost of
living for them has fallen 33 per cent. since 1876.

The Clearing-house of New York passed a resolution in
1878, when the Sub-Treasury was admitted to the Clearing-
house, forbidding the use of silver certificates in settlement
of Clearing-house balances.

The National Banks, in 1878, were bragging about their
having paid 86 million dollars in taxes in 14 years. They
said nothing about having drawn 350 millions of interest, in
that time.

The New York *Tribune* said early in 1879 :—A part of the nation's net earnings, in 1878, was applied to the extinguishment of foreign debt—perhaps $300,000,000. Another part was secured by the Treasury, in preparation for resumption—about $94,000,000. But, if the estimate of Mr. David A. Wells is correct—that the nation accumulates wealth, in excess of all its expenditures, at the rate of about $500,000,-000 yearly,—over $100,000,000 of idle capital must have been stored up during the year 1878 ; and an amount nearly or quite as large in 1877, awaiting a restoration of confidence and prosperity.

FAILURES.—The following table of failures is taken from Hunt's Merchants' Magazine for the years from 1862 to 1870; the rest from other sources ; up to 1871 they are only for Northern States.

Year.	Failures.	Liabilities.
1862	1,652	$ 23,049,000
1863	495	7,899,000
1864	520	8,579,000
1865	530	17,625,000
1866	632	47,333,000
1867	2,386	86,218,000
1868	2,197	57,275,000
1869	2,411	65,246,000
1870	3,160	79,697,000
1871	2,915	85,252,000
1872	4,069	121,056,000
1873	5,181	228,490,000
1874	5,830	159,239,000
1875	7,740	201,060,353
1876	9,002	191,117,786
1877	8,872	190,669,930
1878	10,478	234,363,132
1879	6,658	98,149,053
1880	4,735	65,752,000
1881	5,582	81,155,932
1882	6,738	102,000,000
1883	9,184	172,874,172
1884	10,968	226,343,427
1885	11,211	267,340,264

Mark how few the failures during what the gold-bugs call

"inflation times "; how they climbed toward the panic year,
1873 ; and how heavily they bore during our "return to
honest money!" And how steadily they climbed again in
the ensuing honest money epoch.

ONE SOWETH—ANOTHER REAPETH.—That worst of all
our famine years, 1878, produced the following harvest of
interest, according to New York *Tribune* of January, 1879 :—
Some surprise has been expressed at the fact that, while
many millions of the four per cents. have been taken by
permanent investors, who are not holders of called sixes, the
purchases of railroad bonds, and the safest investment stocks,
have also been very large. During last week, the recorded
sales of railway bonds, in the Stock Exchange, amounted to
about $6,000,000, and during the previous week, to nearly
$5,000,000. It is presumed that the unrecorded sales were
much larger. But it should be remembered that the amount
disbursed in interest and dividends has been very large.
Besides the January interest on the public debt,—about $22,-
000,000,—the interest on bonds of solvent railroads amounts
to about $47,000,000 each half year, the greater part of
which is payable in January. The half-yearly dividends on
paying railroad stock amounts to at least $35,000,000. The
interest on municipal, county and State bonds, which still
pay promptly, must exceed $25,000,000 each half year. The
dividends on National bank stocks, are $14,000,000 half-
yearly. And the dividends on manufacturing stocks, even
in the present depressed condition of industries, must exceed $40,000,000 half-yearly. Of about $161,000,000 thus
disbursed in interest and dividends for the half-year,—exclusive of interest on the public debt,—certainly more than
half is paid in January ; so that the sum disbursed in January, to be reinvested, or applied to the personal expenses of
investors, must be over $100,000,000. As long as United
States bonds, and other first-class securities are offered at
low rates and in large amounts, a large proportion of the
sums disbursed will naturally seek such investments ; the
more because such securities may be expected to advance in
price, before the return of full prosperity in commerce and
manufactures invites enlargement of the capital therein
employed.

1879.

A RESOLUTE START.—The following resolutions of the

New York Associated Banks took effect January 1, 1879—the day of Resumption :—" 1. To decline to receive gold coins as ' special deposits ' ; but accept and treat them only as "lawful money"! 2. To abolish special exchanges of gold checks at the Clearing-house. 3. To pay and receive balances between banks at Clearing-house in either gold or the United States legal-tender notes. 4. To receive silver dollars upon deposit only under special contract to withdraw the same in kind. 5. To prohibit payments of balances at Clearing-house in silver certificates or in silver dollars, excepting as subsidiary coin in small sums (say under $10). 6. To discontinue gold special accounts, by notice to dealers to terminate them on January 1."

Thus in every way they " headed off " gold payments and the use of silver.

———

The New York *Times*, in 1878, had concluded an article on resumption with the following—which is very noticeable from such a paper :—The simple fact is the Associated Banks of New York propose to use their power to exclude the silver dollar from commerce, in defiance of the laws and the will of the people. They must naturally expect stubborn and persistent opposition ; and such opposition will not be carried beyond the bounds of reason, if it shall compel the banks to share in the work of resumption.

A DEVOURING DEMON IN PHILADELPHIA.—Judge Kelley, summing up his speech in Congress on Resumption, February 14, 1879, gives this as the state of things in Philadelphia, in January of that year : "Thus it is shown, Mr. Speaker, that by the erection of 22,111 new buildings ; by the improvement and extension of 7,045 other buildings ; by the opening of more than 54 miles of new streets, and the curbing, paving and laying sidewalks of 99 miles of street, by the laying of 92½ miles of gas-mains, and the erection of 2519 public lamps ; by the addition of nearly 131 miles of water-mains, and the construction of nearly 57 miles of main sewers, and the increase by about 70 per cent. of the foreign commerce of the city, *the value of Philadelphia has been reduced $13,000,000.* Consequently, they who have accomplished this work have not delved and wrought and builded for themselves. No, sir, ruin has pursued, as an avenging demon, enterprise wherever it has engaged in productive business. He only has profited by their toil who has wrapped his talent in a napkin of untaxed government bonds, and brought it forth for use only when the products of labor, energy and enterprise were to be sacrificed at sheriff's or other forced sales.

" But, sir, the sheriff's sale was not the only joyous event with which the stricken people of Philadelphia were made to welcome the great fact of equivalency between our paper money and gold. For on the first day of the 'glad New Year,' the owners of 13,582 properties, within the limits of the city, on opening their morning papers, were pleasantly greeted by name, by the receiver of taxes, with notice that their taxes for 1878 were in default : and that unless they were paid on or before the 15th of the month, preliminary steps would be taken to secure their collection. Living in enforced idleness, as thousands of the most industrious and thrifty of them are, think you that this was a grateful New Year's greeting? "

He shows, then, that immediately after resumption, the following appeared in the organ of the Philadelphia sheriff, the *Record:*

" Sheriff Wright, on January 6, will begin the largest sale of real estate ever held by any sheriff in this city. There are 692 writs, covering about 1,000 properties. The sale on the first day will begin at 4 o'clock, in the new court-house, and extend from No. 370 on the list to No. 692."

About that time in 1879, the Philadelphia *Times* called a halt, in " paying large salaries and erecting costly public buildings, while the money to pay for them can only be got by the seizure of citizens' property at the hands of the sheriff."

Well might Philadelphians ask, with Solon Chase of Maine, " Who gets the hay ? "

This, mind you, was in thrifty Philadelphia, the fountain-head of co-operative building societies—the city of homes—the city where people own their homes.

More or less.

ENGLAND A THOUSAND MILLIONS OUT.—Judge Kelley, on April 17, 1879, quoted Ernest Seyd, " the ablest statistician in England," as saying that demonetizing of silver by Germany had cost England a thousand million dollars of her capital, in three years; and that she was losing in a larger

ratio in 1879. " Her factories and mines are closed. Such
is her immense wealth, that her land is in parks and game-
preserves for the sport of the aristocracy and the gentry.
She looks to us and other nations for most of her food. As
for Germany, after her great victory over the French, her condition is worse than that of England."

CALIFORNIA CLEANSED.—1879 saw a purifying cyclone
sweep over California, the results of which were a new and
better constitution; the driving of the gamblers of the stock
exchange from San Francisco to New York, and the fall of
seats in their stock exchange from $35,000 to $5,000. They
swarmed in New York in the Boreel Building; but did not
succeed, as expected, in teaching all our servant-girls and
longshoremen to gamble in stocks, California fashion.

GOLD BIG-BUG PAPERS. — About this time the N. Y.
Graphic, a silver paper, said:—The New York press does
represent the "syndicate " and the large money-lenders more
than any other class of the community. It is believed, and
stated, without contradiction so far, that the N. Y. *World* is
under the control of August Belmont, and the Philadelphia
members of the syndicate. It is they who are the money-
backers of the paper; and it is understood that it is their
interests, both in politics and business, which are represented
by the course of that journal.

The N. Y. *Times* is supposed to be inspired by ex-governor
Morgan, also a member of the syndicate. Then the other
influences back of the *Times* are the very rich men who have
direct relations with Wall Street, and the leading money interests there.

The *Tribune*, it is popularly supposed, is partially, if not
wholly, owned by Jay Gould. His interests are those of a
" bear ". By insisting upon the gold unit of value, prices
are depressed, and the millionaires have common interests
the world over; being the representatives of the creditor
class, who naturally wish their money to have the largest
possible purchasing power.

The *Herald* is owned by a very rich man, James Gordon
Bennett; supposed to be worth some six million of dollars,
and, of course, his interests are with the creditor class. •

The *Journal of Commerce* and the *Bulletin* are peculiarly subject to Wall Street influences, especially those of the great
creditors.

The *Sun* has lately given some signs of repentance of its golden heresy.

Of course the creditor interests are powerful in the *Evening Post* office, although, we judge, the attempt to pay in gold debts contracted in paper money, in the purchase of real estate, has proven a very serious business for the chief proprietor of that paper. [Poet Bryant.]

Augustus Schell, whose relations to the syndicate are well-known, is a large stockholder in the *Express* newspaper; which accounts for the milk in that cocoanut.

It will be thus seen that, without any actual bribery, the New York press, because of its proprietorship, is on the side of the gold big-bugs, instead of the people. It represents a class that has money out at interest; and wish to get the largest possible return for their investments. We do not say that any editor, publisher or proprietor of any of the New York papers is purchased with money; but, naturally, these organs represent the people who own them, and their interests are very different from those of the great mass of the American people.

———

And now, in December, 1891, a further evidence of the stuff there is in the editors of the "leading papers" is found in this concerning that infamous creature W. H. Hurlbert, now hiding from arrest (for perjury and wronging a woman), in Mexico. This passage is from his old paper, the N. Y. *World:*—At about that time Hurlbert was taken on *The World* by Manton Marble, the editor, as a writer of editorials. Later, when Tom Scott bought *The World* to use it for business purposes, Hurlbert was made editor. He was retained in the editorial chair by Mr. Jay Gould, when the paper passed into Gould's hands. With the advent of the present proprietor of *The World* Hurlbert's services were dispensed with.

THE INTEREST EQUALS THE PUBLIC DEBT.—The interest paid on the public debt, from 1860 to 1879, amounted to $1,916,577,099.35—an amount greater than that of the entire debt in 1864; just before the close of the war. Such facts should be branded into the American mind; and set there " as with lead in the rock forever."

The Congressional Silver Commission estimated the total

indebtedness of our people in 1879 at thirteen billions—
about the same as in 1877. This was one-half the total
wealth of the country.

WHAT GOLD THE BANKS HAD.—Judge Warwick Martin
wrote in 1880 :—

Some bogus statesmen, when it suits their purposes,
insist that nothing but gold and silver coin is capital. The
National banks have existed 16 years. It might be interesting to learn from the reports of the Comptroller of the Currency, how much gold and silver coin these banks have had,
as capital, for the last 16 years. * * From 1864 to 1869 these
banks had no coin capital. From 1869 to 1879, the average
was $26,000,000; nearly all of which was held in the city
of New York. Sometimes these banks have held more, but
often less than this average. * * According to the bullion
definition, for ten years these banks had an average of three
per cent. capital. At another time not one per cent. Now
[1880.] they have $109,000,000 to secure over $1,204,000,000
liabilities. They have aggregated coin capital very slowly;
though in the last 16 years these banks have received from
the Treasury over $300,000,000 in gold : which they sold at a
premium.

BONDS SOLD AFTER JANUARY 1, 1879.—Martin said :—The
four per cent. bonds sold after this date were not purchased
because resumption had taken place. They were purchased
because business was still in a prostrate condition, and was
purposely so kept, the same as before so-called resumption,
so that bonds might be sold. It would not do to permit
business to revive until these bonds were sold. The business of the country had to be kept down, so that there would
be no investments of money in anything but these bonds.
Business, therefore, remained prostrate for more than six
months after professed resumption. There was, up to the
last of July, 1879, scarcely a ripple upon the business waters.
The purchase of bonds for legal-tender notes, was about the
only business being transacted. No other could be permitted, or the bonds could not be sold. On April 18, the bonds
were all contracted for, but they were not paid for until
months after the sales. To permit business to revive and
the money of the country to be employed therein, before this
money for the bonds sold was collected, would have caused
the failure of the banks and bankers composing the syn-

dicate, to whom the bonds had been sold. Time had to be given these banks and bankers to make sales of these bonds in England and in the United States, or they could make no money out of their purchases, and might be ruined. This was done at the expense of the business of the country. The people had to suffer. The syndicate had to be and were protected. So soon as the bonds were all paid for, the money in the banks and in the Treasury, which had been so long locked up, was released.

Resumption was not attempted until legal-tender notes were made equal to coin. This is admitted by Mr. Sherman. If these notes had not been made equal to coin by being received for duties, no resumption, so-called, could have taken place. The whole $346,000,000 legal-tender notes would have gone to the Treasury for redemption, as the law contemplated. There being in the Treasury for redemption purposes only $133,000,000 coin, a failure of the Government would have taken place.

GOLD RUSHES FROM EUROPE.—After the money lords let up on us, in 1879 (as they promised they would, if we paid "the pound of flesh"), and gave us prosperity,—gold rushed hither from Europe. We had been too poor to get into debt to her latterly; and she had shoved the bonds back on us, when they rose to a high figure. So when her poor crops forced her to use our food products, she had to shell out gold for them. The N. Y. *World* said, December 1879:—All Europe said, six months ago, that by the end of the present year, the balance of trade in our favor in merchandise transactions, would become a balance against us. But Europe is changing its mind. The Bank of France alone, since June 1, last, has lost over 54 millions of dollars in gold; which has come to New York; and the drain still continues, to-day, as severe as ever. On August 1, 1879, the Bank of England had more than 35 millions of pounds sterling of coin and bullion. On November 26, 1879, it had but 28 millions. The coin and bullion stock in the Bank of Germany fell between September 1 and October 15, 1879, by at least three millions of pounds sterling. According to the best attainable information, the stock of gold and silver in the principal European banks, in October last, was about 1,000 millions of dollars; of which about 400 millions were in silver.

PAPER MONEY IN THE UNITED STATES FOR 26 YEARS.

Amount of Each Kind of Paper Currency in the United States, each Year for Twenty-six Years, in Millions.

Paper Money in United States for 26 years.	Demand and 1 and 2 year Treasury notes (Acts of March 12, 1861, Dec. 17, 1860, and Dec. 27, 1857) outstanding July 1.	Temporary 10-day loans, and 1-year certificates of Indebtedness, July 1, each year.	Treasury notes, payable in 2 yrs. and in 60 days (Act of March 3, 1863), July 1, each year.	7-30 3 year notes, July 1, each year.	Compound interest notes, July 1, each year.	3 per cent. certificates, July 1, each year.	Non interest bearing Demand and Legal Tender notes (Acts of July 17, 1861, Feb. 25, 1862, July 11, 1862, March 3, 1863).	Fractional currency.	Nation'l Banks.	State Banks.	Total of Bank-notes and of unfunded Government Debt, circulating to any extent as money, each year.
									Bank-note circulation, Jan. 1, each year.		
1854										205	205
1855										187	187
1856										196	156
1857										215	215
1858										155	155
1859										193	133
1860	20									207	207
1861	3									202	222
1862		108		123			151	20		184	445
1863		259	153	140	15		382	23		239	1,044
1864		243	42	109	194		432	25			968
1865		205	3	673	159	50	433	29			1,654
1866		148	1	807	122	52	401	28	67	45	1,804
1867		20	1	489	28	46	372	33	213	7	1,330
1868		14		38	3	32	356	32	291	4	817
1869				1	2	12	356	40	294	3	750
1870					1		356	41	291	2	740
1871							356	41	293	2	734
1872							358	45	302	2	736
1873							356	46	318	2	738
1874							382	42	336		779
1875							376	34	350		778
1876							370		331		735
1877							360		317		677
1878							347		325		671
1879							347		337		684

From Heath's "Labor and Finance."   All but the last column is a quite rough estimate, rejecting all sums below a half-million.

CHAPTER XV.

1880 to 1885.

THE TRIUMPH OF THE PLUTOCRATS.

1880.

PRESIDENT HAYES, in a message in 1880, congratulates the country upon the successful resumption of specie. Judge Martin shows, at length, how and why it has not been successful,—has been, indeed, a farce carried out contrary to law.

———

An article in the *Political Science Quarterly*, in 1890, makes the statement that in 1879–80, one-half of all the mortgages in Indiana were foreclosed.

WHO HELD THE BONDS.—A radical paper said in 1880 :—
They used to sing us such sweet songs about the value of United States bonds as a boon to the savings-banks ; and to the money people, all over the country who wanted a safe investment for their little savings. Doubtless there was considerable truth in the song; but there is much less truth now. The following chunk of solid facts lets daylight upon the whole matter ; and we commend it to the serious attention of our readers :

The *Sunday Herald* claims to have information as to the largest holders of United States bonds. The list of these millionaires, in this country and Europe, is as follows : Mr. Vanderbilt, 37 millions ; Mrs. A. T. Stewart, 30 millions ; Jay Gould 13 millions registered and a large amount of coupon bonds ; an estate in Boston, and three or four persons in New York have 10 millions each ; the estate of Moses Taylor five millions ; D. O. Mills, four millions. These,—with an unmarried lady in New York, name not given [probably Catherine Wolfe], who has eight millions,—are the largest holders in the United States. In Europe the Rothschilds, together, hold the evidences of nearly one-quarter of the bonded debt. They have nearly 400 millions. In England

the Baroness Burdett Coutts Bartlett has 20 millions ; the
Duke of Sutherland five millions, and Sir Thomas Brassey
five millions.—*Boston Journal.*

CURRENCY OF FIFTEEN NATIONS.—B. S. Heath, gives the
following, in 1880 :—Nearly all civilized nations recognize the
sovereign right of Government to make its Treasury notes
legal tender.   In the following table, we follow the figures of
the Director of the Mint ; adding thereto the statement of
the amounts of paper money which is legal-tender in the
countries named :

Countries.	Gold.	Silver Full Tender.	Total Paper.	Paper Legal Tender.
United States...	$205,750,197	$15,206,200	$683,943,799	$346,601,000
Great Britain....	618,619,043	....	209,148,875	200,000,000
Sweden.........	15,000,000	....	11,680,000	11,680,000
Norway.........	10,000,000	....	10,300,000	10,300,000
Denmark........	20,000,000	....	18,900,000	18,900,000
France.........	733,400,000	366,700,000	466,755,000	....
Austria.........	43,200,000	27,360,000	322,938,854	128,993,411
Italy	17,000,000	....	315,000,000	305,000,000
Russia...... ...	108,000,000	....	587,907,562	360,000,000
Spain..........	130,000,000	40,000,000	33,795,000	*40,000,000
Peru	62,000	1,819,900	13,900,000	13,900,000
Brazil	....	....	91,000,000	91,000,000
Canada	6,291,385	....	29,047,742	10,674,850
Japan	30,000,000	10,000,000	143,000	*100,000,000
Turkey.........	... .	....	100,000,000	100,000,000

The following shows how we were frightening Europe
about her gold in 1880 :—Paris, September 10.   The subject
which engrosses public attention here, and throughout the
continent, is the enormous exportation of gold to America.
Notwithstanding the efforts made to arrest its outflow from
Germany, by raising the rate of discount, and the limited
payment of gold to certain centers of disbursement,the exportation is assuming alarming proportions.   The steamer
that left Hamburg on the 4th inst. took out 3,000,000 marks ;
the steamer of the 9th took out nearly 3,000,000 more ; and
Saturday's Hamburg steamer which calls at Havre, will
probably take out between 4,000,000 and 5,000,000 marks.

* As given.

At two Paris banking-houses there are large shippers of gold; and it was stated to-day that they will have shipped this week 3,000,000 francs each. The magnificent cotton crops in America, this season, will no doubt, influence the exchange against France for the next three months.

GREENBACKS AND NATIONAL BANK NOTES COMPARED.— Judge Martin made elaborate comparisons between Green-backs and National bank notes in 1880. Here are some of his points : 1. Since the first issue of National bank notes, the laws have made the legal-tender notes perform for the National banks all the offices which coin did for the two old banks of the United States, and for the State banks. 2. Legal-tender notes were, during the bank suspension in the Fall of 1873, in the city of New York, worth one per cent., and even one and a half per cent., over the notes of National ·banks. They were needed to make up the reserves of the banks, which National bank notes could not do. 3. The legal-tender notes of the United States are now worth one per cent. premium over newly-coined American gold, in all the commercial cities of Great Britain, and on the continent. They are more convenient than coin ; and preferred by travelers. They are current everywhere. 4. These legal-tender notes are worth more than gold in the large cities of the United States—owing to convenience and safety. This cannot be said of the notes of the National banks. 5. In Canada, legal-tender notes are worth two per cent. premium over gold. On the Pacific coast, they are worth from one to two per cent. Why cannot the people be supplied with this money, when they desire it so much ?

The annual meeting of the National Land, Labor and Currency League of Canada, for 1880, was held at Guelph, Canada, Mr. Wm. Wallace, M. P., President, in the chair. Their demands were precisely like those of the Greenbackers of the United States.

THE BONDED DEBTS OF ALL NATIONS.—It is given by Fawcett in his "Gold and Debt" at 32 billion dollars : taking the increase of the United States bonded indebtedness since the publication of that book, it was, in 1880, about 33 billions. The holders of these bonds against the civilized nations absorb from the product of labor an annual income of $1,-700,000,000 ; mostly payable in gold. They, to a very large extent, control the precious metals used as money, and the mines that yield them; and are very generally, in all the commercial centers, advocates of a single gold standard or specie basis money.

To Pay the Bonds at Once.—The following from the N. Y. *Times*, of October, 1880, gives the bullionist aspect of a very interesting piece of financial history. Of course, every one knows that the genuine Greenbacker,—who despises all metal money—sometimes advocates silver, " not because he loves silver more but gold less; " and knows that the more we push silver to the front, the sooner we will be rid of all metal money, except as a commodity. The *Times* said :—On April 5 of this year, Mr. Weaver of Iowa, at present the Greenback candidate for the Presidency, got a vote on certain resolutions brought in by him at the beginning of the session. He had been put off, from week to week, by the Speaker, Mr. Randall, of Pennsylvania, *who knew very well that if his party in the House were let to vote on Mr. Weaver's resolutions they would vote wrong.* The result showed that this fear of Mr. Randall's was wholly just. The resolutions declared—that there should be no further refunding; but that the United States bonds should be paid off as quickly as they could be; and to this end the Mints should be employed, to their full capacity, in coining standard silver dollars. In the 30-minutes debate which went before the vote, General Garfield made a strong speech against the resolutions. Mr. Kelley of Pennsylvania and Mr. Weaver spoke for them. Not a voice was raised on the Democratic side against them. When the vote was taken it was found that 73 Democrats, and only 2 Republicans, with 10 Greenbackers, were in favor of them; 88 Republicans with only 29 Democrats [Eastern] were opposed to them.

Pretty Good Picking.—Here is the logical results to the stockholders of the National banks, as shown by the retiring president, Wm. H. English, of the First National Bank of Indianapolis :—As an evidence of how the banks have been able to get along, in spite of the " ruinous taxation ", we append an extract from the report of Mr. Wm. H. English, upon retiring a few weeks ago from the presidency of his bank, which he says has run 14 years : " *In the meantime it has voluntarily returned $4,500,000 of capital back to its stockholders ; besides paying them in dividends $1,196,250, part of which was* *in gold. And I now turn it over to you with a capital unimpaired and $327,000 of undivided earnings on hand. To this may be fairly added premium of United States bonds on hand —at present prices amounting to $36,000; besides quite a large amount for lost and destroyed bills.*

"May I not safely leave these grand results as a permanent testimonial of the fidelity and careful and judicious management of my administration?"

According to this statement, the profits of this bank for the fourteen years it has been in existence were *Two millions and fifty-nine thousand, two hundred and fifty dollars.*

The capital stock of the bank is now half a million. We venture to assert that no legitimate business in Indiana has paid such profits, during the same period, as this bank; or, for that matter, as any well managed National bank. The banks have been carried forward upon the prosperous tides of privilege and subsidy; and to these they would now add immunity from taxation. This they are likely to secure; for they are almost all-powerful with Congress. But, woe to the Congressman who serves them in this last scheme of extortion! A day of reckoning comes.—*Terre Haute Express.*

COMPOUND INTEREST.—Occasionally a strong proof of the consuming power of interest reminds one of the impression made upon Napoleon by the study of a compound-interest table. He said: "There is one thing, to my mind, more wonderful than all the rest: viz., that the deadly fact buried in those tables has not before this devoured the whole race."

Here is a specimen: On Oct. 6, 1854, Geo. T. Walker of Santa Clara, Cal., gave Wm. Hood a note secured by a mortgage, for $1,850, for six months; interest at three per cent. a month, to be compounded if not paid at the end of each month. Mr. Walker went to Mexico before the note came due; and when he returned, in or about 1880, his creditors sued him and got judgment for $9,000,000.

Tilden was nominated in 1880, on a Wall Street platform. The Democrats had not done this since 1828, except in 1877.

GOULD BECOMES RESPECTABLE.—About 1880, Jay Gould, who began his large operations, by stealing nine million dollars from the Erie RR. (which he refunded in preference to going to jail, and covered back into his pocket, by the rising of Erie), forced himself into the "highest financial circles." We then, at length, find such men as Moses Taylor, Robt. Lenox Kennedy, J. P. Morgan and Saml. Sloane associated with him, as Western Union directors—not to mention Schell, Sage, Cornell, Dillon, Field and Huntington, who were associated with him in various enterprises.

The fountain of gambling in the United States is Wall Street. Is it honest gambling, or dishonest? Is the game "straight" or "crooked"? Mr. Henry Clews in a recent work maintains that it is "straight".

"I recollect the time," he says, "when men in the higher walks of life would have been ashamed to be seen in Wall Street. Now men in the same sphere are proud of the distinction, both socially and financially."

ANOTHER STRAW IN 1890.—Sumner, of Yale, lately came down from his high-horse, and lectured to the boys about the good and bad gambles of Wall Street. But he is too prosy and antiquated, and now they have a fresh young man right from the spot—F. W. Hopkins, Yale, '80. "Mr. Hopkins is with the brokerage firm of S. V. White & Co., of New York; and has chosen for his subject a course on 'Investment Securities.' The different forms of securities will be described and distinguished from one another, with illustrations —and the advantages and disadvantages of each for investment will be explained.

"With the exception of a few general remarks on the subject in the political economy classes, this topic has been rigidly suppressed; and never before has the open discussion of Wall Street methods been allowed in the classic precincts of old Yale."

THE TONNAGE OF THE LAKE PORTS.—One great cry of the gold-bugs is that we need a coin basis, because our foreign trade, as Garfield falsely stated, is "transacted in coin." If this were true it would not offer a weighty reason in view of such facts as this given by Alex. Mitchell's son-in-law, at the Bankers' Convention of 1880:—The tonnage annually entered and cleared in the Milwaukee Custom House district is larger than that in either Boston, Philadelphia or Baltimore. The commerce of the ports of Lake Michigan, judged by the tonnage of vessels entered and cleared, is almost as large as the whole of the foreign commerce of New York

City. The commerce of the lake ports is as large as the whole foreign commerce of the United States.

A BRIGHT IDEA—WHOSE?—Dr. E. P. Miller keeps a hygienic institute in New York City. He is an indefatigable worker and writer for what he considers true currency reform, but has not as yet (1880) been converted to the "fiat" idea. He had much influence over Peter Cooper, but has been generally at loggerheads with the leading brains of the Greenbackers. He is credited with the following, which seems a truthful view of the main obstacle to paying off the bonds that existed in the darkest times—1873 to 1880 ; and one not suggested, as far as I know, by any one else. Having usually disagreed with Dr. Miller, I gladly credit him with this idea :—Now, the charges made against these papers in that issue were these : That by advocating the issue of Greenbacks enough to pay off the bonds, they were knowingly or ignorantly working in the interest of the bondholders. They are doing so in this way : It would be necessary to nearly treble the volume of money to pay off the bonds, and the effect of trebling the volume of money would evidently be trebling the value of property. To have the Government issue 1,800 millions of Greenbacks, and put them into the hands of the bondholders, when property is depreciated in value as much as it is now, *would enable them to invest that money in real estate*, which, in less than four years, would be worth more than 5,000 millions of dollars, and would establish *one of the worst landed monopolies in the world*. We challenge any one to refute this argument.

The true policy would be, if more Greenbacks are to be issued, let them be used to start public improvements ; to employ our idle workingmen ; to promote the industries of the country ; and let the people who now hold the property have the benefit of the rise. If the money is issued, people employed, business restored and the country made prosperous, the payment of the bonds will be a matter that will not be difficult to accomplish or burdensome.

Immediately after writing the above, I found an extract from Dr. Miller's paper, giving an interview with George Francis Train, during the hard times, which looks as if the bright idea came from that erratic seer. If Train was then demented, we need a few more of the same style of dement.

He said:—Some Greenbackers begin to see that success this fall would have been a terrible defeat. To give bondholders, who have been twice paid already, Greenbacks for their bonds, would be equal to making them a present of all the mortgaged property in the land. Shylock, with a couple of thousand millions in hand, could foreclose the whole nation; and two hundred thousand Alabama bondholders and National Bank shareholders would own 48 millions of slaves.

THE OHIO IDEA.—The N. Y. *Tribune* said, after election in 1880:—"The defeat of Ewing will finally dispose of the Ohio Idea. Only the tail-end of it is alive in this canvass. After a year of successful resumption, with gold pouring into the country at the rate of two tons a day, the irredeemable currency notion will speedily expire. The Ohio Democracy will be reorganized on the basis of State Rights, and a hard-money currency supplemented by redeemable Green-backs."

Ewing has, indeed, given up the fight, and is trying to " make money " in New York. But the Ohio Idea, at this writing—1890—is a very lively corpse.

In 1880, when Gen. Weaver was running for the Presidency, there was a lively fight in Maine, which is thus spoken of in the N. Y. *World* in September, 1892, by a man named Frank A. Barr, a neighbor of Blaine:—McKinley's political career was practically born in that old homestead when Blaine brought him to Augusta in 1880, when the biggest fight of his life was on hand. Twice during that battle, when Blaine was beaten by the Greenback craze, and an ordinary man by the name of Gen. Plaisted was elected Governor, Mr. Blaine took McKinley under his arm and spoke from the same stump with him. It was practically his start in national life. During that battle there were scenes which have never been repeated in American politics. Every cross-roads was picketed with workers, and every schoolhouse was filled with a speaker. A dozen times during the combat, which threatened the destruction of Garfield's chances for the Presidency, there were more than 150 meetings a day in the State of Maine.

Those were the years when the primest powers of the Republican party were centered in that September election, and Mr. Blaine dominated every feature of it, bringing to his side not only money without stint, but men of the highest distinction, many of whom have passed to the great unknown, but whose lives are a part of the mighty history of this Republic.

Did I say pathos? Yes. For not long ago the great Secretary of State, when speaking of the wonderful events which gather like shadows and sunshine over his life, said in one of those moods which indicate fatigue · "Politics is a Vanity Fair, of which I have been only a part."

[All of which shows that Blaine was a politician rather than a statesman, and a politician on the wrong side. That disgust with his work never comes to the patriot who feels that he is fighting for the right.—S. L.]

1881.

THE CARLISLE REFUNDING BILL.—January 19, 1881, the Carlisle Refunding Bill, refunding the 202 million six per cents and 470 million five per cents, at three per cent., passed the House. Efforts were made to put the rate of interest back to three and a half per cent., and to strike out the prohibition against receiving other bonds as security for circulation; but they did not succeed. With one or two trifling amendments, the Senate on February 18, approved the bill and returned it to the House. The banks pretended to believe that they would have to change the bonds at once, and tried to get up a panic. In a week they gathered 14 million dollars; and sent it to Washington to deposit — against their bonds.

The Stock Exchange collapsed; many stocks falling rapidly. Secretary Sherman tried, in vain, to stop the panic; but nothing but the knowledge that they would ruin themselves,—as well as cause universal bankruptcy,—stopped the crazy course of the bank officers; and they quieted down— apparently assured by Hayes that he would protect them. At all events, though the bill finally passed the House on March 1, it was promptly vetoed by President Hayes, the next day but one, in a message which took the ground, fairly and squarely, that the measure was detrimental to the banks; and therefore was disapproved by him. Secretary Windom came into office March 5, and he has been much praised by some for the way he handled the refunding. The banks were chuckling—feeling sure of their five and six per cent. for another year. Windom, who really had not 150 millions in any shape for refunding, played sharp. Acting on the idea that one man with a pistol is a match for ten unarmed ; he announced on April 11 that on July 1 he would pay the 202 million sixes then maturing ; or so much of them as were not, in the mean time, presented for extension at the pleasure of the Government at 3½ per cent. With characteristic cowardice the holders rushed for the 3½ extension. In a month all the sixes were sent in and stamped with an agreement binding the Government to nothing, but obliging the holders to accept 3½. The same game was played with the fives ; and by August 12, they too were covered in. These fives and sixes were, in 1882, regularly converted into three-per-cent bonds ; payable at the pleasure of the Government ; and bond-holders are anxious for a two-per-cent. bond to run twenty years.

The report of the Controller of the Currency, for 1879, shows that the profits of the First National Bank of New York Syndicate was $2,153,959 in distributing $738,000,000 of bonds. Windom distributed the above $672,000,000 for $10,500.

On February 26, 1881, the N. Y. *World* said of the above bank panic : " It is a terrible power which the banks possess of throwing everything into sudden unhingement and confusion, when everybody was expecting financial fair weather."

THE BANKERS' REBELLION.—Congressman E. H. Gillette, of Iowa spoke of the " Bankers' Rebellion " thus in 1882 :—
This bill went into the Senate, and as soon as it got there we found that the stand we had taken had disturbed proud Senators a little ; for they began to write letters to the Greenbackers, asking for copies of their speeches ; and the result was they did not try to modify the bill materially ; but passed it substantially as it came to them. Then the bankers were furious and said they would rebel. They began to carry out their threat ; and in a few hours contracted the currency 18 millions, and produced a panic which reduced values in New York City alone 100 millions of dollars. They came down to Washington,—whole train-loads of them.—filled our halls and lobbies, and blackened the air with their threats. The Republican leaders said they would filibuster to prevent the Senate amendments being considered in the House ; and we had to sit there for a day and a half and vote on motions to adjourn. I don't want any of you to understand the Greenbackers voted for that bill ; we always voted against the bill,

and against any issue of bonds; but did all we could to modify the bill. [Applause.]

These bankers also went up to the President (Hayes) and threatened revolution. They said, "We have destroyed 100 millions of values already in New York; and we propose to withdraw 200 millions if necessary; and we will produce a panic such as was never heard of." What did your President do under those circumstances? What did he do? Did he call out the troops? Did he say, "We will see whether this rebellion will be triumphant or not?" Oh, no!

We have had a great many rebellions in this country. There was one in Rhode Island, one in Massachusetts, and another in Pennsylvania. We have put them down. When a half million of men sprang to arms in the South, to overthrow this republic, a million men in the North, thank God, rose up to put that rebellion down. And then came a little rebellion in Pennsylvania. A few men at Pittsburg broke into cars and stole some provisions for their starving families; and in the riots that followed two millions of property were destroyed. But it was nothing but a poor man's rebellion; and we sent troops to put it down. But when the bankers rebelled in 1881, and destroyed 100 millions of values, what did the President do? Did he call out the troops to suppress that rebellion? Oh, no; he said "Don't! don't! we will surrender!" And without a struggle, without a blow, without one drop of blood, your country's flag was hauled down in the mud; and you were surrendered into the hands of the bankers,—more dangerous foes than fired on Sumter.

In 1881, Californians,—having gotten a little over their speculative fever, and seeing how they had kept population out and business down by fighting paper money, and nickels, etc., are in a more reasonable frame of mind generally.

Gold was becoming a burden in Boston in 1881. The Clearing-house committee of the banks held a meeting, and voted to recommend making the Boston Safe Deposit Vaults, on Milk Street, the depository for gold coin, used in settling balances between banks: Clearing-house certificates being used.

GOULD MUST BE SUSTAINED.—August 20, 1881, when the stringency of the morning, at six per cent., changed to two and three per cent. in the afternoon ; it was charged that the dubious Mercantile Trust Co. was offering ten millions at three per cent: and there was much head-shaking at the statement that the money came from the " Equitable Life " to help Jay Gould.

SENATOR JONES SAW A GREAT LIGHT.—In an interview in the Cincinnati *Enquirer*, on November 11, 1881, Senator J. P. Jones of Nevada, so noted as having become a Greenbacker, though interested in silver mines, said :—I came to the Senate a victim or a convert to the writings of the old financial authorities, like Adam Smith, Amasa Walker and Stuart Mill. It was after that that I became illuminated by a study of the actual facts of exchange, panic and currency. I saw property reared by the work of men's hands,—towns, farms, mines, mills, railroads, all shrink to be next to worthless : while this medium of exchange, gold and silver, began to mount up and up in value. Whatever made life interesting was without a market, and that which had no use whatever, except to be hoarded and handled by Jews, was the master of the times. I said to myself there is injustice in this. We want a money that shall not leave the country, as soon as we get into a tight place.

On another occasion, Senator Jones said :—Gold had been set up as the sole instrument of valuation, but the masses of this country, who were accustomed to doing their own thinking, and did not rely for that purpose on the creditor classes, either of the United States or England, had made up their minds that, instead of being an instrument of valuation, gold was an instrument of confiscation and of spoliation. The people of the United States could not prevent the creditor classes of England from robbing and despoiling the Canadian, the Australian, the Egyptian, the Hindoo, and the Turk, but it surpassed his comprehension why an American Congress in 1873, or at any other time, should assist the English creditor classes—and, for that matter, the American creditor classes, also—to rob and despoil the debtors among our own people.

The single gold standard men attempted to brush aside the equities involved by sneering at the debtors. Who were the debtors in this country? They were the aspiring, the hopeful, the energetic, the audacious—they were the up-builders, the designers, the men of initiative, of executive power, and of achievement. They were the constructive

force in every community. As probably nine-tenths of the
business of America depended in one form or another on
credit, any system which made the dollars of a debt more
valuable at the date of payment than at the date of borrowing was a system of robbery. Machiavelli, describing a certain period in the history of Italy, had said of it, the "people
perished, but the brigands throve."

In October Folger took charge of the Treasury ; and, Garfield having been shot, Arthur reigned in his stead. There
is fanaticism among silver as well as gold men. An outbreak of it is seen, at this time, in the absurd proposition of
Californians to Arthur and Folger, to replace one, two and
three bank and Treasury notes by silver.

SILVER CERTIFICATES PREFERRED TO GOLD.—Senator
Teller, in his Congress speech of May 14, 1890, said that
"On September 18. 1881, the Secretary of the Treasury gave
notice that he would receive gold for silver certificates. For
some reason, I do not know what, he revoked that promise
November 1, 1881. And during that time $30,000,000 of
silver certificates were exchanged for gold." One explanation of this the Senator would have found, if he searched the
record, viz., Windom was Secretary in September, Folger in
October. Windom then had more of the courage of his convictions than he showed in 1890.

KEENE ON GOULD.—It was apparently about this time,
that James R. Keene, the California speculator, talked in
this way about his ups and downs :—According to Gould's
fables, I lost some four millions in wheat ; while, in fact, I
lost only a million and a quarter : half of which loss I recovered, at one stroke, in a speculation in lard ; and more
than the other half in stocks. Did it ever occur to you why
Gould seeks the malarious banks of the Hudson ? No ? Well,
he cannot stand the pure, bracing air of the seaside : it is too
healthy for his constitution. He lives on malaria, and other
people's misfortunes. If the Government were to put him
in a Florida marsh he would absorb every taint of miasma in
it, so that not even an alligator would be left.

THE ST. LOUIS REPUBLICAN—had an article on November
8, 1881, that treats of the successful attempt of the banks to
defeat the three per cent. refunding bill. It continues
thus :—President Arthur takes a more just and patriotic

view of the subject. Instead of approving the conduct of the banks, he exhibits alarm at it, and recommends that Congress take measures to prevent a repetition of it in the future, by prohibiting the National banks to recall their notes, without giving due notice of their intention to do so in advance. Secretary Folger speaks still more emphatically. He says: " Should many of the banks through apprehension of adverse legislation, or from any other cause, desire to retire their circulation, the deposit of such amount with the Treasurer might cause a serious and sudden contraction of the currency, and grave embarrassments in business. That the apprehension of such action is not groundless, is shown by what took place on the passage of the refunding bill by Congress at the last session." He, therefore, favors a law prohibiting the banks to call in their notes, except on giving due notice: and in a period fixed by statute. There are so many good reasons for the legislation recommended,—and the need of it is so apparent,—that we may take it for granted the present Congress will promptly provide for it. Not only is such legislation needed, to protect the country from bank intermeddling with public affairs ; but it is needed, also, as a rebuke to the amazing executive folly, which took sides with the banks and against the country, in the refunding bill of last season.

AN ELASTIC CURRENCY.—An article in the *International Review* for October, 1881, quotes the testimony of U. S. Treasurer Gilfillan against the idea that the National banks furnish an elastic currency. It says : " Within his observation, the National banks do not retire any of their circulation when currency is redundant, or increase their issues when there is a stringency. A bank which would retire $90,000 of its circulation when funds are in excess, would receive $100,-000 ; say in four per cent. bonds ; which it would immediately sell at $113,000 ; and find itself with $23,000 more than when it endeavored to get rid of its surplus. Should it prefer to hold the bonds, without selling, it might as well let them rest in the Treasury, and hold the notes instead, subject to any possible demand. In case of a stringency, likewise, the straightened bank will hesitate before drawing $113,000 from its available cash in order to get $90,000 in its place. The interests of the country and the interests of the banks work inversely, in the expansion and contraction of the bank currency."

GOLD STICKING IN THE WEST.—A new trouble, that began
now to worry the honest-money gold-bugs, is thus voiced by
the N. Y. *Tribune:* "Accumulation of grain at Chicago and
other interior points, necessarily involves the use of increased
sums of money ; while the *comparative immobility* [.'] of gold
which, when once paid out in the producing regions, seem
to stick there, most pertinaciously,—almost wholly prevents
that return of money to the East which used to appear about
Oct. 1. If the grain speculation continues, therefore, still
larger sums are likely to be absorbed in the interior : while
the curtailment of exports will limit our power to draw gold
from abroad."

Really, now, how sad. Ask Prof. Sumner what to do about
it !

———

The famous " Rigolo " talked thus in Nov. 1881, in the
N. Y. *Sun :*—Inflation and overspeculation seem to be the
order of the day all over the globe ; and *people who now pay
$50 a share for stocks like Wabash, St. Louis and San Fran-
cisco, or Missouri, Kansas and Texas,—which but two years
ago sold at a dollar a share.*—can console themselves with the
fact that the *Union Générale* in Paris rose from 125 to 2,350
francs per share. The grain speculation seems also to turn
against New York. The "boys" here have oversold the
wheat and corn market : and have been squeezed to the extent of two or three cents a bushel. But most of them must
have *made a pile of money on the upward track ;* and ought
to be able to stand the loss.

WM. H. VANDERBILT SELLS HIS FRIENDS.—Here are two
1881 items from Wall Street and conservative journals, that
are very historical. The *Public* said :—We regret to hear from
some of Mr. Vanderbilt's nearest and dearest friends, that
he has lied again. Accusations of this sort should not be
thus lightly and loosely tossed about the Street. It is not
right that the character of a great man, who owns 100 millions
should be spotted by unfriendly criticism or indecorous
rumor, It is asserted that Mr. Vanderbilt assured his friends
that the railroad war was settled ; and proceeded to buy
stocks. But if he did, the man certainly had a right to sell
both his stocks and his friends, as usual. At any rate, he
has not settled any railroad war thus far ; and his friends and

followers wish that they had been the friends and followers of somebody else.

Again,—the *New York Banker and Broker* insists that Mr. Vanderbilt is determined, in his own interests, to show that his roads can make dividends on rates which would not pay new roads. He has been convinced that a check in railroad building and subscriptions to construction companies will ruin Mr. Gould ; and next to his desire to maintain his roads as the standard of solidity and regular income, is his desire to break Mr. Gould ; whom he regards as a wrecker and a parasite.

EIGHTY-SIX NATIONAL BANKS, with an aggregate capital of $9,651,056, and to which $5,233,580 in circulating notes were issued, were organized in 1881 ; being a greater number than in any year since 1872.

STOCKS UP TWO BILLIONS.—1881 was truly a marvelous year for financial history : in fact the last of our marvelous years ; though others in the '8os have been quite eventful. In it we saw the climax of the reaction from the panic and famine years in the '70's. Two thousand millions were added to the nominal values of stocks, which were afterward unloaded upon the " lambs ". It would be very interesting, could one learn how many of the fortunes of one to five millions, upon which Americans are disporting themselves the world over,— were founded in that year, by the smart Alecks, who unloaded in time ; and invested in real estate and various industries. The work that went on was thus described by the N. Y. *Indicator :*—The stock market showed a capacity equal to that of the Mississippi Valley for taking water this year. The following graphically describes the situation : Why should not the cliques in Denver and Rio Grand, Missouri Pacific, Texas Pacific, Western Union *et id omne genus,* strive hard to sustain the stock market ; as their schemes are yet incomplete ? They have filled up to overflowing with watered stocks, which are worthless without a market on which to dump their load. The crowd sustaining this class of stuff, —and incidentally the whole market,—are by no means poverty-stricken. They control large amounts of money made in previous ventures,of a like kind ; which they freely use in support of their present endeavor to flood the country with bastard securities. It remains to be seen if a credulous public is to be deluded into coming to their relief.

SEVERE ON SECRETARY FOLGER.—A Philadelphia paper said, in December, 1881 :—Henry Carey Baird lectured at Greenback Hall last night, on "Some Thoughts on Political Economy and Social Science." He said that the idea that there was no further need for Greenback organizations was a delusion. He was more than ever convinced of this by reading the report of the new Secretary of the Treasury. "Secretary Folger," said the speaker, "has shown himself to be utterly incompetent at the outset. He proposes to stop the coinage of silver, now being turned out at the rate of $2,000,000 a month ; and also favors the retirement of silver certificates, of which there are 66 million dollars worth afloat. Let him try it : and such a disturbance will be created that he will be driven from his office in 48 hours." Mr. Baird then proceeded to argue for the necessity for the issuance of more money by the Government.

1882.

JESUITICAL NONSENSE.—Although the financial excitement was milder in 1882, there was much hot discussion. Here is an item from the N. Y. *Sun*, which is Jesuitical nonsense; inasmuch as it ignores the labor cost of gold and the interest on its intrinsic value, and the larger denominations of notes: "The relative cost, in wear and tear of gold coin, as compared with bank notes, has lately been investigated in England ; and the advantage has been found to be largely with the coin. To manufacture a million of sovereigns costs $10,000 , or about a cent apiece. In fifteen years they lose in weight one-half of one per cent., or about $25,000. This makes their total expense, as currency, for the fifteen years, $35,000. The paper and printing of a million one-pound notes would cost, it is estimated, four cents apiece, or $40,000 at the out-set ; and during fifteen years they would have to be replaced at least three times, or, with active use, six times : thus requir-ing an outlay of $160,000, and perhaps $280,000, for the same period that a million sovereigns would remain in circulation."

One piece of Jesuitism in the above is, the ignoring the fact that a ten-thousand-pound bank-note costs no more to print than a one-pound note. Again there is no such expense in printing bills here as in England ; and no such fool way of de-stroying them, and reissuing them when they return to their source, as occurs with Bank of England notes. With such rubbish do the gold-bugs retain their hold upon simpletons.

In 1882, the famous Prof. Soetbeer wrote an article upon, THE GOLD DRAINAGE FROM EUROPE TO AMERICA.—He thought that it would last for some time; but that no evil result need be apprehended; "that the American banks will tire of having so much gold; and that the American people will show their old preference for paper money." Wise man!

F. B. THURBER AND HIS ANTI-MONOPOLISTS—were largely with us in the fight for Government paper money in the early '8os. Here are some of his utterances upon railroad monopoly when he was fighting Vanderbilt, Depew and Co: —We believe that these encroachments were never contemplated by our forefathers, who rebelled against unjust taxation, and threw the tea into Boston Harbor, upon which it was sought to levy taxes. We believe that the men who abolished primogeniture and entail—in order to ensure the more equal distribution of wealth—would not justify a system of freebooting under the guise of law, which places the production and commerce of a continent at the mercy of a few men, who recognize no principle of action but personal or corporate aggrandizement.

Again: Unless charges for transportation are based upon *cost of service, and regulated by law,* the railroads are virtually owners of the country. Indeed it is more advantageous to the railroad managers than if they had a proprietary interest in all property: for with charges for transportation based upon the principle of *"what the traffic will bear,"*—and the railroad managers sole judges of that question,—they can tax production and commerce at will, without the trouble or responsibility of ownership.—*Report of N. Y. Board of Trade.*

INTEREST COMING DOWN.—Matthew Marshall, the conservative old gent who took the place of the late lively "Rigolo", in writing the Monday finance articles in the N. Y. *Sun,* had this in 1890 :—As we know, the fives and sixes thus extended at 3½ per cent by Secretary Windom [in 1881] were converted in 1882 into 3 per cent. bonds, payable at the pleasure of the Government. And it is worthy of note that the same bank officers who, in February, 1881, were ready to ruin the business of the country, rather than accept at par a 3 per cent. bond,—having five years to run,—absolutely sent their clerks August 1, 1882, to stand in line at the Post Office, to get in the earliest application for 3 per cent. bonds; which could be paid off at any time; and which were, in fact, paid off in part within a year; and were finally extinguished in less than five years.

KNOX KNOCKED OUT.—It was in 1882 that the *South Bend Era* thus exposed J. J. Knox :—General J. B. Weaver's exposition of the clause in the National Bank law granting 90 per cent of the current market value of the bonds, alarmed the philanthropic gentlemen engaged in the banking business; and brought from them an instant denial, supported by the testimony of John J. Knox, Comptroller of the Currency.

No sooner was the denial uttered than General Weaver and the Greenbackers confronted the bankers and the Comptroller with the plain words of the statutes. The law was as distinctly in favor of the Greenbackers' position as the English language could make it. This was a point clearly scored for the new party.

After being convicted of garbling the law, and attempting to deceive his countrymen, Comptroller Knox is driven to admit that the law does grant to the banks 90 per cent. of the current market value of the bonds, but claims that he and another inferior officer had an informal consultation some years ago; and decided to place a different construction on the law; so that banks, at present, can only receive 90 per cent. of the par value of the bonds, in bank notes.

Knowing that Comptroller Knox falsified in one instance, —in defence of the banks,—we received his new statement with some doubt; and at once proceeded to investigate as to the correctness of it. And what do we find? We find that only a few months ago Comptroller Knox furnished to the *Bankers' Magazine* the following statement:

Washington, D. C., January 1, 1882.—The Treasury holds the following bonds to secure bank circulation :

Currency 6's.....................	$3,536,000
5 per cents	144,000
4½ " "	32,117,500
4 " "	93,190,000
3½ " "	243,262,500
Total........	$372,250,150
Total circulation outstanding currency notes................	362,792,292

A moment's use of the pencil demonstrates that 90 per cent of the par value of $372,250,150 of bonds is just $335,-

025,135, whereas, according to the testimony of Comptroller Knox himself, the circulation issued to the banks on these bonds is $362,792,292, or $27,767,157 more than 90 per cent. of the par value of the bonds.

Convicted of falsehood and deception,—first by the law under which he holds his office, and now by the logic of his own official statistics,—Comptroller Knox stands before the country as the contemptible lackey of the National banks; while the Greenback party has proven anew the correctness of its position on this point of the financial question.

But all that does not prevent Knox from being president of a New York National bank at this writing, in 1891; and continuing to vent owl-like wisdom as such.

In 1882, Judge Warwick Martin printed his " Financial History of the Democratic Party "—a very strong work; showing that all the first leaders of the party were practically Greenbackers; and that Belmont, Tilden, Hewitt and English have entirely repudiated Jeffersonian Democracy.

ON JULY 12, 1882, THE BANK CHARTER BILL WAS PASSED. Section 13 provided that " any officer, clerk or agent of any National banking association who shall wilfully violate the provisions of an Act entitled ' An Act in reference to certifying checks by National banks,' approved March 3, 1869; or who shall resort to any device, or receive fictitious obligations, direct or collateral, in order to evade the provisions thereof, or who shall certify checks before the amount thereof shall have been regularly entered to the credit of the dealer upon the books of the banking association,—shall be deemed guilty of a misdeameanor," etc. There was a fine of not more than $5,000, or imprisonment not more than five years.

The bankers smiled at this; and simply "accepted" checks instead of certifying them; and everything was lovely again. Not one of them even went to jail, to say nothing of the $5,000.

On that same July 12, 1882, John Sherman worked another of his cunning tricks and deep-laid schemes in getting this seeming innocent proviso passed relative to the deposit of gold coin in the Treasury, and the issue of coin certificates therefor. Here is the gem, with comments by P. Prentiss, of Cleveland, O :

" *Provided*, That the Secretary of the Treasury shall suspend the issue of such gold certificates whenever the amount of gold coin and gold bullion in the Treasury, *reserved for the redemption of United States Notes*, falls below $100,000,000."

Notice carefully the above words in italics, for they are the ones that Sherman says authorizes the Secretary to maintain, as a reserve for redemption purposes, a minimum amount of $100,000,000 in gold. The act speaks of the " reserve " as though it was a thing already established by law, and there is where the craftiness comes in, for it never was established by law at all. It is solely and entirely a scheme gotten up by our gold-bug Secretaries of their own volition, and maintained by every one of them—the Democrats as well as Republicans—to this hour.

The law does not authorize or require any reserve of gold, silver or anything else to be established or maintained for $100,000,000 or any other amount. It simply says nothing about it. But it does require him to redeem the Greenbacks in coin and authorized him to sell bonds for coin for that purpose.

The words, " reserved for the redemption of United States notes," so interloped into the said Act of July 12, 1882, were cunningly devised and put in for the purpose of making a show of a base and support for their claims of a $100,000,000 gold reserve—as being established by law ; and John Sherman is now putting it to that use, as intended from the beginning. The Secretary institutes the " reserve " on his own motion and order, without authority of law, and the next step of the conspirators is to refer to it in the Act of 1882 as though it had been established by law. And the next and last step is to now refer to the Act of 1882 as " an act authorizing the Secretary to maintain a minimum reserve of $100,000,000 in gold." How is that for a scheme by honest (?) men for honest (?) money ? But further, he is only authorized to sell bonds for coin, " to the extent necessary," to redeem the greenbacks in coin—for that purpose and no other—to that extent and no further.

But the Secretary is using the gold reserve to redeem Treasury notes issued under the Sherman Act of 1890, which

17

Treasury notes the law says he shall redeem in gold or silver coin, at his discretion, and that he shall coin, of the silver bullion purchased under the act, as much as may be necessary to redeem the Treasury notes issued under said act.

Does the law command him to coin the silver bullion as may be necessary to redeem them and, at the same time, authorize him to sell bonds for gold coin with which to redeem everyone of them ? Certainly not ! But that is just what he is doing or says he will do if necessary.

Who wants the bonds ? The national banks, to enable them to issue more of their notes as money, and draw interest on the bonds at the same time.

Who wants the gold coin ? De Rothschilds & Co., to put poor, poverty-struck Austria-Hungary on the gold standard, and so make lower prices and lower wages for the producers and higher money for the Shylocks.

Then the Secretary must pay out, in the usual course of business, the Greenbacks and notes so redeemed, which must again be redeemed on presentation, and so, round and round, ad infinitum; and the amount of gold coin that could be demanded of the Treasury would be unlimited.

[France redeems her " coin " obligation in silver or gold, choosing the metal she has most of.—S. L.]

Henry Appleton (Honorius) had this in the *Irish World* in 1882 :—And then, just think of the big boss food-thieves ; compared with whom, your family grocer is but an innocent babe. According to the official statistics, the corn crop in 1881, was sold four times through speculative purchases ; the wheat crop ten times, and the cotton crop 172 times. In cotton the speculative trading amounted to $1,729,000,000, in wheat $600,000,000, and in corn $133,000,000. The statement is unblushingly going the rounds in the prominent news and commercial papers, that the price of the necessities of life has been enhanced, on an average, 50 per cent. higher than what a normal profit would warrant. Yes, the world stands amazed when it is stated that 12 men own one-half of Scotland, while a few hundreds own four-fifths of Ireland.

But right here in free America, 12 men, to-day, dictate that a poor working man shall pay 20 cents for a pound of meat that would furnish a handsome profit at ten cents ; and are standing despotic guard over the stomachs and backs of fifty million of free men.

BANK PROFITS.—Banks usually try to conceal their profits. But in the Saratoga Bankers' Convention of 1882, Mr. A. D. Lynch, of Indiana, gave a paper on " Banking in the West," containing this : ' The profits of National banking in the middle Western States cannot be said at this time to be extravagant, though satisfactory. The time has been, within the last 20 years, when the semi-annual dividends of the banks of the States named have been *such as to have satisfied even that voracious old usurer who demanded the pound of flesh.* For the close of the year 1881, the reports of these States spoken of, as shown in tables made by the comptroller of the currency, evince that the dividends to capital were 8½ per cent; and earnings to capital and surplus were 9 1-10 per cent.

" This is the average ; while in individual instances we still find the old 8 and 9 per cent, semi-annual dividend ; where the capital has been thrice paid back to the shareholders in dividends in the past 20 years ; all costs and losses properly charged out. This will represent about 700 National banks ; with capital of \$175,000,000 and deposits at least \$500,000,-000."

1883.

TRADE DOLLARS IN SIAM.—During the Trade-Dollar excitement, this came from Siam :—The King is buying American trade-dollars, at about 90 cents on the dollar, and coining new Siamese *ticols.* The new coin is very handsome and much sought after by the native traders. These *ticols* pass current for 60 cents within the kingdom : but at Singapore, Senang and Calcutta they are accepted at a discount of 20 per cent., so that their actual value is not more than 48 cents. It is said at the British Consulate, that one trade-dollar produces two *ticols ;* so it will be seen that the Siamese Government is doing a profitable business by debasing the coin.

THE WATER AND GAS GONE.—By 1883, the gas and water had gone out of so many American enterprises, that had been unloaded upon the "lambs",—that our fellow "skins" of Europe began to give us the cold shoulder. Rigolo said, in his Monday article, in the *N. Y. Sun :*—Business men, returning from Europe, say that the moment an American comes to any broker's or banker's office in London and Paris, —and attempts to talk business,—everybody runs away. They are willing to meet well-introduced and polished

Americans on social terms,—as they are willing to marry handsome American girls,—but they won't have anything to do with any kind of American securities.

THE " SENEY CROWD'S" HIGH KICKING.—In 1883 came the high-kicking of the " Seney Crowd ", which is thus described in the N. Y. *Times :—*

*How Securities are Piled up and Marketed by Christian Financiers :—*The well-known and philanthropic banker, Mr. Seney, is the recognized head of a group of financiers and railroad constructors which Wall Street has dubbed " The Seney Crowd." The crowd, as a collective substantive, exists for the purpose of issuing securities. This is the function of its being. It has introduced " the Seney method," of railroad financiering,—the like of which was never seen in Wall Street before, and it is to be hoped, will never again be seen. The reasoning on which the method is based is simple —plenty of securities, and if you make them cheap enough the people will buy ; they won't buy 1,000,000 at 50, but give them 50,000,000 at 10 and they will take the lot. Had the " Seney Crowd " acquired the New Orleans line they would first have formed a syndicate among themselves, and bought up the property for cash at the lowest price obtainable. They would then have made some necessary repairs, got some equipments on car trusts, and made a traffic agreement with the road it was intended to work with. Having thus put things into shape, the members of the syndicate would organize themselves into a railroad company, with a high-sounding name ; and proceed to divide the profits. The printing press would go to work with energy. First mortgage bonds, second mortgage bonds, terminal bonds, consolidated bonds, income bonds, preferred stock certificates, and common stock certificates, would be rolled off by the ream. First mortgage bonds would be issued in amount nearly enough to cover the cost of the property ; of second mortgage bonds there would be issued as much ; consolidated bonds to cover mortgages already resting on the road ; income bonds and common and preferred stock *ad lib.* The terminal bonds would cover the terminal property ; the argument of the Seney financiers being that terminals are really real estate, not railroads ; and real estate always has its value, and should be covered by a real estate bond. Equipment, also, is not road, so that must be got on car trusts. First mortgage six per cent. bonds may be held at 90, and the terminal bonds also ; the seconds may bring 75 ; income bonds, 40 ; the preferred stock may be sold for 25 ; and anything over 10 for the common is unexpected gain. Having worked off these alleged securities on the public ; the " Seney Crowd " would leave them to be kicked about Wall Street, for any price they could fetch.

Recently the East Tennessee company (which is theirs) held a meeting ; and authorized the issue of an additional $10,000,000 of bonds ; $3,000,000 of preferred stock, and $13,000,000 of common stock,—the bonds to be issued only on newly-acquired property. The trifle of $16,000,000 of stock will be loaded on to it in addition. As the East Tennessee company has only $83.000,000 of securities now outstanding (exclusive of car trusts), the new issue will bring its obligations up to the respectable figure of $109,000,000. This is in the true Seney style.

[But the Seney Crowd could not long emulate Gould,—who is his own crowd ; and great was the fall thereof.—S. L.]

Here is another version, from Henry Clews' book. Henry's stomach is not easily turned ; but he draws the line at Seney and Eno ; he thinks them "crooked",—in fact, "not respectable." After showing that Seney helped to bring on the panic of 1884, he gives particulars :—

Seney was a great patron of churches and religious institutions. He was probably the most eminently respectable financier in Wall Street ; where he carved out an original course for himself in speculation—so original, in fact, as to stamp a number of enterprises with his name. The Seney properties became almost as familiar to the financial world as the Goulds, the Vanderbilts, and the Villards.

Mr. Seney's chief securities (so called through the courtesy of speculative parlance) were Ohio Central, Rochester and Pittsburgh, East Tennessee, Virginia and Georgia, and the celebrated " Nickel Plate " Road. These were known as the Seney Syndicate properties, and the system of handling them was entirely novel in the history of Wall Street ; causing the financial veterans of Wall Street to stand and stare at the boldness and rapidity of the Seney movements.

Instead of starting with moderate issues in amount,—as has usually been the custom of most men handling railroad and telegraph properties,—and doing the watering process by degrees, Mr. Seney boldly began the watering at the very inception of the enterprise ; pouring it in lavishly and without stint. There was nothing mean or niggardly about his method of free dilution ; the sight of which threw some of the old operators into a fit of consternation. The stocks were strongly puffed ; and as they were so thoroughly diluted, their owners could afford to let them get a start at a very low figure. The future prospects of the properties were set forth in the most glowing colors ; the public took the bait, and the stocks became at once conspicuous among the leading active fancies of the market.

The cause of the vigorous life and amazing activity so suddenly imparted to the stocks of the Seney Syndicate, can only be revealed by a careful perusal of Mr. Seney's checkbook ; which, if still in existence, will show commissions paid for the execution of the orders to buy and the orders executed to sell,—both by the same pen and in the same handwriting.

These transactions, in the language of the " Street ", are called washed sales. In this way, Mr. Seney was understood to have made a very large amount of money ; and from being almost one of the poorest men in Brooklyn, he soon became marked as the richest. While he continued to thrive, it was a singular fact that the majority of his financial friends seemed to fall into a decline.

When the affairs of the Seney enterprise were wound up, it was discovered that these people had little left, except the certificates which bore the high-sounding term of the Seney Syndicate Property.

One peculiarity about Mr. Seney, in his social relations, was, that while he appeared almost bereft of sympathy for used-up friends,—whom his schemes had ruined,—he drew largely on his immense gains for philanthropic purposes ; and, in the aggregate, must have distributed over two million dollars in a very magnanimous manner.

" It would seem," adds Mr. Clews, " that Mr. Seney at one time aspired to be a great philanthropist ; and had it not been for the *exposé* which was the result of the panic ; he might one day have stood in as high and lordly a position as the renowned Peabody,—with even a greater reputation as a financier. It is sad to picture the contrast presented by the dénouement, with what might have been, in a career which began with so much promise ; dating from the time that Mr. Seney was installed as president of the Metropolitan Bank,— whose standing and credit were the highest in the State. Mr. Seney's speculative career affords an example of the way in which this kind of speculation reflects on the stability of our best banking institutions. The lesson is one that should be carefully taken to heart, by the financiers of this country."

After these moral reflections, Mr. Clews proceeds to sketch the career of another estimable financier,—Mr. J. C. Eno, the former president of the Second National Bank.

Most of the money lent by that bank was upon collateral securities ; which,—for convenience as well as for safety,— were kept, not at the bank, which was situated under the Fifth Avenue Hotel, but in a vault down town.

· The capital stock of the bank was $100,000 ; and it had $4,000,000 of deposits ; all of which was appropriated to speculative use by this smart young man ; who decamped to Canada in company with a Roman Catholic priest.

Instead of loaning the money to Wall Street brokers,—as he represented to the directors,—he placed it as margin with his own brokers, in various speculative ventures ; and in that manner he made away with the entire $4,000,000 of the bank's deposits, without exciting the least suspicion in the confiding breasts of the directors.

" Such another instance," says Mr. Clews, " of a clean sweep of the deposits of a bank, by any of its officials, is probably not on record, in the whole history of this kind of manipulation."

But Mr. Clews makes a curious omission. Who were the brokers that received Eno's stolen money ? Did they know it to be stolen ? If they did, were they not as culpable as the thief ?

A somewhat celebrated case is now [1890] before the New York courts. It is that of Eno *vs.* Seymour, Baker & Co. In bringing this suit, Mr. Eno alleges that the frauds of Seymour and Baker, the brokers who transacted his business, were the cause of his ruin.

Were these brokers exceptional, Mr. Clews ? Would many firms in Wall Street have rejected the business which Eno brought them ? Did Eno have to go far afield before he found two men of his own kidney ?

Eno swindled his depositors. His brokers swindled Eno. Is the case so unusual?

VANDERBILT GETS PALACES AND RESPECTABILITY.—Wm. H. Vanderbilt was in high feather in 1883. In that year, he built his Fifth Avenue palaces ; and had the great masquerade ball, at which Abram S. Hewitt appeared as " King Lear before he was crazy." This was the first step toward " complete respectability," on the part of the Vanderbilts. It was a success. Their sins are already forgotten by most people ; and only the virtues of their bank accounts are remembered. But we, who don't forget, will take a few peeps at them. Here is a spring item of interest, about this royal personage.

The *Wall Street News* of New York says : " W. H. Vanderbilt's check for April interest, on Government fours, was $402,000 ; or interest on $40,200,000 of bonds." This is quarterly interest. So our Lord Vanderbilt practically receives an annual pension from the people,—for no service whatever,—of $1,608,000. We say no service. What has he done for us ? He has exchanged our non-interest-bearing notes for our interest-bearing notes. In other words, with unlimited power to issue all the non-interest-bearing notes we need, we have, instead, to form an excuse for supporting our rich loafers, issued interest notes, and then made an even exchange. We cannot blame Vanderbilt. We have offered him a million cows that give milk, for a million cows that don't give milk ; and he has accepted our offer,—upon condition that we shall shelter and feed them.—Indianapolis *Globe.*

And here is a summer item, from cynical Rigolo of N. Y. *Sun* :—

It looks as if business would be uncommonly dull in Wall Street, all through the summer. Mr. Vanderbilt has returned from Europe ; but he ignores the Street, drives Maud S., and concentrates all his energies upon beating Frank Work's team. He even refuses to go to Saratoga ; and the stockbrokers, who have summer offices there are in the depths of woe ; as there will be no one on the piazza of the United States to give valuable friendly points. For several years past, Mr. Vanderbilt has divided with the congress water and the roulette and faro tables, the honor of being one of the main attractions to the Springs ; and it will be highly interesting to watch his old torpid-liver chums, who will now be de-

prived of their only intellectual and conversational resources,
—the repeating of what "Bill" says about stocks, Maud S.,
Frank Work and the "common people"; who take the liberty
of criticising anything with which Vanderbilt's name is connected.

The original Vanderbilt had "wanted the earth," and felt
that he had it. The brutal ways of the old commodore are
thus described :—The despotic will of the old sailor,—disre-
garding everything except his personal comfort and aims,—is
still on the surface. Speaking a short time ago on the subject
of "rapid transit", he said in the rudest tone it was ever my
lot to listen to: "I will have nothing more to do with it;
and I don't care what New York wants! I was willing once
to give rapid transit to the city I have met opposition, and
there is an end of it! And no member of my family shall
ever have a hand in it, as long as I live."

This was in Democratic America. And the old *highway
robber* died unpunished, and, in fact, in the odor of sanctity.
Is it any wonder that the Democratic Republic is practically
dead?

THURBER ON THE LARD FAILURES.—Here is plain talk
from F. B. Thurber's Anti-Monopoly *Justice*, on the "Lard
Failures" in 1883 :—A Chicago press dispatch says : "Every
creditor of the late suspended firm of McGeoch, Everingham
& Co.,—who failed for $6,000,000,—has, it is said, signed the
50 per cent. compromise ; and the $450,000 cash to pay un-
secured creditors is to be sent here Tuesday. It is expected
that the firm will be reorganized, and resume business in
about a month. Its commission business, before the failure,
was worth $300,000 a year." When one firm makes $300,000
per year in commission, it shows what a nation of gamblers
we have become. The above firm had no legitimate business; they were simply speculative gamblers—public enemies ; who ought to be drummed out of town to the tune of
"The Rogues' March ;" And yet, very likely, they stand
high in the Church ; and contribute as regularly to its revenues as do the pious Sicilian brigands. The only way to
reach commercial gamblers, who manufacture and trade upon
false reports (as gamblers do with marked cards), is to put
them in the same social and legal category,—make their acts
unlawful, and disreputable. That they are equally unscru-
pulous every one knows ; and that they are more dangerous

to the community, is indicated by the following from the Chicago *Tribune:* " No mere blunder, commercial or otherwise, could entail such widespread disaster in two hemispheres, as followed the collapse of the lard corner in this city. The act must take high rank among the crimes which are committed against society. Human greed,—seeking riches through the means of an unnatural inflation,—has entailed severe loss upon hundreds directly ; and upon scores of thousands indirectly. It led to the blocking up of the channels of trade ; to a forced production of material ; and fostered a perversion of commercial ethics ; the last being not least among the evils which followed in the train of the movement."

The Trade Dollar Nuisance.—There was much trouble from the trade dollars this year, that were everywhere thrust upon innocent people ; and refused by the sharp ones. July 23, 1883, Secretary Folger replied, at length, to a Dr. James C. Halleck, of Brooklyn, N. Y., who had urged the President to order the receipt of the coin at the Treasury, the same as the standard dollar. He enclosed a letter from John Sherman, setting forth how this dollar having become of less value than Greenbacks in 1877, he had stopped the coinage ; and that since then it had been worth only the bullion price of its silver.

The Greenbackers at this time had the laugh on the " intrinsic value " bullionists : since the trade dollar has 8 grains more of silver than the standard dollar. Again we remark " The law creates money."

" These be Your Gods, O Israel ! "—We finish this year, 1883, with another " elegant extract " about Vanderbilt and Gould :—

The *Herald* hit the nail on the head, when it said yesterday, that last week's events in Wall Street hardly bear out the official utterances of Mr. Vanderbilt, that Lake Shore was cheap at 120 ; and of Mr. Gould that Western Union would certainly be advanced, on its merits, to par. So, at least, think a great army of martyrs, who bought these stocks on these gentlemen's representations, and now find themselves minus their money. Mr. Vanderbilt has built himself a big house, and seeks to purchase or force himself into social recognition. Mr. Gould is, perhaps, satisfied with having simply skinned the Street. Neither one nor the other is likely, in the long run, to secure either social or financial advantage from the very questionable proceedings which have attached to their former stock deals ; and which have been especially prominent in the present one. *Lying, trickery and device are gradually becoming the sine qua non of a successful stockbroker : and it is lamentable to say that the instruction comes from the head men and the wealthiest operators.*

1884.

A WALL STREET PANIC.—The year 1884 is noted as that in which occurred a Wall Street panic, that would have spread over the country, if it had not been for the increased currency through the silver legislation, and for the fact that resumption had been accomplished by yielding largely to the demands of the Greenbackers.

Noticeable among the failures this year, were those of Grant and Ward, James R. Keene, Commodore Garrison and the Metropolitan and Marine Banks.

———

Boston despatches of Feb. 27, 1884, complained that now, for the first time, Boston banks were "compelled to yield to the silver policy of the Government. On account of a great output of silver certificates among the banks, by the Boston Sub-Treasury, the Clearing-house had been driven to admit them for the settlement of balances."

A GREAT VICTORY.—One of the greatest victories obtained by the Greenback Labor party, was the second endorsement of the Greenback by the Supreme Court, in March, 1884. This decision declares the constitutionality of the act of March 31, 1878, reissuing Greenbacks in time of peace. Space will not permit the quoting of long opinions about this important matter. Geo. S. Coe considered it "The most disastrous thing that has happened in the country since the beginning of the war." Since the *beginning*, mind you !— worse than any rebel victory. That is what one might expect from Coe. On the other hand, banker A. S. Hatch says, "My general conviction is that the decision is a good one." The *Times* thinks it "a proof of demoralization." The *Tribune* sneaks right up onto the fence.

MANY MARVELOUS FACTS are hinted at, in the following, of April, 1884, by Rigolo, of New York *Sun*. Among these is the fact that there were few failures during the great come-

down in stocks in 1883-4: and that the few leading speculators held up prices so long. If Rigolo could have got pay
for telling all he knew, what a tale he would have unfolded!
He said :—

The stock market is in a condition analogous to that of a
man in the last stage of Bright's disease. The patient does
not suffer much pain, but the speedy approach of death is
evident in the pinched nose, the hollow cheeks, and the livid
tint of the skin. The collapse is likely to come at any
moment, and the sooner it comes the better it will be for
everybody. The Wall Street organism has shown remarkable staying powers. There were no failures, with all the
tremendous decline that has taken place within the last three
years, and there are no big failures to be apprehended at
present. Consequently, everything is to be gained by a
speedy settlement of the agony. Since the patient is in-
curable, the sooner he dies the better it will be for the sur-
vivors.

Another ten or fifteen points' drop in prices, will revive
Wall Street business, to an extent which will astonish and
attract into brokers' offices everybody who has any spare
cash. But neither investors nor speculators will appear there
before the sick man is actually dead. Those who are interested in the revival of Wall Street business (and there are
several thousand men who are so, besides the 1,100 brokers)
must try to bring things to a focus as fast as possible. It
would be preferable to settle the whole thing before Summer
fairly sets in, instead of dragging it for another four or five
months, till the moneyed people come back from Saratoga,
Newport, and Europe. If men like Gould, Sage, Cyrus
Field, Vanderbilt, and a few of the speculative bank directors,
had courage enough to see a temporary loss (on paper) of a
few millions of dollars, and leave the market to itself, a complete revolution would take place in Wall Street in a few
weeks ; and they would have a chance to make up, several
times over again, the temporary loss which their books might
show during the drop. There are fair indications that Mr.
Gould shares this view; for he evidently does not protect
his stocks. But the action ought to be a concerted one on
the part of all the magnates, if it is to be made a success of.
No new life is likely to be infused into stock speculation
until Erie is below $10, Wabash and Denver below $5, Read-

ing and Jersey about $25 and $50 respectively, the Grangers about 10 points down, and the ex-Villards and the rest of the list in proportion. At something like such figures, a very fair speculative demand could probably be created both at home and abroad.

April 13, 1884, George Ticknor Curtis,—an alleged constitutional lawyer,—appeared before the House Committee on the Judiciary, to argue for an amendment to the Constitution, that would upset the recent decision of the Supreme Court in favor of the Greenback.

HE BUCKED AGAINST THE WIZARD.—May 1, 1884, Keene suspended payment, after a furious career of speculation in California and New York. He got in with Gould, soon after coming from San Francisco ; and made money till he broke with the wizard, in 1877. Here is an epitome of his after career : Gould is reported to have said, as an excuse for the dissolution of their friendship, that Keene had played him a shabby trick, and he was done with him. Keene, on his side, asserted, according to friends, that Gould had gone back on his friends and sold them out.

As one of the results of this little misunderstanding, Major Selover, who had been Keene's broker and admirer, picked Mr. Gould up from " the Street " by the collar, one afternoon, in August, 1877, and deposited him with great energy into an Exchange-place area, greatly to the personal surprise of a good-natured barber, who was shaving a customer. Keene said he was rejoiced that retribution had overtaken Mr. Gould ; on the ground that Mr. Gould was the wickedest man in the world.

The two men never spoke after that ; but Mr. Keene, as a result of his conflicts with Mr. Gould as a rival, dropped a pile that was reported to contain $6,000,000. He lost it in trying to get up a corner in wheat, and to fool with Jersey Central stocks. He held on to Jersey Central grimly, until it ran down forty points in a single week at a breakneck pace.

Just before this little experience, he was known to be worth $9,000,000 in cash ; and Isidor Wormser, his broker, said that one day he saw in Mr. Keene's office as much as $2,400,000 in cold cash.

He got all he had lost back again, and more too, with a

rush of his old luck; and in 1880, during the big boom in stocks, he was reputed to be the possessor of $20,000,000.

It was at this period,—the acme of his success and fame,—that the white ribbon with the blue spot, floating above American horseflesh, brought the name of Keene into the mouth of everybody who was a lover of the turf. The millionaire was kept busy spending some of his ducats for champagne, to celebrate the victory of his stable abroad and at home. In 1881, Foxhall amazed the world by carrying the white with the blue spot to the front in the race for the Grand Prize; and Keene was king of the turf as well as a king of the Street; and a fusilade of champagne corks testified to his popularity.

The see-saw of the Street brought him down again; and when Guiteau's shot paralyzed the country, he was reputed to be pretty nearly gone up financially. Again he rallied, however, and went on see-sawing till he got overwhelmingly swamped by the great Northern Pacific and O. T. downfall. Bad luck followed him, until it ended yesterday with his announcement of " Suspension of payments."

" He lies flat on his back," said an old broker, "a victim to the folly of trying to be a bull on a falling market. He probably hasn't $5,000 left. His fall won't affect the market in the slightest. It was known for months that it was coming."

COMMODORE GARRISON—one of the leading millionaire speculators of the country, failed in the spring of 1884. He was heavily interested in Western railroads, and a man of striking appearance. His face, massive and foxy, seemed a cross between that of Daniel Webster and Martin Van Buren. The lying and cheating of big speculators had not then ceased to be remarkable. Here is what Rigolo of the *Sun* said :—If something more was wanted finally to disgust everybody with Wall Street, and frighten him away from it, this something was admirably done last week. The failure of men reputed to be arch millionaires, is in itself a strong disturbing element. But when the very possibility of their failure is indignantly denied by the failing men themselves, within a few hours of their making an assignment, the business community is placed in the position of a paymaster's heavily-laden chest carried into the camp of cowboys and road agents. The commotion produced by the circumstances of Commodore Garrison's failure, was of the most alarming character.

When confidence in public statements of facts is gone, the whole business edifice of a community falls to pieces. When it becomes evident that no plain, truthful statement of facts from any millionaire, bank president, or railroad president can be obtained, every man of sound mind locks up in his safe the ready cash he has got, and sends to Jericho every business except that of which he has absolute control himself. It is the fault of lying millionaires, lying bank Presidents, and lying railroad magnates, that the denials are now accepted as confirmations. The momentary flurry created in the stock market on Saturday morning has, it seems, also postponed the collapse of two or three important Wall Street firms. But the last hour of business fairly suggests the probability of our hearing of them to-day or to-morrow ; unless, of course, the Gould-White-Morgan combination have money and courage enough to try once more to put prices up by means of the squeezing artifices in which they are adept.

THE BLASTED SILVER DID IT.—The St. Louis *Republican* said on May 23, of this bankers' panic of 1884 :—If there is any one thing of more smiting brilliancy than the financiering of New York bankers and brokers, it is the reasoning of a New York newspaper. The New York *Tribune* solemnly tells us that "there is not a competent student of financial questions in the country who does not see, that among all the causes of the present disturbance and peril, the continued coinage of silver, with the issue of paper certificates against coined silver, is the most potent. All about us lie financial wrecks, caused by this mischievous policy."

What a pity we ever revived the coining of good, hard silver dollars ! Had we not done it, the GRANTS would have kept their fortunes, the flabbergasted millionaire presidents of broken National banks would have remained exemplary observers of the law, and Mr. FERDINAND WARD would have lived and died a paragon of honesty.

The old N. Y. *Journal of Commerce*, is still occasionally worth quoting. It said during this panic :—A large volume of call loans hanging over the market are as dangerous as a dynamite cartridge, when the shock of a rude awakening comes ; and no one can tell how far, or in what direction, the explosion will make itself felt. The danger is greatly increased by the custom of allowing interest on deposits.

THE BEY OF TUNIS HAS COUPON BONDS.—For a temporary rest, we fly across the ocean, and, as misery loves company, we take a laugh at the old-time pirates of North Africa ; when we find them under the rack of that most relentless and cruel of pirates, the modern Shylock. In the London *Weekly Intelligencer*, we find that, pursuant to the decree of His Highness, the Bey of Tunis, of May 27, 1884, Consolidated four per cent. bonds; etc., etc., amounting to many million francs are to have their coupons paid in Paris at Messrs. Rothschilds Brothers, etc., etc.   This reminds one of a picture in *Redpath's Weekly* where John Bull stands in full regimentals over a prostrate Egyptian, who is all tied up with " bonds ", while a Jew bondholder asks him, " How you like dese bonds of Egypt ? "   The Oriental tyrant now, instead of raiding his own or the neighboring peoples, borrows money in England or France, and gets the English and French to collect it at the point of the bayonet.

BACK TO STATE BANKING.—The Mechanics and Traders' Bank of New York, which was organized in 1830, changed back to a State bank in May, 1884. The cashier said: "The reason that the large down-town banks continue as National banks is, because they carry the deposits of out-of-town banks : which are allowed to return, as part of their legal reserve, their deposits in the city banks."

JUST THE OTHER WAY.—In June, 1884, Henry Kemp made this statement in Bradstreet : " It may be asked, how are you to economize the use of money in a country ? I answer, simply by increasing the number of good banks of deposit and discount.   It is the small number of these banks in France, as compared with England and this country, that makes the former require thrice the amount of currency per capita of her population, that the two latter countries require. Banks collect and loan the money that would be stored away in the strong boxes of merchants and others, for deferred payments and purchases ; and thus the money is kept in circulation until wanted by the BANKS.   Hence the deposit and discount bank is the economizer of the amount of money required in a country."   Greenbackers take just the opposite view.   They glorify France for having enough money to do its business without so many banks.   So France never has a disastrous panic.   Its money is not only abundant and widely circulated, and kept passing from hand to hand, but also it is not gathered by banks in money centers to lend to speculators on call ; and then be missing when a panic comes.

BANKS RETIRING CIRCULATION.—Here is the status of the National banks June 30, 1884 : At the close of June, 1883, there were 2,417 National banks in existence. The number at the termination of June, 1884, was 2,625, an increase over the previous fiscal year of 208. Not only have the National banks increased in number, but their capital stock has like-wise increased. On the 30th of June, 1883, the aggregate capital was $500,298,312. One year later the aggregate was $522,517,411, a growth of more than twenty-two millions in a single year. Notwithstanding the increase in the number of banks and banking capital, there has been a steady fall-ing off in bank circulation since 1881. At the close of that year the circulation put out by the banks was $325,000,000. The following year it was $315,000,000. At the close of June, 1883, it had fallen to $311,000,000, and at the close of the fiscal year ended June 30, 1884, it had decreased to $295,175,334. The cause for this retirement of bank circu-lation is to be found in the forced withdrawal of bonds de-posited with the government to secure circulation.

THE COMING DELUGE.—In July, 1884, the N. Y. *Even-ing Post* was wailing thusly about the coming deluge of silver, and flight of gold :—That the steady drain of gold, which has been going on for the last six months will, if con-tinued much longer, force the Government to using silver in making its payments, either through the Clearing-house of this city or over the counters of the Sub-Treasury, was the universal opinion among many prominent bankers whom a reporter of the *Evening Post* visited this morning. Since January, the Treasury has lost about $50,000,000 of gold ; the decrease having gone on almost without interruption. At the end of May, the gold balance stood at $140,000,000 ; at the end of June it was $133,000,000 ; on July 19 it was $122,000,000 ; and on last Saturday it had fallen to $118,-000,000 only $18,000,000 more than the Secretary of the Treasury is required by law to keep as a reserve, to offset the circulation of National bank-notes. [!] No one wants to take silver ; but with a decreasing reserve of gold and an increas-ing stock of silver, supplemented by a coinage of $2,000,000 a month, there can be no escape from coming down to sil-ver, unless there is a turn in the tide.

18

The President of the Gallatin Bank said, that if the Government began to pay out silver, the banks, would have to take it. The Clearing-house tried to bar out silver ; and the Government forbade banks so doing to belong to the Clearing-house. Hitherto the Government's daily debt to the Clearing-house, of about $500,000, had been paid in gold. Silver was cumbersome. A million dollars took a space eight by five by four feet.

GODKIN'S GHOULISH GLEE.—On July 28, 1884, that gold maniac, Godkin, had an editorial in the *Evening Post* headed " The End of Bi-Metalism." He was in ghoulish glee over a gloomy letter from H. H. Gibbs, a silver leader of England, and called it "a sort of obituary notice of bi-metalism in the Old World."

WM. H. VANDERBILT was still, in the summer 1884, making the hay on which his high-toned offspring are now gently and genteelly browsing. Here's a love-tap from the N. Y. *Sun :*—The little performance with the new issue of New York Central bonds, after interminable public denials that such an issue was ever contemplated, put an extra bright feather in Vanderbilt's veracity cap. The mental process which makes a man hoard up millions upon millions, and build for himself the reputation he does at home as well as abroad, is really incomprehensible.

THE CLEARING-HOUSE AND THE TREASURY.—This is the way in which the N. Y. dailies were talking about the relations of the U. S. Treasury and the N. Y. Clearing-house, in the summer of 1884 :—The relations of the Treasury and the Sub-Treasury to the New York Clearing-house have never been thoroughly understood, and have frequently been very different from the relations of other Sub-Treasuries to the Clearing-houses in their respective cities. For instance, although Sub-Treasuries have never received any instructions upon that point, it is the custom at nearly, if not all, of the other Sub-Treasuries, to tender one-half or less of the balance due from the Treasury to the Clearing-house in silver certificates. This has come to be recognized as one of the unwritten Treasury regulations for those cities ; but in New York, although the Sub-Treasury is generally a debtor to the Clearing-house, of from half to three-quarters of a million dollars daily, all settlements have been made by the Sub-Treasury with the Clearing-house in gold or gold certificates. This is entirely voluntary on the part of the New York Sub-Treasurer; but, of course, the practice has not grown up without the approval of the Secretary of the Treasury. There has recently come a rather earnest demand that the New York Clearing-house should be treated as the Clearing-houses of other cities are; and that the spirit of the law which forbids discrimination against silver certificates should not be violated. Attention has been called to the fact, that while it is true that the New York Clearing-house has rescinded its order refusing to take silver certificates, in view of the enactment of the law of July 12, 1883, which forbids National banks to be members of Clearing-houses which do so discriminate, it is reported that the members of the New York Clearing-house have a tacit understanding that silver certificates shall not be tendered. But whether the members of the Clearing-house effect their settlements with each other with gold or silver certificates, or any other currency, is a matter of no concern to the Government. [!] In view of the fact that the Sub-Treasury is nearly always a debtor to the Clearing-house, the voluntary tender by the Sub-Treasury of gold certificates, in each case, is something which the banks do not rightfully control. There are those who think that gold had better be in the Treasury and silver in circulation, if the Secretary of the Treasury has to choose between these two alternatives; and that the National banks would pursue a wiser course not to insist upon a policy which continually depletes the Treasury reserve in gold; as the greater the impairment of the Treasury gold, the greater is the probability of coming to a silver basis.

TIMES AND WE CHANGE.—The Chicago *Tribune* of September 24, 1884, quotes a long article from the *Wall Street News*, beginning thus, under the heading. "The Union of the Puritan and the Blackleg": —"The formal alliance of Mr. Jay Gould and Mr. Charles Francis Adams, Jr., is one of those strange sights which the whirligig of time sometimes presents to a wondering world. The most telling exposure ever made of the Erie rascalities, was made by the Massachusetts gentleman, who gained great fame thereby. His pen-portrait of his present partner, has passed into literature as one of the best of its kind. It is quoted now from time to time, when some peculiar performance of Mr. Gould makes it appropriate. To-day the firm of Gould & Adams is regularly advertised. as one of the prominent partnerships of financial circles."

The article goes on to show that Mr. Adams will come out with a total loss of reputation; and that those who thought that Mr. Adams' puff of Michigan Central was a result of inexperience, will see,—in the light of his puff of Union Pacific,—that both were stock-gambling dodges.

In October, 1884, Secretary Gresham left the Treasury, and Hugh McCulloch,—about whom such very contrary opinions are expressed,—took hold again, under President Arthur.

GOULD'S GREATNESS.—1884, finds Jay Gould thoroughly "in touch" with all the other great American financiers. Some other monopoly paper said, apparently, in 1884:— It is a sign of the times that even New York newspapers, which have been unanimous in assailing Jay Gould, as the wickedest man in Wall Street, are finding that he is no worse, after all, than a great many of his associates and competitors in speculation ; and that he is even better than some of them. It is a new thing to find a good word for Jay Gould in a New York paper. The *Sun* of yesterday has this fair-minded statement : "Gould is a schemer of immense genius, and a financier of amazing abilities. He builds up immense systems of railroads and telegraphs. He is the head and soul of innumerable corporations; some of which are of national importance. He is a public man in the broadest sense of the word. His name and his works will live in the history of the progress of this country. The way in which he did and still does his work may be objectionable, even unjustifiable, but that is another question. *He may be a bad man, but he is a great man.* Posterity will decide whether he was as bad as his contemporaries assert that he is."

It seems that there was a desperate and old-fashioned scheme seriously considered by the British ministry in 1884, for retaining gold. The *Troy, N. Y. Telegram* said :—The proposition of the British ministry to degrade the gold coin of England by increasing the alloy, is a scheme to retain the gold in that country by legislation. If a given amount of gold bullion will make more legal money in England than elsewhere ; that country will have no difficulty in retaining

as much as it wants. The proposition is meeting with decided opposition on all sides.

In 1884, J. J. Knox published a book claiming to give the
history of "United States Notes." Whoever reads this book
should read that one; and determine, for himself, as to
which gives the truer account of American paper money.

NOT USEFUL CITIZENS.—It is always pleasing to find
admission made by the enemy. Hear what the N. Y.
Tribune—the monopolist's own—said in 1884:—"Within
a few years the number of brokers in this city has increased
immensely," said an old-time "Street" operator to a
Tribune reporter. "There are, without the least exaggeration, three or four times as many brokers now as there were
ten or twelve years ago. There are about 11,000 brokers in
the city; and they must average $5,000 a year each; or they
could not pay clerk hire, office rent and other necessary expenses. Here you have about $50,000,000 taken from the
producing classes to support these non-producers; who
chiefly act as middlemen for others who want to gamble.
The number of speculators is also multiplying. Twenty
years ago, speculation outside of stocks and gold, was scanty.
Now look at the array of articles, such as cotton, wheat,
corn and other cereal products, lard, pork, bacon, butter,
cheese, oil, iron, steel, copper, etc., etc., which have been
added to the list of things bought and sold on margins.
There are 3,000 members of the Produce Exchange. If each
article sold on that floor was actually delivered, it would require many times the amount of cereals now shipped to this
market. Forty-nine out of fifty ' sales ' are simply bets, nothing more. The loser pays the difference in price, and does
not deliver the goods. I allude to the 'reported' sales
only. The unreported sales are no doubt very large. Three
hundred members could actually do the legitimate business
of this Exchange—the actual buying and selling of cereals
in this market. But business must be made for the extra
large number of members; and each article of produce
shipped to this market is bought and sold forty or fifty times,
—but it is only delivered once. The Petroleum Exchange,
finding there is not enough oil in the country, is now gambling
in railroad shares: perhaps it will next take ' pools ' on horse-
races. The lowest limit of shares in the Petroleum Exchange

has been reduced to ten ; so that even the comparatively poor can enjoy the luxury of putting up a margin on railroad stocks. This shows that the passion for gambling is increasing year after year.

" But the increase of this large non-producing element of brokers—who merely act as stakeholders for those who gamble,—adds nothing to the industry or development of the country. Not one bushel of grain or pound of metal is added to the resources of the country."

CHAPTER XVI.

1885 to 1892.

THE BEGINNING OF THE END.
1885.

BELMONT-HEWITT-TILDENISM.—The year 1885 opens with the reign of Cleveland in the White House, and Manning in the Treasury. Mr. Cleveland could not wait until he had taken the oath of office, to vent his Belmont-Hewitt-Tilden Democracy. On February 24, 1885, he wrote to A. J. Warner, and others, who had admonished him about silver. He demanded that we should get rid of the silver coinage act at once; otherwise we would be on a silver basis; and the gold obligations of the Government could not be met. He exclaimed that a financial crisis was close at hand. Gold was being expelled! Mark in his conclusion, the old gag about an honest dollar for the dear workingman. He said :—Such a financial crisis as these events would certainly precipitate,—were it now to follow upon so long a period of commercial depression, would involve the people of every city and every State in the Union in a prolonged and disastrous trouble. The revival of business enterprise and prosperity,—so ardently desired and apparently so near,—would be hopelessly postponed. Gold would be withdrawn to its hoarding places ; and an unprecedented contraction in the actual volume of our currency would speedily take place. Saddest of all, in every workshop, mill, factory, store, and on every railroad and farm, the wages of labor, already depressed, would suffer still further depression, by a scaling down of the purchasing power of every so-called dollar paid into the hands of toil. From these impending calamities, it is surely a most patriotic and grateful duty of the representatives of the people to deliver them.

I am, gentlemen, with sincere respect, your fellow-citizen,
GROVER CLEVELAND.

Albany, February 24, 1885.

The enemies of U. S. notes never relax their efforts against them.   April 16, 1884, the House Committee on Coinage, Weights and Measures, unanimously instructed representative Lacy to report favorably his bill to prohibit the issue of Treasury-notes of less than five-dollar denomination ; and to provide for the issue of one, two, and five dollar silver certificates.

———

On the same day, Boards of Trade from various cities were nagging at Congress to stop coining silver and " save the country."   " Why do the heathen rage ? "

MANNING PANIC.—By July, 1885, the money-lenders got poor little Manning worked up to such a frenzy, that he began to buy millions of gold with his silver,—" to get ready for the panic."   Here is what Senator Teller said, in his speech of May 14, 1890, about that absurdity :—

Mr. Teller.—It is pretty well known that in July, 1885, Mr. Jordan, who was then Treasurer of the United States, was present at a congregation of bank presidents in New York, who got together, ostensibly, for the purpose of sustaining the credit or the American Government ; which was on the verge of bankruptcy !   The new Administration had just come in.   The President had appealed to his party associates to demonetize silver.   They had told him,—in terms polite but emphatic,—that they would not do it ; that the Democratic party was not in favor of the single standard of gold.   And then this remarkable convocation of bankers in New York City got together, to prevent the Government of the United States from paying its obligations in what ?   In silver.   Every obligation that the Government had out was by law payable in silver. It was the money of this country, and of the contract ; and not even the gold barons had any right to complain that they were getting silver ; for they had stipulated that they would have silver or gold.   It was on the face of the bond. They had put it in the bond themselves ; and demanded that it should be put there before they would take the bond.

Mr. Stewart.—It was printed on every bond.

Mr. Teller.—It was printed on every bond, that it was payable in coin of the then standard value silver of July 14, 1870.   Now, that was the dire calamity that might overtake the Government.   So they got together and said, " The Government is in danger."   Of what ?   Disgracing itself by paying according to its contract. The next morning, every financial region of the earth contained the statement that the Government of the United States was on the verge of bankruptcy. Had there been any executive officer in that meeting officially, he ought to have been impeached. A more shameless attack upon the public credit has never been known in the history of the finances of this country.

Was the Government in danger of bankruptcy? I demonstrated in a speech that I made here,—but I will not go over it,—that there was an abundance of gold to pay every maturing obligation of the Government. There was not the slightest suspicion of danger of paying a silver dollar; and the Treasurer, and the Secretary, and the Chief Executive knew it. They said that they were not responsible for the transaction. They said they did not get it up; it was these loving bankers who were anxious to give the Government a lift and keep its credit at par. And Mr. Jordan, the Treasurer, said he was only a looker-on and not there officially.

Mr. Teller then went on to show that there was abundance of money in the Treasury—gold, Greenbacks, National bank notes and silver; and all could have been turned into gold. He said, "That, I assert, was a combination and conspiracy of the bankers of New York, to frighten the American people, —to compel them to·bring the influence of public opinion upon the legislative department,—to compel the suspension of the coinage of silver."

"GREAT HEADS" RATTLED.—It is interesting to watch some of our "great thinkers and leading economists," floundering through the years. Here is the immaculate and vociferous Edward Atkinson, saying, in Aug. 1885, "Witness the effect of the great mass of gold which was suddenly placed at the disposal of Germany by the payment of the French indemnity. It may be questioned whether the disasters which ensued from this sudden accretion of wealth in Germany, were not greater than the burden imposed upon France. It precipitated the one country into disastrous speculation; while the other went quietly to work to replace the devastation of war." He thinks that the thousand million dollars indemnity was paid in gold; whereas only two hundred and fifty millions was paid in money of any sort; and the rest in French goods, which, through a wise use of paper money by the French, were made to utterly swamp the same sorts of German goods. Hence the German misery; which was only in a small degree from " disastrous speculation."

Another and a ludicrous slip up, is seen in the following from the N. Y. *Journal of Commerce* of Oct. 1885, concerning the wording of the U. S. 4 per cent. bonds of 1907. Editor Stone, that fossilized Wall Street oracle, says: " We drew up the clause in question to be engraved on the first bonds upon which the promise was made; and wrote it 'gold coin of the standard value,' etc. Some time afterward, when there was a question about the matter, we stated that they were payable in gold coin; supposing that our suggestion had been adopted, precisely as we wrote it. In reply, a Wall Street broker brought in a bond; and we found, to our great surprise, that the word ' gold ' had been omitted."

What an outrage! It is enough to make all the plants in Editor Stone's celebrated Brooklyn greenhouses and gardens turn white with wrath. It would be interesting to learn how much more gold-bug mischief, " we " had a hand in. Fortunately, on this occasion, "we," did not " get there."

A CURIOUS PROPOSITION was made to the United States in 1885, by the noted English economist and bi-metalist, Morton Frewen. He said :—

And it seems to me that you might throw open your Pacific ports, and trade freely through them with all nations : while continuing the existing tariffs on your Eastern seaboard. For, if you did this, none of our manufactures could be sent round the world as it were, to Pacific ports ; there to make a profitable entry; but, on the other hand, China and India would send you tea, rice, coffee, jute, etc., in exchange for the silver of Colorado, Nevada, and California. And in this way you would encourage the building of a mercantile marine in the glorious harbors of your Pacific coast,—and such a trade would spring up at free-trade England's expense, across the Pacific, as would force England to buy and monetize silver on your terms. There can be no question that if, as we are now told, China is waking up from the sleep of centuries, she is destined to absorb silver in such quantities, that ten years hence the ratio of 1 to 16 may be altogether against gold. As a nation, therefore, you have everything to gain by continuing to support silver.

Judging from present appearances, the gold-using nations are insolvent. The tide of their currency requirements is retreating, and leaving them stranded high and dry on the mud banks of a contracted currency.

1886.

A Coon Treed.—Whenever an ex-Treasury official wants to get a bank presidency, or to please the money-lenders generally,—he begins to shout for gold payments. A coon of that sort was thus handled by the N. Y. *Sun* February 23, 1886 : " The proposition that good faith requires the payment of the outstanding United States bonds in gold is elaborately supported by Mr. Charles E. Coon, lately Assistant Secretary of the Treasury, in a letter to the New York *Herald*. Mr. Coon bases his argument upon the use of the word 'gold' by members of Congress and public officials, in speaking of the bonds at various dates, down to June 19, 1877." The *Sun* says that if he had followed the record a few months further, viz., to January 25 and 28, 1878, he would have come upon the Congress resolution of that time, declaring that all the outstanding bonds, except 200 million of 4½s and 75 million of 4s, are payable in silver dollars.

The Ways of the Robber Nation.—The following from Senator Teller's Congress speech, of May 14, 1890, shows, that England, the great robber nation, legislates only for her money-lending class and Government officials of late ; and robs her own producers as brutally as those of other nations, by maintaining the gold basis :—

The American farmer has suffered because of the mistaken financial policy of England, followed by the United States with slavish subserviency,—the English farmer, not having the many natural advantages possessed by the American farmer, has suffered much more. I have here a statement made in March, 1886, by the senior land commissioner of Great Britain, Sir James Caird, before the Royal Commission of Trade and Industry, which I have had copied. I do not desire to read it, but I desire to put it in the *Record*. I desire that the American people may see what this financial policy, with reference to silver, has done for the agriculturists of Great Britain, as well as this country. Mr. Caird came before the commission and said he was the senior land commissioner of England ; that he had prepared himself to give his testimony before the commission as to the condition of the agriculturists of that country. His statements were quite startling, and can be found in the second report, on page 293 and the subsequent pages to, and including, page 308. One member of the commission spoke of the statement as "having regard to the very fearful condition of things as shown by you." The condition of 1886 was compared with ten years before, and it was stated that, on an average, the landlords had lost 30 per cent., the tenants 60 per cent. and laborers 10 per cent., or a total loss to tenants, laborers and landlords of spendable income of £42,800,000 during the last year ; and in this estimate Ireland was not included. He declared that the price of wheat had been less each year (except the year 1877) ; and the loss to farmers on wheat, comparing prices with the price of 1874, had been, ten years, £97,100,000, or nearly $500,000,000. He declared that the Irish agriculturist no longer "farmed for profit, but simply for bare subsistence."

*   *   *   *   *   *

" Do you suppose that the depression in agriculture has been greater in degree than that of other British interests of great magnitude ? "

" I am speaking before gentlemen who are very much better informed upon that question than I am, and I can only venture to offer a calculation which has been made by a gentleman who placed it before me ; and which shows that whilst the fall of price in all kinds of food up to 1885 was 25 per cent., the fall in iron, copper, tin, lead, and coals was 35 per cent. ; in textiles, cotton, flax, hemp, wool, and silk, 32 per cent. ; in sundry materials, hides, leather, indigo, and other things 26 per cent. ; and therefore it would appear that many of those great British interests are suffering from the fall of price quite as much as agricultural interests."

LORD CHANCELORS' GOLD PENSIONS.—An English Royal Commission was appointed in September, 1886, " to inquire into the recent changes in the relative values of the precious metals." It worked two years. Edwards Pierrepont, in the *North American Review*, says :— " The report is inconsistent in its parts, fertile in untenable objections, inconsequent in its conclusions, proposing plans of relief quite inadequate to the conditions ; wholly impracticable, and absolutely bewildering to any honest seeker after light upon this recondite [?] subject. From its scope and drift, one might easily imagine that the six commissioners were all retired Lord Chancelors, intellectually convinced that international bi-metalism was the only remedy for the evils under which Great Britain and her Indian Empire now suffer ; *but dreading lest the introduction of silver might diminish the purchasing power of their gold pensions."*

The scoundrels !

WHAT THE SOLDIERS LOST.—Mr. Weaver, Greenback labor candidate for the Presidency in 1880, was for several terms in Congress. He was most noted as a skillful congressional fighter—generally on the side of the people. One of his most unique efforts is thus described by the St. Louis *Republican* in 1886 : " Mr. Weaver (Greenbacker) of Iowa, has introduced in the House a bill to appropriate $300,000,000 to indemnify the soldiers of the Union army, for the losses they sustained in the depreciation of the Greenbacks they were paid in during the war. This bill, or one just like it, has been offered in almost every Congress, for the last eight years : but little attention has been paid to it, and it is not probable that it will receive consideration now. The soldiers of the late war do not have the good fortune to belong to the favored class of American citizens. The Greenbacks they were paid in were worth 37 to 80 cents on the dollar in coin ; and the Greenback bonds sold by the Government during the war, were bought at the same rates. But while a Republican Congress gratuitously turned a profit of 20 to 40 per cent. into the pockets of the bondholders, by making their Greenback bonds payable in coin, it has repeatedly refused to extend similar favor to the soldiers."

A specimen of the tone of the gold-bugs in 1886 is seen in an editorial by Horace White in the N. Y. *Evening Post* of January 13. This deluded mortal who had joined himself to two " others worse than himself," Carl Schurz and E. L. Godkin, makes his severe criticism on Senator Beck's silver speech. The only fresh point he makes is that the money reformers find their argument for paying the bonds in Greenbacks on the BACK of that money, while the FRONT promises to pay a dollar ! ! !

1887.

A DELUGE OF TRUSTS AND SYNDICATES.—The year 1887 shows no very marked financial events. Everything drifts toward trusts and syndicates ; and these hold the public attention. English capital pours over here—absorbing our best-paying industries. The continued effort of the money-lenders to suppress silver and Greenbacks is shown by the following editorials of our pet British daily—the N. Y. *Times*. In one article it commends the noble efforts of Hugh McCulloch under Arthur, and Manning under Cleveland, to withdraw the legal tenders; and wails thus at the effect of their patriotism :—But in the country at large, there was no response to these suggestions, so clearly and forcibly sustained. On the contrary, they were regarded as propositions actually to destroy something accepted as real money. Had Congress been asked to sink $346.000.000 of gold or silver in the bottom of the sea, the proposition would not have appeared more absurd to the general mind.

*   *   *   *   *   *

The Supreme Court has decided, on grounds that we believe to be logically unsound, historically false, and in economy mischievous—that these legal tender issues (forced loans in fact and in effect), can be increased at any moment, by any amount, at the whim of a chance majority in Congress, with the consent of the Executive ; or, if the majority be two-thirds of a quorum, without that consent. Against this monstrous and grotesque theory, which is the law of the land, there is absolutely only one defense; it is to pay the legal-tender notes ; and thus to free the public mind of familiarity with the power whose exercise is allowed.

"WHO MAKE LIES THEIR REFUGE."—In another article, it commends Professor J. L. Laughlin (of Harvard, I believe) for his painstaking effort in the *Quarterly Journal of Economics*, to prove against all the facts—that the fall in prices that has taken place since 1873, cannot be traced to the scarcity of gold and demonetization of silver. Laughlin funnily and cunningly slurs over the demonetization of silver ; and dwells on the idea that the supply of gold has not greatly diminished ; that checks and notes are more used, and that manufactures have been cheapened, to explain the situation. He coolly denies the well-established fact that prices of commodities fell at least 33 per cent. from 1873 to 1890.

THE OLD, OLD STORY.—The needless loaning of Government money to banks in 1887, was thus tersely rebuked by the N. Y. *Sun* :—

Favoring the Banks.

The Secretary of the Treasury has resolved to increase both the number of depository banks and the amount of public money put into their keeping. The maximum for each bank is to be $1,100,000, and the security required is to be $1,000,000 in United States four per cent. bonds.

The practical result of this measure will be to make a gift to each of the favored banks, of nearly the whole of the interest on the bonds required from it. The four per cents. are selling at 125, and $1,000,000 of them would cost $1,250,-000. Supposing each depository bank to' purchase this amount in bonds, and then receive $1,100,000 of public money; its net investment will be $150,000; while it will draw the interest on the full $1,000,000 of bonds, amounting to $40,000 a year. Deducting the interest on the $150,000 margin, its net profit will be $34,000 a year; less a small deduction for a sinking fund for the premium on the bonds.

If, on the other hand, the Secretary should purchase the bonds himself,—as he has the right to do under the act of March 3, 1881,—the people would gain the interest instead of the banks. It is not pretended that any more depository banks are needed for the convenience of public business, or that any increase of the money deposited with them is required. The Secretary's scheme is purely one of favoritism to the banks, at the expense of the taxpayers.

The Treasury has plenty of money to spare; and it should be employed in buying bonds and stopping the interest on them.

JOHN THOMPSON said to me :—I find the following was going the rounds of the money-reform papers in 1887. I am of that opinion still.

" The mono-gold advocates are doing their best to monopolize the money of the world. Their measures are admirably calculated to sweep into the hands of the millionaires the assets of the industrial classes, at very disastrous prices.—

" John Thompson, President

" Chase National Bank, New York."

STOCK SWINDLES.—A reform paper says :—In 1887, an Arizona mine was placed on the list of the Stock Exchange. It was capitalized at five hundred thousand dollars, in five hundred thousand shares of one dollar each. It was probably worth just that amount. Nevertheless, by flaming advertisements, by lying opinions of experts, by the process known as " Washing ",—that is, by hiring one set of brokers to buy and another set of brokers to sell,—the price of shares was forced to fifteen times their value. Then, when the public was safely trapped, the operators allowed the stock to tumble into the cents. Thousands were ruined. They were nearly all people of small means.

Now, with one exception, the people who planned this cruel swindle were people of the highest respectability. They were church-goers, deacons, leading lights of the Masonic fraternity. They knew precisely what the mine was worth; they prepared for the reception of the experts who visited it; they saw that it was properly " salted "; they even tampered with the specimens which the experts brought away. They deliberately set their snares for waiters, washerwomen, elevator-boys, anybody, in short, who would invest the saving of a lifetime in their nefarious enterprise.

The swindle made them rich; and to-day they laugh at those who seek redress from them. One of them had even the effrontery to prosecute the unspeakable Henry S. Ives, for schemes far less heartless and far less successful.

" The case is wholly exceptional," Mr. Clews would say. Not at all.

If the financial writers of the daily newspapers cared to speak frankly on the subject, they would say that there is hardly a stock on the list which is not being " manipulated " like this Arizona mine. There is hardly a stock that is not being daily made the subject of the " deal." And a " deal " is a Wall Street euphemism for a swindle. The dealer is playing with marked cards.

1888.

BLAINE RIGHT THIS TIME.—The most interesting financial matter in 1888, outside of the rush into trusts and syndicates, was the trick of loaning Government money so largely to banks, which was made a double-leaded outrage by Mr. Blaine, because it was done by Democratic secretaries. After a short term as Secretary, Mr. Manning made the usual rush into bank presidency, in company with Jordan the great gold borrower of the Treasury.

In 1888, Mr. Blaine paid off the democrats for rattling his friend Sherman, by getting this point on them. I have something more to say on that point; for I have learned something since I spoke on it. Not only have they taken 60 million dollars and loaned it to banks in the United States; but they have done that through the agency of the bank established by Mr. Jordan, and by the late Mr. Manning. They have made them a sort of Government bureau; have given them $1,100,000 as a fixed balance to call their own, and then they have allowed them to peddle out this 60 millions to other banks; and, by that means, to get a large number of banks throughout the country, to give them their entire business. And I say here, that Louis XIV. of France, or Peter the Great of Russia, or Napoleon, at his most absolute period, would never have dared to treat the Treasury of their respective countries in that way. Never!"

The *Sun* said:—Secretary of the Treasury Fairchild, in his Wall Street speech on Saturday, tried to break the force of Mr. Blaine's Detroit argument against loaning the surplus to the banks without interest. In this attempt, he made use of a characteristic Democratic wriggle.

Mr. Blaine had estimated that a deposit of one million dollars would be worth $50,000 to the depository in a year. Secretary Fairchild, in answering this, immediately assumes that the $910,000 of bonds which he would have required as security for the deposit would have cost the bank a premium of 25 per cent., or a total purchase price of $1,137,500; which, at five per cent., would have given the bank $56,875 interest, even if it had not became a depository.

Now, nobody knows better than Secretary Fairchild, that many, if not most of the banks, that have borrowed the Treasury surplus, have used as security the bonds on which they had been securing their circulation. They did not have to buy bonds at 125 to offer as security for the loan. They simply retired their circulation, which was only 90 per cent. of the face value of the bonds, and used the same bonds to borrow 110 per cent. of their face value on. A safe loan, undoubtedly, when the bonds were selling at 125; but for all that it gave the banks 20 per cent. more money to lend, than they derived from the use of those bonds as security for circulation.

As the bonds that have been serving as security for circulation, were bought at varying prices, and at different times within the past ten years, it would have been a good deal fairer to· estimate their average cost at 110 or 115 than at 125. But it was still more unfair to ignore this increase of more than 20 per cent. in the principal of the amount that the banks were enabled to loan.

19

HIGH TREASON.—In 1888 the Controller of the Currency made a proposition that was enough to make the old departed Greenback leaders rise from the dead. It is described by a pseudo-Democratic paper; and Democrats should do some hard thinking, when they reflect how far from the doctrines of Jefferson and Jackson their leaders are leading them, by writing such articles as the following :—The most striking feature of the report of the Controller of the Currency, is his recommendation that the Greenbacks be funded in 2½ per cent. bonds, available only as a basis for National bank circulation. This would, at least, save the Government from further infraction of the constitutional principle, against issuing paper money in time of peace. It is true that the Supreme Court has sustained the legality of reissuing Greenbacks after they have been redeemed ; but, in so doing, it did more to hurt its reputation, than in rendering almost any other decision in its history. Perhaps, if the case were to come up before it again, the result would be different. There are more Democrats on the Bench now.

A POOR CREATURE.—David A. Wells,—who has been wandering in the Serbonian bogs of false economics ever since he deserted his first master, Henry C. Carey, to try to boss the Free Traders,—has, of course, something to say about " the fall of prices ; " and vents the same sort of wisdom in 1888 as Prof. Laughlin did before him. The *N. Y. Record and Guide* handles him thus :—The articles contributed by David A. Wells to the popular *Science Monthly*, purporting to explain the causes of the fall in prices since 1872, are about to be republished in book form, and will in that shape be very widely read. Mr. Goschen, the British Chancelor of the Exchequer, gave the results of his study of this subject in several well-considered speeches a few years back. He attributed the rapid fall in prices to the demonetization of silver by the leading commercial nations. Other causes were, of course, at work to depress values. But the measuring of prices by one instead of two metals was sufficient to account, in his estimation, for the depression of industries the world over. Mr. Wells' contention, however, is, that the adoption of the gold unit has nothing to do with prices. It is true these have fallen in a most remarkable way ; but, according to Mr. Wells, it is because of improvements in machinery, new inventions, increased production, and an extension of steam transportation to distant regions : thus utilizing the products of the earth in a way that would not have been possible twenty years ago.

The *Financial Chronicle*, however, takes Mr. Wells to task, and shows that the figures and facts he gives are fallacious. He picks on the wrong years with which to make comparisons ; and, in the case of wheat and cotton, for instance, the facts lead to the very opposite conclusion to that he draws from them. Mr. Wells is, however, a *doctrinaire* of the most pronounced type. It is quite evident from the tone of his articles, that he cares less about getting at the facts, than he does about using them to establish a foregone conclusion.

IN A NUTSHELL.—I venture to say that nowhere in writings upon economics, is there a more pregnant paragraph than the following. It gives proof positive, from all sorts of economists, that demonetization of silver has caused,—all through the civilized world,—a fall in the values of the great human products (except that one selected for petting—gold) of at least 33 per cent. Read and be convinced :—

The *Economist* of London gives prices in 1873 at 134; in 1888 at 101, a decline of 33 per cent. Dr. Soetbeer gives in 1873, 138 ; in 1887, 103, a fall of 35. Mr. Palgrave gives in 1873, 104; in 1887, 73, a fall of 31. Mr. Sauerbeck gives in 1873, 111 ; in 1887, 68, a fall of 33 per cent. Mr. Giffin gives prices of British exports in 1873 at 132 ; in 1886, 82, a fall of 50 per cent. The same author gives British imports in 1873 at 107 ; in 1886, 74, a fall in prices of 33 per cent.

Most, if not all, of these statisticians are advocates of the gold standard. Their figures cannot be claimed as having been brought forward by silver advocates.

1889.

"FAIR GAMBLES."—There is increasing talk and action in connection with trusts this year. "Matthew Marshall", who succeeded the late "Rigolo" in writing the N. Y. *Times*' Monday article on "Finance", gives a lucid article on trust stocks from his stand-point, that of a mere sharp money-maker and seeker. He makes no complaint against trusts—says that they are all right and inevitable. They are blind pools; and he won't invest in them, because they make no clear reports.

Like a fly-wheel, they equalize the motion of the industries they control. He concludes :—

Of the liability of these trusts to injury from hostile legislation I do not make much account. If the Western Union Telegraph Company can, without interference, own all the telegraph lines in the country ; and the Standard Oil Trust all the petroleum wells and refineries ; I do not see why other combinations, of a similar nature, should not find a way to carry on their business with equal impunity. Of course, laws may be made and lawsuits may be begun, which, for a while, will be troublesome and even embarrassing ; but, sooner or later, the ingenuity of skillful lawyers will circumvent all obstacles, as the water of a brook finds a course past all the stones that may be heaped in its bed. So long as partnerships and corporations are permitted, there can be no prevention of trusts, and partnerships and corporations cannot be prohibited without putting a stop to all enterprises which require large amounts of capital. This objection to investing in trust stocks is, therefore, entitled to little or no weight.

On the whole, I am inclined to regard industrial trust stocks as fair GAMBLES, for those who can afford to risk their money in them ; but not as sound investments for people out of business. Probably, after a while, time will so consolidate and strengthen the best of them, and so much may become known of their affairs, that even cautious buyers may be induced to regard them with favor. But they have not reached this state yet.

ABUNDANT SILVER HELPS PRODUCERS.—Senator Jones gives this, in 1890, in rebuttal of the statement that remonetization of silver would only profit the mineral states. Of course abundance of paper money would have the same effect as abundance of coin : "The price of cotton for the year 1873, in gold or silver (then of equal power), was 16.4 cents per pound. The price in 1889 was 9.9 cents. The yield of cotton for 1889 was 7,000,000 bales, or 3,500,000,000 pounds. Had not silver been demonetized that cotton would have brought as good a price to-day as it did in 1873. At the price of 1873, the account would have stood 3,500,000,-000 pounds, at 16.4 cents, $574,000,000. At the price of 1889 the account stands 3,500,000,000 pounds, at 9.9 cents, $345,500,000 ; showing a loss in debt-paying and tax-paying

power on cotton alone (only one article of merchandise) in
the single year 1889,—by reason of the fall in prices caused by
the demonetization of silver, of $227,500,000. Having shown
that the loss to the silver miners by the discount on silver,
for the seventeen years from 1873 to 1889, was less than
$130,000,000; it will be seen that the loss in one single
year to the cotton planters of the United States is greater,
by $90,000,000, than the total loss for the entire seventeen
years to the silver miners of the country.

" A like computation with regard to wheat, will show a loss
in debt-paying and tax-paying power of not less than $1,000,-
000, a year to the farmers of the north and west; [much
more.—S. L.] by reason of the demonetization of silver—a
total of $1,700,000,000 in the article of wheat alone in seven-
teen years."   **1890.**

From Mr. George O. Jones' chart I clip the following
paragraph, which shows the true relative interests of silver
miners and other producers :—

The Director of the Mint reports our present production
of silver at about 52,000,000 ounces a year, or at the rate of
520,000,000 ounces in ten years. Twenty-five cents per
ounce loss on these amounts would be $13,000,000 a year, or
$130,000,000 in ten years, leaving the account as between
American farmers and American silver kings as follows :

Relative value of certain American farm products, compared
with the value of all silver produced in this country, when
silver is selling at par with gold :

Products.	Per year.	Ten years.
Cotton........	$ 390,000,000	$ 3,900,000,000
Wheat.................	495,000,000	4,950,000,000
Corn.................	712,000,000	7,120,000,000
Oats and dairy products..	920,000,000	9,200,000,000
Total...	$2,517,000,000	$ 25,170,000,000
Silver total............	52,000,000	520,000,000
Difference	$2.465,000,000	$ 24,650,000,000

Loss on the above-named farm products, caused by a decline of 25 cents per ounce on the price of silver, compared with a like decline on all silver produced in this country :

Products.	Per year.	Ten years.
On the farm products named	$637,000,000	$6,370,000,000
On all silver............	13,000,000	130,000,000
Difference........	$624,000,000	$6,240,000,000

The above table shows that the American farmers, in the last ten years, have lost, by the demonetization act, nearly fifty times as much as the American silver miners.

GOVERNMENT LOANS ON LANDS AND GOODS.—1890 shows a great extension of the demand in the West and South for these loans. The following from a book called, "The Three Americas," published in 1890, has this :—It is not uninteresting, in this connection, to state an instructive fact touching the subject of Government loans, or loans guaranteed by Government, to Brazilian coffee planters. Under the recent Curo Preto ministry, the sum of 100 contos of reis (about $54,500,000), in aid of the agricultural interests, was lent to farmers through the banks. The statement is made, in the first annual report of the minister of finance, issued December 31, 1889, that this sum has to be spent during the various terms ; the Government having authorization to suspend such contracts if judged to be useless. It is the opinion in Brazil,—among that very enlightened people, the descendants of one of the oldest and most refined of European nationalities,—that *the Government will not lose* the interest, if the farmers derive no result from it ; as on the contrary, *the interest will enter the coffers of the Treasury*, under the form of importation and exportation taxes on agricultural products ; of lands whose taxable value is enhanced by the loans. Our statesmen must go to France and Brazil ; not England, to learn financial wisdom. Yet England, by act of parliament, has aided Irish farmers to the amount of £50,000,000. Prussia has made the same salutary experiment; and the state of New Jersey is not without a beneficent precedent. The class which feeds and clothes mankind, is of all others, the most entitled to the fostering care of Government. In the United States it has ever received the least consideration.

In them now reposes the power to enforce attention to their necessities. "They know what they want and are going to have it."

RATIO OF SILVER TO GOLD.—Senator Jones, in 1890, had a computation made of the alleged ratios of gold and silver from the foundation of society, and the beginning of history. Much of it is fanciful. But the general tenor seems to bear out his claim that the ratios have ranged, wherever apparent, from 1 to 10 to 1 to 16. A great part of the record is 1 to 10. His data from 1873 to 1889, are strictly reliable, and quite significant. Here they are :—

Table showing the ratio of silver to one of gold since the demonetization of silver by Germany and the United States, and the closing of all mints of the Western World to its free coinage :

1873	15.72	1882	18.19
1874	16.17	1883	18.64
1875	16.59	1884	18.57
1876	17.88	1885	19.41
1877	17.22	1886	20.78
1878	17.94	1887	21.13
1879	18.40	1888	21.99
1880	18.05	1889	22.10
1881	18.16		

THE SUN INCONSISTENT.—The following from the N. Y. *Sun*, in 1889, is probably to corroborate what I lately quoted from that paper about Gould's being "a great man" :—

The growth of the Missouri Pacific under Mr. Gould's management is shown by the fact that, in 1880, the gross earnings from 879 miles of road were $4,161,671, and in 1888 the gross from 1611 miles was about $6,000,000. The increase of business has come chiefly from the Texas lines ; as the Missouri Pacific has taken it away from the upper portions of the road, especially in Kansas. There is this to be said about a property or corporation that becomes bankrupt in Mr. Gould's hands ; as, in fact, nearly every property he manages does ; that the wreck he leaves is so complete that reorganization is most difficult. The Wabash furnishes irrefutable evidence of this statement ; and the Missouri, Kansas and Texas will supply additional proof. The concern has been insolvent for nearly a year, yet very little progress has been made toward improving its affairs. A good deal of investigation has been done ; but as yet no one has been able to furnish the actual dimensions of the hole that Mr. Gould has made in the property. The foreign security holders have, according to all accounts, been systematically misinformed as to the condition and value of the property ; and each interest has, if anything, become more self-sufficient and determined to have its own way. In the meantime, disinterested receivers are demonstrating what the property can earn.

TRUST COMPANY PROFITS.—In the following, from that reliable statistician, Marshall of the *Sun*, we catch a glimpse of how such palaces as that of the Union Trust Co. can be built. That company failed in 1873 :—The expenses, also, of a bank, for rent and salaries, are immensely greater, in proportion to its profits, than those of a trust company; while a trust company has sources of income—from commissions for accepting and executing mortgages and other trusts —which are denied to a bank. The usual fee for accepting a railroad mortgage trust is one dollar per $1,000 bond ; so that on a 10 million mortgage, it amounts to $10,000. Besides this when a trust company acts as agent for the reorganization committee of a bankrupt railroad company,— and advances the cash needed to facilitate the operation,—it charges a commission, as well as six per cent. interest on the money. These profits count up rapidly : so that I can well believe the story that the Central Trust Company made, in this way, $80,000 in one month, last year.

In his speech in the Senate, before the Silver Bill was passed, Mr. Jones said :—

I will read a cable dispatch recently addressed to me by Mr. Henry H. Gibbs, formerly governor of the Bank of England, and now president of the bimetallic league, of Great Britain :

"LONDON, May 6.—The friends of silver deeply regret the death of Senator Beck, whose services in the cause of monetary reform are most warmly appreciated on this side of the Atlantic. The bimetallist party of the United Kingdom now including over 100 members of the House of Commons, attach the greatest value to the debate about to commence in your illustrious chamber. We fully recognize not only that the support afforded to silver by your legislation,

during the last twelve years, has helped to protect the industrial world from an acute monetary crisis; but also that
the debates in Congress have served, more than all else, to
educate our people to recognition of the important issues
involved. We believe also that the increase and coinage of
silver contemplated by Congress will restore, wholly or considerably, your coinage rates; and will thus make international settlement of this complex question comparatively easy.
We anticipate further, and with much confidence, that the
advance in the price of silver which must follow your action,
will stimulate both the export and the other trades of your
country; and, while tending to the prosperity of your agricultural classes, will also assist the manufacturing industries
of the United Kingdom, and the whole body of our wage-
earners."

Mr. Moreton Frewen, of London, an able writer on economic subjects, whose recent work on "The Economic
Crisis" I commend to the careful perusal of senators, says:

"It may, indeed, be affirmed, without fear of contradiction,
that legislation arranged in the interest of a certain class,
first by Lord Liverpool in this country, and again by Sir
Robert Peel at the instigation of Mr. Jones Loyd and other
wealthy bankers,—which was supplemented recently by simul-
taneous anti-silver legislation in Berlin and Washington, at
the instance of the great financial houses,—this legislation
has about doubled the burden of all national debts, by an
artificial enhancement of the value of money.

"The fall of all prices induced by this cause, has been on
such a scale that, while in twenty years the national debt of
the United States, quoted in dollars, has been reduced by
nearly two-thirds; yet the value of the remaining one-third,
measured in wheat, in bar iron, or bales of cotton, is considerably greater—is a greater demand draft on the labor and
industry of the nation, than was the whole debt at the time
it was contracted. The aggravation of the burdens of taxation induced by this so-called 'appreciation of gold', which
is no natural appreciation, but has been brought about by
class legislation, to increase the value of the gold which is in
a few hands; requires but to be explained to an enfranchised
democracy; which will know how to protect itself against
further attempts to contract the currency; and to force down
prices to the confusion of every existing contract.

" Of all classes of middle-men, bankers have been by far the most successful in intercepting and appropriating an undue share of produced wealth.   While the modern system of banking and credit may be said to be even yet in its infancy ; that portion of the assets of the community which is to-day in the strong boxes of the bankers would, if declared, be an astounding revelation of the recent profits of this particular business.   And not only has the business itself become a most profitable monopoly ; but its interests, in a very few hands, are diametrically opposed to the general interests of the majority.   By legislation intended to contract the currency and force down all prices,—including wages, the price paid for labor,—the money owner has been able to increase the purchase power of his sovereign or dollar, by the direct diminution of the price of every kind of property measured in money."

Mark the words of the British Chancelor, April 18, 1890. Even the Britons sometimes realize the gold slavery. The Chancelor of the Exchequer, said in the House of Commons :—I admit that, as interested in the commerce and monetary system of this country; I feel a kind of shame that on the occasion of £2,000,000 or £3,000,000 of gold being taken from this country to Brazil,—or any other country,— it should immediately have the effect of causing a monetary alarm throughout the country.

SILVER BUGABOOS.—The following extracts from the speech of Senator Teller, of May 14 and 15, 1890, in the U. S. Senate, are very pertinent to the silver excitement. Speaking of the Windom Bill he said :

P. 7 :—Mr. President, that scheme, as I said, met the approval of the gold monometallists everywhere. I have found one thing pretty safe, in my practical life : that when my enemies want to do a particular thing and are anxious for it, look out.   When I found all the monometallists everywhere singing praises to this bill ; when I found the press that had been denouncing silver, and denouncing every man who supported the free coinage or even the limited use of silver under the Bland bill as money supporting it, and all gold monometallists clapping their hands in glee over the prospect of this bill becoming a law,—then I had reason to suspect that it was a Trojan horse. It was pretty certain, in a week, or I will say in a month, it was morally certain that that scheme could not succeed.

P. 15 :—There has never been a Secretary of the Treasury,—except it might have been a few months when somebody was accidentally there,—but there has been no man in charge of that Department for any considerable length of time, who has not been determined that silver should not go to par; and anything that would put it to par he was opposed to.

.P. 16 :—They said we were threatened with the increased mintage of silver ; with such a redundancy of silver certificates that the people would not want them, and they would come into the Treasury in payment of duties on imports, and the Government would have no gold with which to meet its obligations. Let us see how much we have received since 1887. That is, as far as I have got the statement.

In January, 1887, there were 16.2 per cent. of silver certificates ; in February, 10.1 ; in March, 11.4. These are the silver certificates paid in for duties on imports that thus found their way back to the Treasury. In July, 1888, these fell to 8.3 per cent.; in August, to 5.5 per cent.; in September, to 4.4 per cent.; in October, to 3.6 per cent.; in November, to 5.4 per cent.; in January, 1889, to 6.2 per cent.; in February, to 5.3 per cent.; and in April, 1890, to 1.6 per cent.

. The certificates are redeemable, according to this bill, in lawful money. They are not legal tender ; they cannot perform the highest money duty; they cannot discharge debts. " Oh," it is said, " everybody will take them." Mr. President, everybody will take them when they do not need the legal-tender quality; everybody will take them when business is all right. But what you need the legal-tender quality for is the time of distress, of financial convulsions and panics.

I have heard it said recently that there has been no trouble about legal tenders. We people of the West know better. I have seen in the State in which I live telegrams to send legal tender from Omaha by special train to Denver more than once. I know two parties left New York with the legal tenders for the city of Denver in 1873, to meet demands for legal tender during the panic of that year. Why should this not be legal tender for all parts of the country ? These notes are practically legal tender for New York City, for Philadelphia, and for the city of Washington ; because they have a Government agency with money stored, of a legal-tender character, to which they can go and exchange their certificates for legal tenders; but in the city of Denver, in the city of Omaha, in Kansas City, no man can exchange these certificates for legal tenders ; and if he wants legal tenders, he is at the mercy of banks that have them. Or, more likely, the banks will not have them ; and he is at the mercy of his creditors.

P. 30 :—If there is this great store-house of silver some-where, why has it not gone to India ? Why is it that India takes less silver now than she took years ago ? India from 1856 to 1870 took more than the entire production of the world of silver. She took last year $46,000,000 of silver. She has taken on an average for the last six years $35.000,000 of silver. Now, the mints are open, India is full of goods, India is full of everything that people want. Why has not all the silver of the world found its way into India to be coined ? The mints of Mexico are open, the mints of Japan are open ; and they have been open all the time, for silver, in Mexico, at a little more than our ratio ; and in Japan at still a little more than that ; and now even China has opened her mints to the silver of the world.

THE SILVER BILL OF JULY 14.—After many weeks of wrangling, this is the bill that finally passed :—

An Act directing the Purchase of Silver Bullion and the Issue of Treasury notes thereon, and for Other Purposes.

Be it enacted by the Senate and House of Representatives of the United States of America in Congress assembled, That the Secretary of the Treasury is hereby directed to purchase, from time to time, silver bullion to the aggregate amount of four million five hundred thousand ounces, or so much thereof as may be offered in each month, at the market price thereof, not exceeding one dollar for three hundred and seventy-one and twenty-five hundredths grains of pure silver ; and to issue, in payment for such purchases of silver bullion, Treasury notes of the United States to be prepared by the Secretary of the Treasury, in such form and of such denominations, not less than one dollar nor more than one thousand dollars, as he may prescribe; and a sum sufficient to carry into effect the provisions of this act is hereby appropriated out of any money in the Treasury not otherwise appropriated.

SEC. 2. That the Treasury notes issued in accordance with the provisions of this act shall be redeemable on demand, in coin, at the Treasury of the United States, or at the office of any assistant treasurer of the United States, and when so redeemed may be reissued; but no greater or less amount of such notes shall be outstanding at any time than the cost of the silver bullion and the standard silver dollars coined therefrom, then held in the Treasury purchased by such notes; and such Treasury notes shall be a legal tender in payment of all debts, public and private, except where otherwise expressly stipulated in the contract, and shall be receivable for customs, taxes, and all public dues, and when so received may be reissued; and such notes, when held by any National banking association, may be counted as a part of its lawful reserve. That upon demand of the holder of any of the Treasury notes herein provided for the Secretary of the Treasury shall, under such regulations as he may prescribe, redeem such notes in gold or silver coin, at his discretion; it being the established policy of the United States to maintain the two metals on a parity with each other upon the present legal ratio, or such ratio as may be provided by law.

SEC. 3. That the Secretary of the Treasury shall each month coin two million ounces of the silver bullion purchased under the provisions of this act into standard silver dollars, until the first day of July eighteen hundred and ninety-one; and after that time he shall coin of the silver bullion purchased under the provisions of this act as much as may be necessary to provide for the redemption of the Treasury notes herein provided for; and any gain or seigniorage arising from such coinage shall be accounted for and paid into the Treasury.

SEC. 4. That the silver bullion purchased under the provisions of this act, shall be subject to the requirements of existing law and the regulations of the mint service governing the methods of determining the amount of pure silver contained, and the amount of charges or deductions, if any, to be made.

In an article on " Exchange with India," in Blackwood's

Magazine, for July, 1890, Lt.-General Gray says : " Experts and scientists on currency are too apt unconsciously, from the peculiar tendency of minds so exclusively employed and trained, to evolve from an irresistible inner current of thought, *a state of chaos* of the subject-matter taken up and dealt with by them, agreeable to individual prepossessions."

PENSIONS FURNISH CURRENCY.—It has been well said, in 1890, that but for the pensions, large parts of the United States would be vastly more destitute of currency than they now are. Ben Colvin, a Western Reformer, said :—I would ask what would the people do if it were not for the pensions the poor soldiers get? Can the National banks answer? This condition of pensioning must gradually leave us; probably in a few years it will all be gone. Then what will we do for money? I suppose borrow of the banks, and thus increase usury and consequent slavery. About $100,000,000 are now paid annually for pensions ; if it were not for that what would the people do? It certainly is a condition that confronts us. Where would be our circulating medium? We should do all we could to keep the soldiers alive ; for when they all die our hopes of a circulating medium will be buried with them. You take $100,000,000 from the business of this country annually and the people are ruined, under the present financial system.

JONES ON INTRINSIC VALUE.—This report of an interview with Senator Jones by " Ben Abou " of the N. Y. *Press*, August 5, 1890, is very significant, coming from the man who is now " on top " in currency discussions : I think him in error about the imbecility of the Farmers' Alliance :—

Senator Jones of Nevada represents a constituency which has so little of the farming element in it, that he can look with complacency on the rise of the Farmers' Alliance ; and, like a man up a tree, watch it from the purely indifferent standpoint. I was chatting with him a day or two since, when he remarked that he thought the farmers might secure twenty or thirty or even forty Alliance members in the next Congress. " Then the end of the movement will come," said he, " because when they are there they will have nothing for which they can unitedly ask, or which they will demand to have done that is not now being done. The part of their movement on which I look with most interest is their demand for the issuance of money upon

products—corn, wheat, oats, etc. It is going to make the
men who have been crying for years that money must
have intrinsic value take a new view of things. If the gold
men are right, then the farmers are right. There is more
intrinsic value in wheat, corn and oats than in gold : because
these products supply and sustain life, whereas gold will not.
If it was left to a man's choice to take wheat or gold on
which to subsist for a number of years on a barren island,
how quickly he would choose the wheat! But, while it will
awaken the gold men to the foolishness of their position, in
reference to what money should be, it will awaken intelligent discussion and understanding of the real basis of money,
which should be *quantitative*. No matter what the medium
of exchange between the people, it is patent that if population increases three per cent. or five per cent. it will require
three per cent. or five per cent. more money to effect exchanges,—that is, to transact business among the people,—if
the money condition is to remain unchanged. This is why I
and many others believe that the medium of exchange, once
decided upon, may be anything which the Government
selects, and gives the name of money ; and its value will always be relatively determined by the ratio of its units to the
population and the demands put upon it."

BEECHER'S DEACON WHITE.—That sharp, jolly Wall Street
speculator, S. V. White, let off an unusual quantity of truth,
for a Wall Street man, one day in August, 1890, as follows :—

You men of the Fifty-first Congress have builded better
than you knew : and better than you dared to hope for.
Cereals are up, and men say it is because of a short crop in
the world. For myself I do not think so. There is no surplus crop ; but counting the surplus of past years there is an
abundant supply. Cereals are up, in my humble judgment,
in a large measure because of the beneficial results of the
silver legislation of the Fifty-first Congress. When this session convened, the Mark Lane grain dealer bought his wheat
in India, where they have the misfortune to have a mono-me-
tallic circulating medium, which happens to be silver. At
the same time that he bought wheat in India, he bought
silver in America at 92½ cents per ounce ; and paid for Indian wheat with silver rated at the gold value of 129½ cents
per ounce. He " had the drop " on the American farmer to
the extent of that 37 cents per ounce. But the 37 cents has

dwindled to 9 cents on the passage of the Silver bill ; and is still dwindling. Boys, you have done well enough! Don't try experiments! There is too much danger of a mistake.

[They will try the experiment of free coinage next. Result—no dropping back of silver to 1.00.—S. L.]

Here is a condensed, accurate statement of the fact that in all our laws about payment, treasury notes, etc., from 1860 to 1876, no payment in gold is called for :—The laws relating to issues of bonds, and of legal tender treasury notes, including provision for payment of duties on imports, beginning with the act of June 2, 1860, and ending with act of July 13, 1876, are thirty in number. While "silver" is mentioned many times and "lawful money" many times, the term "coin" is used throughout when referring to metallic money, in relation to any of the obligations of the United States, and "gold" not in a single instance is used in relation to those obligations. The word "gold" is mentioned in but three of all those acts and joint resolutions. The first one is in the act of March 3, 1863, where provision is made for receiving deposits of that metal upon which certificates might be issued for circulation. The second is in joint resolution of March 17, 1864, whereby any gold in the treasury not needed in coin payments of interest on the public debt, might be disposed of. The third is in act of July 14, 1870, whereby coins of that metal may be received and certificates issued. Even the assumption of an obligation on part of government to redeem legal tender notes is in these words, found in act of March 18, 1869 : "And the United States also solemnly pledges its faith to make provisions at the earliest practicable period for the redemption of the United States notes in *coin*."

1891.

Early in the winter of 1891, still expecting this work to be printed in connection with "Sixty Years in Wall Street," which gives the career of John Thompson, the banker, I wrote the following account of THE PANIC OF NOVEMBER 1890.

This book was to be printed in November, 1890. A delay consequent upon the final illness of Mr. Thompson, gives opportunity for some mention of the memorable Panic.

It much resembled that of 1884 in being mostly a Wall Street panic. But it is wider and deeper in its causes and effects than that of 1884. Men who understood the situation, like John Thompson, had been warning the people for a year that panic was close at hand, for want of sufficient currency. But it was left for the suspension of the Barings in London to start the ball.

History repeats itself very literally in this case. Nearly every article in this book about the disturbance of 1884 is applicable to this one. Let us revert and see.

We find, looking back, the statement that the panic of 1884 would have spread from Wall Street all over the country but for "the increased currency through silver legislation; and for the fact that resumption had been accomplished by yielding largely to the demands of the Greenbackers."

Then as now there were not many more failures than usual; but enough to *check business* considerably: so that, after it was over, "Conservative bankers", could congratulate the country that "money was now plenty again." Good reason: because so many industries had been checked, and men thrown out of work, who should be earning this plentiful money.

In 1884, as now, we find leading speculators buying stocks when they thought they were hammered as low "as the traffic would bear!" and thus preventing a general smash.

In 1884, as now, we had the owlish *Tribune* and such papers saying: "There is not a competent student of financial questions in the country who does not see that among all the causes of the present disturbance and peril. the continued coinage of silver [a pitiful two million a month] with the issue of paper certificates against coined silver, is the most potent. All about us lie financial wrecks caused by this mischievous policy.

In 1884, as now, call loans of banks to speculators was a destructive element, against which even the gold-bug *Journal of Commerce* raised its feeble whine.

In 1884, as now, as soon as the worst is over, the cry is raised that we do not want more money, but more banks of deposit and discount "to economize the money." "We do not want more money, but more credit."

In 1884, as now, our British papers, fiercest of gold-bugs—

20

the *Times* and *Evening Post*—were wailing about the flood of silver and "the flight of gold." The *Post* told us in July, 1884, that the Treasury had lost 50 millions of gold since January. "There can be no escape from coming down to silver," howled the *Post*. That same month Godkin was in ghoulish glee over the "End of Bi-Metallism."

But in 1890, as not in 1884, there is a cloud much bigger than a man's hand in the West. The Farmers' Alliance has elected many Congressmen ; pledged *before all else to more currency*. Ingalls has been dethroned in Kansas—Ingalls the leader of the Senate—and things are on the move generally in the West toward A GLORIOUS SUNSET FOR THE NINE-TEENTH CENTURY !

REVIEW OF 1891.—In March, 1891, I came to Chicago as an editor of the Chicage *Sentinel* and the Chicago *Express*, leading papers in the reform movement now called The People's Party.

In May came the wonderful convention of all sorts of radicals at Cincinnati, who so peaceably formed the new party. Through the summer and fall I was writing for these papers, and lecturing for the party as occasion offered in Illinois, Indiana, Nebraska and Missouri.

The fall elections were such as were to be expected, though we did not gain such victories in Kansas, Nebraska, and South Dakota as we hoped for. Yet we made gains in all those States, and elected hundreds of officials ; and ten thousand more votes properly distributed would have enabled us to beat the combination of the Republicans and Democrats in them.

Very much of the immediate future of the People's Party depends upon the South. If those who sympathize with us there can get over their fear of Negro domination, and their hope of salvation through the Democratic Party, we may throw the next Presidential election into the House and elect the President. Or we might even have a universal political cyclone like that of Kansas in 1890, and elect him in a straight contest.

All our party and a majority of the Farmers' Alliance, are in favor of the plan in the Ocala Platform to loan money on land. But Northern men are generally dubious about the loans on imperishable produce—not so much because they think them impracticable, but because other plans seem less risky and cumbrous.

As I write, the situation in Congress is very interesting to our people. The election of Crisp to the Speakership, though he is a mere politician, seems to make it certain that the Democrats will make silver rather than free trade the leading·issue.

Nine Congressmen and two or three Senators stand squarely for our party, and 38 Congressmen, called " Alliance men ", are on trial there. It is claimed that they will show up bravely for the Ocala Platform when occasion offers ; but many of them talk as if they considered that their duty and inclination lies in working with the Democrats. Time will show.

. On Nov. 21, I summed up the situation, as far as radical progress is concerned, in the following editorial in the Chicago *Express*, which would make a suitable closing chapter for this book.

DO YOU THINK, O FOOLS ?

There is high jubilation among some short-sighted, low-minded people, over the fact that the Alliance and the People's Party have not done so well politically this year as last.

Do you think, O fools, that the existing political, industrial and social systems, all tending to centralization of power, are not to be changed ? That because Tammany spoils and the lost World's Fair were the bones of contention in New York, the whole country is to sink to the level of New York ? That all the past progress of this country in freedom and scientific ways is to count for nothing ?

Do you think that the Alliance and the People's Party will now vanish like the hoar frost before the rising sun of your stupid, malevolent reaction ? That the money reform begun thirty years ago by such heroes as Thaddeus Stevens, Benj. Wade, O. P. Morton, Henry Wilson, Wendell Phillips, Henry C. Carey, Judge Kelley and Thomas Ewing, is to be at last put down by usurers led on by Jew Shylocks ?

Do you think that the stern, earnest farmers who met at Cincinnati last May, with all the solemn, religious decorum of Cromwell's Ironsides, will now settle back to be contented

serfs of Wall Street and the multi-millionaires? That the im-
pulse toward freedom and human rights that is stirring all
the wise-hearted of this and other lands, is now to be hushed
by your venomous lies and trickery? That the men of the
forest and hill country and prairie, who have been meeting in
their groves this summer, by the ten thousand, to consult
about the righting of their wrongs, are now to be quelled by
a good crop, and the billingsgate of hireling editors and demagogues?

Do you think that the corruption in all high places of trade,
politics, legislation and social life, will not work its legitimate
fruits, in total demoralization and the Mexicanizing of this
Republic, if not stopped? That the despair in the hearts of
all wise, thoughtful people over our present industrial and
commercial rottenness, will suddenly be turned to jubilation,
by the magic of your devilish spells? That when the great
railroad, telegraph, oil, mining and manufacturing trusts are
showing us what government should take hold of, it will be
allowed to keep its hands off much longer?

Do you think that your little spurt of reaction, by a combination of Reps and Dems at the polls, is turning back the
hands of progress on the dial of this epoch? That Europe
and European ways are now to be invited to finish their damnable work, by taking complete possession of this country?
That Europe is to be urged to set up her usury pumps here,
in harmonious unison with those of our own blood-suckers?
That Europe is to be encouraged to seize, wherever possible,
our lands, mines and best-paying industries? That while
England is beginning a tardy justice to Ireland, by buying
the land for the soil tillers, all sorts of monopoly is to ride
rampant here? That when England has just put thirty workingmen into Parliament, and is preparing to overthrow her
House of Lords, our " nobility ", now uncoroneted, are soon
to bloom out with coronets? That when the Social Democracy of Germany is filling up the Reichstag, the American
Congress is still to be run by millionaires and corporation
lawyers? That when scores of towns and cities in England are municipalizing gas, water, street cars, coal, etc.,
we shall still allow packs of thievish corporations to run
our cities?

Do you think that because John Sherman—may his tribe

decrease—sits grinning on his throne of Ohio Republican
majorities, he will never get his deserts? That the people
will not resent the dictation of Wall Street that induces
"great" Democratic leaders to back Sherman? That the
railroad, mining and manufacturing barons, aided by the politicians, are to have henceforth free swing? That trusts are
to concentrate our industries until all come under one industrial czar? That Bean-Soup Atkinson, Sumner of Yale
and John Sherman are to guide our economic thought? That
editors who confess that they only run their papers "to sell
news and get ads" are to furnish our future literature? That
the sham of the two old parties pretending to fight over tariff
and silver and temperance is to go right on? That we will
always permit our predatory classes to bring over European
serfs by the million, to crowd our native Americans, while
they howl about excluding the pauper products of Europe?
That, in a word, you "who call good evil and evil good" will
always be allowed to run riot over this glorious land?

Do you think that because Shylock has got our Eastern
and Middle States bound hand and foot, the West and South
will tamely submit to the shackles? That the multi-millionaires, scoffing at the graduated property tax, will be let grow
to be billionaires? That the United States will much longer
pay the Vanderbilts thirteen million dollars a year salary for
robbing it, and the Astors, Rockefellers, Goulds and the rest
of the 7,000 millionaire robbers in proportion? That in accord with the "Hazzard circular", white slavery has permanently taken the place of black slavery in this land? That
the American people will be much longer fooled by small con-
cessions from their tyrants—such as a little increase of currency? That when foreign noblemen tell us our commercial
barons are far more powerful and oppressive than theirs, we
will continue under the yoke? That when we find the misery
of our city poor as great as that of European cities, we will
take no steps to abate it?

————

O fools, you are reckoning without your host! You want
to join the innumerable caravan of American plunderers, who
are astonishing Europe by their lavish riot there. By clinging to the coat-tails of big monopolists, you little monopolists
want to get to Newport, Saratoga, Washington, New York,

London, Paris, Venice, Rome, Naples. You want city palaces, rural villas, palace cars, yachts, opera boxes.

But beware !

" Dinna ye hear the slogan ? "

THE FARMERS ARE COMING !

AND THE WAGE-WORKERS !

1892.

AFTER THE ST. LOUIS CONVENTION.—Another delay in publication brings me to March, 1892. Here is what I said in the *Express* about St. Louis :

WELL.

It is spring time.

The sowers have gone forth to sow.

What shall the harvest be ?

An ear-piercing bugle-call has gone forth from St. Louis, for the gathering and marshaling of the armies of freedom, and a movement all along the line against the enemy.

Will the movement be grand, general, disciplined, irresistible ?

Or will the village oracle at the village store be heeded, who has " done pretty well, thank you " this year ; and don't see any wrongs to be righted, except that " there should be more hard work done and less sitting around on dry goods boxes ? "

Even the most conservative and stupid see that the United States are in a very critical condition.

Of course the old party papers will cluck it out,—as they do in regard to Governor Fifer's Jeremiah cry,—as long as there is anything to be got from their rich bosses.

But all thoughtful people, in their inmost souls are asking, Whither are we drifting ?

What shall the end of this century see in America ?

To all such the voice of the St. Louis Conference comes with no uncertain sound.

"'This is the way—walk ye in it."

The way out.

We need a way out.

We are drifting into a maelstrom very rapidly.

To the time foretold by Macaulay, when the " hungry

fellows " would undertake to settle all our political, financial and social questions.

The time foreboded by the California millionaire, who did not want to build a palace in New York, and thus make himself a conspicuous mark for the hungry fellows.

St. Louis was grand,

Unique,

Magnificent !

The men meant it,

The women meant it,

The leaders mostly meant it.

But the movement is stronger than its leaders.

If any of them try to monkey with the buzz saw while in motion, they will be sorry.

They are not likely to. They will be like the unruly boy in the factory who touches the big fly wheel, and concludes not to try to stop it.

Or the tough boy in the great public school, who tests the great machine at some points, and concludes it is too strong for him.

What a pentecostal time at St. Louis.

All at length spoke one language—Parthians, Medes, Elamites and them of Georgia.

"Multitudes, multitudes in the valley of decision."

And the decision was right.

The chance of the century is now open to us.

If we make good use of it, the country may very speedily recover its liberties.

If we don't—

Woe! woe! woe!

Here now in this month of March, 1892, the irrepressible conflict between Shylock and the money reformers goes on apace. The money power in Europe and America is fighting tooth and nail against silver. But it is significant that Secretary of the Treasury, Foster, writes in surprise from London, that he finds all England, outside of London, favoring the remonetization of silver.

Here is a specimen of the conflict raging on the more money question. The gold bugs say, we have over 24 dollars per capita " in circulation ". The money reformers say about 5.00.

The statement of the Chicago *Tribune* is, December 1, 1891, population, 64,680,000 ; circulation per capita, $24.38 :

	Gen. stock coined or issued.	In treasury.	Amount in circulation
	$	$	$
Gold coin, including bullion in Treasury....................	677,774,595	271,843,193	405,931,402
Standard silver dollars, including bullion in Treasury.....	461,205,960	398,508,756	62,697,204
Subsidiary silver.............	77,235,022	14,389,585	62,845,437
Gold certificates.............	161,852,139	19,202,170	142,649,969
Silver certificates...........	324,274,918	3,401,308	320,873,610
Treasury notes, act July 14, 1890.....................	72,959,652	1,976,366	70,983,286
United States notes..........	346,681,016	13,316,707	333,364,309
Currency certificates, act June 8, 1872....................	10,135,000	370,000	9,765,000
National bank notes.........	172,993,607	4,841,754	168,151,853
	2,305,111,909	727,849,839	1,577,262,070

That looks clear but is totally misleading—ignoring as it does the money that has been lost and destroyed in 30 years, and that hoarded as reserves in banks and elsewhere. The method in use in the Treasury department, to ascertain the volume of currency in circulation is, to add to the amount of all the coin minted, all the paper money that has been issued, and from this sum substract the amount held in the Treasury, and assume that the balance is in circulation.

For instance, Government statistics ask us to believe that every silver dollar coined since 1878 still remains in the country, either in the banks, treasuries or among the people. We are also asked, to believe that all the subsidiary coin that has been minted since 1878 and $68,418,371 ; a considerable portion of which was coined previous to the war, is still in use as currency.

Since that is their method of handling the computation of gold and silver extant, imagine the same rule applied to paper money. Even if they wished it, they have no facts upon which to base an estimate of the loss by fire, wreck, flood or other accidents, including the lost and worn-out bills.

So careful a statistician as N. A. Dunning, author of

"The Philosophy of Price," gives the following estimate, under date, August 3, 1891 :

Amount outstanding as per Treasurer's
statement...................................... $1,666,094,420.47

Amounts to be deducted :
Loss in gold coin....................... $200,000,000.00
Loss in silver coin.................... 20,000,000.00
Loss in paper currency................. 50,000,000.00
Loss in fractional currency.............. 6,916,690.00
Held as reserves total.................... 603,008,707.00
Held in U. S. Treasury................. 337,144,089.36
Coin sent abroad this year.............. 61,695,504.00
Bullion counted as currency............ 76,439,588.00

$1,355,204,578.36

Deducting this last sum from the Government statement above, we have $310,889,842.11, or about $5 per capita of population—against $24, claimed by the enemies of the plain people.

The following is an able statement of the situation in 1892 from Chicago *Western Rural :*

INDUCTIVE METHOD WITH SILVER.—England, Germany, Holland, Belgium, and other nations of Europe, can buy a given amount of tea in China and Japan, with a given number of grains of silver bullion ; whether they buy their silver bullion at a low price or at a high price. Hence it is for the financial advantage of the nations of Western Europe, to get their silver as cheap as possible. The same rule holds good in the purchase of cotton, wheat, silks and spices in India, of spices and medical supplies in Ceylon, Sumatra, Borneo, and all the Islands of the Indian Ocean ; and of tin ores and ores of other metals from the same quarter of the globe. The cheaper the price of silver, the greater profits European merchants make, and the more easily they can control the trade of the United States, and all other countries on the Western Continent. The reason ought to be plain to every one, why bankers and merchants of London, Paris, Amsterdam, Berlin and other money centers of Europe, are deeply and actively interested in the monetary affairs of all the silver-producing countries ; such as the United States, Mexico, Peru, and others this side of the Atlantic. The reason ought to be plain why they can afford to enlist, intimidate, bribe or hoodwink bankers, merchants, Congressmen, Senators and Secretaries in the United States, and even to spend money like water in controlling nominations and elections of Presidents in this country. The bankers and merchants of the chief European business centers, control and draw profits from almost the entire trade of Asia, Africa and Oceanica. They are almost as successful to-day in taking unlimited tolls out of the earnings of Americans, as of the earnings of Hindoos, Chinamen, and New Zealanders.

North and South America embrace the leading silver mines of the earth. When an Englishman or a Dutchman gets control of this silver product, he holds the key by which he can dominate at will the merchandise of more than half of the inhabitants of the entire world. The reason can easily be seen, why the United States Government has been led to place its silver interests in the hands of an International Monetary Conference, now in session at a European capital; and which is controlled by a large majority of European diplomats. * * The Chicago *Inter-Ocean* of November 30, expresses aptly the theory of the conspirators on both sides of the Atlantic. It says: " It will thus be seen that the whole subject of the monetary system of the civilized world, is in a fair way to be thoroughly overhauled and readjusted." This is terribly true ; and it will be thoroughly overhauled and readjusted to suit the money mongers of Europe ; and by methods among the most damaging to the business interests of the United States that could be devised ; and by the methods that will serve most successfully to make interest and dividend bearing securities continually enhance in value, while the money with which they are to be paid becomes continually scarcer and dearer,—continually costing more labor and products of labor than these securities were worth when issued. Thus the people of the United States, with all their conceited notions of their own intelligence, are placed by foreign intrigues on a level with the Mongolians and Malays. Doubtless, our Congress will be asked to register the decrees of the coterie of foreign gold and bond gamblers, and our people will be asked to sanction the conspiracy by their votes. Shall the American voter always continue to swindle himself under the delusion that he must do it in order to be honest ?

So STUPID.—The bottom facts of the silver war, as discussed in 1892, are well illustrated in the following, from Senator Teller's speech delivered in the Senate, April 20th.

Mr. Gray.—I ask the Senator whether he will explain what the mechanism of the process is, by which the vitiation of silver has brought the large export of wheat from India in competition with the grain grown in the United States.

Mr. Teller.—I will explain that to the Senator, and it is not difficult of explanation. I will take as an illustration the price of silver to be 90 cents an ounce. It costs to ship wheat from Bombay, Calcutta, and other places in India, to Great Britain, just about twice what it costs us to ship it from New York. It passes through a region of country hot and unhealthy even for wheat; and when it reaches Great Britain it is not the best of wheat, and not as good as ours, but it comes in competition and fixes the price of American wheat. Now, let us see how it is done. The India shipper can buy wheat for $1.20 a bushel, and he can send it to Great Britain and sell it for 90 cents a bushel, gets 90 cents and no more.

The English shipper, who takes it from India to Great Britain and sells it, gets gold for it. He takes the 90 cents and buys an ounce and a third of an ounce of silver. That costs him $1.20. What does he do with that silver? He takes it back and puts it into rupees at $1.38 an ounce. He has got from $1.84 to $1.85 for his wheat, while the American wheat-grower, owing to this beautiful system of finance of ours, has got his 90 cents. He gets a little more than that, for wheat has been worth a little more than 90 cents. I only use this as an illustration.

Does the Senator understand now how that is done? If not, I will explain further.

Mr. Gray.—I should like to have the Senator explain further.

Mr. Teller.—The Senator does not see it yet. Let him take a pencil and a tablet; let him put down the price of wheat in Bombay at $1.20; let him add to it the 14 cents, the cost of transportation, and he has got $1.34. That is what it will cost when it gets to England, and he realizes $1.84 or $1.85, according to the market price of silver, for his wheat. Can the Senator make the subtraction of $1.85 and find a fair margin for the Indian exporter?

Mr. Gray.—I do not want to interrupt the Senator; but

in both cases, both for the bushel of wheat shipped from this country and the bushel of wheat shipped from India, the producer is paid in London or in Liverpool in gold, is he not ?

Mr. Teller.—Certainly, and if the American wheat-grower buys silver he brings it back here, and it is still at the same price it was when he got it in London, and it will not buy any more than his 90 cents of gold. But if the Indian merchant takes it back to India, it buys as much, ounce for ounce, whether it is in coin or in bullion, as it did thirty years ago. That is, the purchasing power of an ounce of silver is in India $1.38, and it has cost him 90 cents.

Mr. Gray.—I will ask the Senator whether the 90 cents which the American grower gets for his wheat in Liverpool, when it comes back here is not equivalent to 90 cents in gold ?

Mr. Teller.—Certainly it is.

Mr. Gray.—Then, what right has he to complain ?

Mr. Teller.—Mr. President, he is so stupid in this country that he does not complain. [Laughter.] The American wheat-growers have sat by and clapped their hands for both of these great political parties, who have been cutting their throats. They will complain after awhile. But still the fact is, our producer has for his bushel of wheat 90 cents and the Indian has for his $1.84 to $1.85. Liverpool price in silver.

In the year 1873, when silver was demonetized, India for the first time sent wheat to the market ; she sent then 290,-000 bushels. This year, in eleven months, she has sent 50,000,000 bushels of wheat, to compete with the wheat-growers on American soil. At the time silver was demonetized here, Russia had never put into the markets of the world more than twenty-five or twenty-six million bushels of wheat. In less than six months now, with a famine in one-third of her land, she has put 100,000,000 bushels of wheat in Europe.

India had never sent any wheat ; she never could send any wheat while silver was at par.

Another item from Henry Carey Baird, in answer to the wonderful Mr. Harter of Ohio, is full of meat on the gold question. He said :

GOLD IMPORTS, 1878–1892.—Being desirous of reaching sound conclusions as to the effect of silver legislation on the movements of the " metal ", let us now rather attempt to form them from the longer period of fourteen years, which has elapsed since the attempt to restore silver to its Constitutional position of a "money metal".

On February 28, 1878, the so-called "Bland bill" became the law of the land, and on May 31 of the same year a permanent stop was put to the contraction of the Greenback circulation. Now, what has been the result? In the fourteen years commencing July 1, 1878, and ending June 30, 1892, while producing (January 1, 1878, to December 31, 1891), $486,000,000 of gold, we have actually gained by import $108,837,000 of that "metal". The extent of the workings of this "vast engine" of civilization, not of "contraction", in adding to our gold resources nearly $595,000,-000 is indeed great; but in addition, up to November 1, 1892, we had added over $500,000,000 in silver dollars, silver certificates and silver Treasury notes, to the circulation, outside of the United States Treasury. These are great sums, but they are not all. While on March 15, 1878, the loans and discounts of the national banks were but $854,750,000, and their deposits but $613,000,000; by September 30, 1892, the loans and discounts had swollen to $2,153,498,000 and their deposits to $1,779,295,861. What a vast addition to the instrument which mobilizes the services, commodities and ideas of the people.

1893.

PANIC OF MAY.—Again the solemn horologe of the years strikes; and we are in the May panic of 1893, not to mention the Fair.

The Wall Street men admit that they permitted the panic because Secretary Carlisle dared to propose to do right, and "redeem" Treasury notes in silver.

Deep thinkers are still very much occupied with the basic facts concerning the rise of gold, while silver and all staples have remained about stationary for 20 years.

Henry Carey Baird has this about

INDIA AND AMERICA.—The imports of raw cotton into the United States are not for the South the only or the most alarming feature in the cotton situation to-day. Not only do Egypt and India compete with the South in Europe, but since the depreciation of silver the development of cotton manufacturing in India has become a fact of great, indeed marvelous, import. The depreciation of the rupee without any material appreciation in prices, has acted as a prohibitive tariff against the rest of the world, in India, China and Japan, with cotton goods. With this has developed a wonderful export trade of India with China and Japan, especially in cotton yarn.

In a speech by Mr. John A. Beith, delivered at a town meeting at Manchester, England, called by the Mayor, October 27, 1892, the following statement is made:

" But if we go more deeply into the matter, we find that during the period when there were exceptional causes for its expansion—such as the opening of the Suez Canal, the quadrupling of the railway system of India, and a reduction of steam freights almost as low as sailing vessel freights, through the discovery in engineering of the triple expansion system—not only has our Eastern trade been retarded, but the practical refusal to take payments in the money of the East, except at an enormous discount, has diverted the channels of trade; and silver-using countries, such as China, have felt themselves compelled to go past Manchester and to trade with silver-taking countries. Now the figures on this question are absolutely appalling. Indian mills did not begin their existence with this change in the currency. For ten years before this change came, Indian mills were in existence and were working vigorously, and making progress in India; but during the whole of that ten years were practically able to export nothing. Manchester had, up to that time, always ' taken the cake' in the neutral markets.

" In 1874, the total exports of yarn from the Indian mills to China and Japan amounted to only 1,000,000 pounds. It was only in 1875, and when silver had fallen 3 pence per ounce, that the 1,000,000 pounds of exports, which it had taken Indian mills nearly ten years to get up to, at once expanded, as if in obedience to the wave of an enchanter's wand, into 5,000,000 pounds. In 1880 there was a further fall of 5 pence per ounce; and consequently a further advantage to the silver of India and China, as compared with England, accepting only gold payments, and so, then, the 5,000,000 of exports from India became 25,000,000. In 1885 another fall took place, and the 25,000,000 became 75,000,-000. In 1889 there was a further fall of 5 pence in silver, and the 75,000,000 became 127,000,000. In 1891 there was still a further fall, and the 127,000,000 of exports of yarn from India to China became 165,000,000; so that in seventeen years, through the operation of this cause chiefly, 1,000-000 pounds of yarn exports per annum had risen to 165,000,-000 pounds per annum.

"These are very large figures, but if you look a little more into the details they become even more appalling. One hundred and sixty-five million pounds of yarn, sent from Bombay to China and Japan, means that India is sending six times as much as the United Kingdom sends to China and Japan, twice as much as the United Kingdom sends to India, China and Japan together; and is indeed very fast approaching the figure of Lancashire's total exports of yarn to the whole world. If the ratio of increase continues as hitherto, the shipment from India will exceed in from three to four years, the total shipments of yarn from the United Kingdom to the whole world, including India, China and Japan."

Verily, verily, the South must soon revive its political economy; and the hour when this people ceases to be dominated by cotton, will mark as great an advance in our progress and civilization, as does the first day of January, 1863, when slavery was, by proclamation, abolished. The disadvantages that have grown out of the belief of the Southern people in the domination of cotton, during the past seventy-five years, have vastly outweighed any national advantages arising from the cultivation of that staple in the United States.

The dethronement of the American cotton tyrant will therefore, be one of the grandest and most beneficent events, in all our history. May it therefore come, and come quickly!

HENRY CAREY BAIRD.

Philadelphia, March 21, 1893.

BOOKS

BOOKS

From the Press of the Arena Publishing Company.

The Dream Child.

A fascinating romance of two worlds. By FLORENCE HUNTLEY. Price: paper, 50 cents; cloth, $1.00.

A Mute Confessor.

The romance of a Southern town. By WILL N. HARBEN, author of "White Marie," "Almost Persuaded," etc. Price: paper, 50 cents; cloth, $1.00.

Redbank; Life on a Southern Plantation.

By M. L. COWLES. A typical Southern story by a Southern woman. Price: paper, 00; cloth, $1.00.

Psychics. Facts and Theories.

By Rev. MINOT J. SAVAGE. A thoughtful discussion of Psychical problems. Price: paper, 50 cents; cloth, $1.00.

Civilization's Inferno: Studies in the Social Cellar.

By B. O. FLOWER. I. Introductory chapter. II. Society's Exiles. III. Two Hours in the Social Cellar. IV. The Democracy of Darkness. V. Why the Ishmaelites Multiply. VI. The Froth and the Dregs. VII. A Pilgrimage and a Vision. VIII. Some Facts and a Question. IX. What of the Morrow? Price: paper, 50 cents; cloth, $1.00.

For sale by all booksellers. Sent postpaid upon receipt of the price.

Arena Publishing Company,

Copley Square, BOSTON, MASS.

BOOKS

From the Press of the Arena Publishing Company.

Jason Edwards: An Average Man.

By HAMLIN GARLAND.   A powerful and realistic story of to-day.   Price: paper, 50 cents; cloth, $1.00.

Who Lies? An Interrogation.

By BLUM and ALEXANDER.   A book that is well worth reading.   Price: paper, 50 cents; cloth, $1.00.

Main Travelled Roads.

Six Mississippi Valley stories.   By HAMLIN GARLAND.

"The sturdy spirit of true democracy runs through this book."— *Review of Reviews.*

Price: paper, 50 cents; cloth, $1.00.

Irrepressible Conflict Between Two World-Theories.

By Rev. MINOT J. SAVAGE.   The most powerful presentation of Theistic Evolution *versus* Orthodoxy that has ever appeared.   Price: paper, 50 cents; cloth, $1.00.

For sale by all booksellers.   Sent postpaid upon receipt of the price.

Arena Publishing Company,

Copley Square,   BOSTON, MASS.